Approaches to Teaching
Austen's *Emma*

Approaches to Teaching
World Literature

Joseph Gibaldi, series editor

For a complete listing of titles,
see the last pages of this book.

Approaches to Teaching
Austen's *Emma*

Edited by

Marcia McClintock Folsom

The Modern Language Association of America
New York   2004

© 2004 by The Modern Language Association of America
All rights reserved. Printed in the United States of America

For information about obtaining permission to reprint material from
MLA book publications, send your request by mail (see address below),
e-mail (permissions@mla.org), or fax (646 458-0030).

Library of Congress Cataloging-in-Publication Data

Approaches to teaching Austen's Emma / edited by Marcia McClintock Folsom.
        p. cm. — (Approaches to teaching world literature ; 82)
            Includes bibliographical references and index.
ISBN 0-87352-912-X (hardcover : alk. paper) — ISBN 0-87352-913-8 (pbk. : alk. paper)
1. Austen, Jane, 1775–1817. Emma. 2. Austen, Jane, 1775–1817—Study and teaching.
            I. Folsom, Marcia McClintock. II. Series.
                    PR4034.E53A67 2004
                823'.7—dc22   2003026996
                    ISSN 1059-1133

Cover illustration of the paperback edition: sketch of Steventon Parsonage,
the birthplace of Jane Austen. From *English Literature: An Illustrated Record*, vol. 4.,
                    by Edmund Gosse (1904), p. 94.

The two essays "Jane Austen, Slavery, and British Imperialism" and
"The Sexual Politics of *Emma*" © 2004 by Ruth Perry.

Published by The Modern Language Association of America
        26 Broadway, New York, NY 10004-1789
                    www.mla.org

For Jamie and Raphael

CONTENTS

PREFACE TO THE SERIES

In *The Art of Teaching* Gilbert Highet wrote, "Bad teaching wastes a great deal of effort, and spoils many lives which might have been full of energy and happiness." All too many teachers have failed in their work, Highet argued, simply "because they have not thought about it." We hope that the Approaches to Teaching World Literature series, sponsored by the Modern Language Association's Publications Committee, will not only improve the craft—as well as the art—of teaching but also encourage serious and continuing discussion of the aims and methods of teaching literature.

The principal objective of the series is to collect within each volume different points of view on teaching a specific literary work, a literary tradition, or a writer widely taught at the undergraduate level. The preparation of each volume begins with a wide-ranging survey of instructors, thus enabling us to include in the volume the philosophies and approaches, thoughts and methods of scores of experienced teachers. The result is a sourcebook of material, information, and ideas on teaching the subject of the volume to undergraduates.

The series is intended to serve nonspecialists as well as specialists, inexperienced as well as experienced teachers, graduate students who wish to learn effective ways of teaching as well as senior professors who wish to compare their own approaches with the approaches of colleagues in other schools. Of course, no volume in the series can ever substitute for erudition, intelligence, creativity, and sensitivity in teaching. We hope merely that each book will point readers in useful directions; at most each will offer only a first step in the long journey to successful teaching.

Joseph Gibaldi
Series Editor

PREFACE TO THE VOLUME

Many Austen scholars consider *Emma* (1816), Austen's fifth novel, to be her greatest book, the one that most fully matches performance with intention. On the hundredth anniversary of Austen's death, in July 1917, Reginald Farrer contrasted *Emma* with *Pride and Prejudice*:

> While twelve readings of *Pride and Prejudice* give you twelve periods of pleasure repeated, as many readings of *Emma* give you that pleasure, not repeated only, but squared and squared again with each new perusal, till at every fresh reading you feel anew that you never understood anything like the widening sum of its delights. (366)

Farrer's comment resonates powerfully for the many Austen readers who return to her books over and over, but it suggests the kind of difficulty that teachers introducing *Emma* to students reading it for the first time may face. If our first eight or ten readings of the novel are doomed to be incomplete, if we are constantly realizing that we did not fully understand "its delights" in prior readings, how should the teacher welcome new readers to Austen's brilliantly created world?

Because students who read *Emma* in English courses are usually reading the novel for the first time, teachers have the challenge of introducing the work to those who may not initially see the "widening sum of its delights." How do we help students move from feeling impatient to finding their "pleasure squared and squared again"? Many readers become enthusiastic as they proceed, but teachers can assist new readers in discovering the novel's pleasures. I hope this volume of approaches to teaching *Emma* will give instructors fresh ideas about how to help students experience the delights of reading it.

A remarkable quality of Austen's novels—particularly *Emma*—is their responsiveness to various critical approaches and their resistance to final interpretation. Lionel Trilling, quoting the passage from Farrer, makes this observation about those "twelve readings":

> The difficulty of *Emma* is never overcome. We never know where to have it. If we finish it at night and think we know what it is up to, we wake the next morning to believe it is up to something quite else. It has become a different book. . . . None of the twelve readings permit us to flatter ourselves that we have fully understood what the novel is doing. The effect is extraordinary, perhaps unique. The book is like a person— not to be comprehended fully and finally by any other person.
>
> (Introduction viii–ix)

This quality makes the novel especially rewarding for teachers whose students will uncover interesting aspects that the instructor hasn't noticed. Insightful questions about the book often yield untapped layers of richness. At the opening of his chapter on *Emma*, John Wiltshire deftly summarizes the oddly responsive quality of the book: "There is hardly a critic who, once having entered the close and intricate world the novel constructs, has not found it hospitable to a coherent and plausible reading, or who has not found something new and interesting to observe in Highbury" (*Body* 110). Since students who enter the novel's "close and intricate world" can also find it "hospitable to a coherent and plausible reading," the present volume, which includes essays from different interpretative vantage points, attempts to illuminate this very quality of the novel's hospitality to various readings.

Interestingly enough, thoughtful readers are themselves drawn to different interpretations at different times, as has certainly been the case for me. As a young teacher, I often taught *Emma* as a book about a young woman growing up. "The education of Emma" was the theme I found in criticism, and since my students were mostly young women, this approach seemed appropriate. And, of course, the novel is about Emma's moral and emotional growth during a momentous year of her life, and Emma is educated by her mistakes, by the discoveries she makes about the behavior of those around her, by Mr. Knightley, and by her capacity for thought, remorse, and resolution. But I am now amazed that I thought of Emma's education mostly as the quelling of her desire to control others and that I taught that lesson as a main theme of the book. I was more rigid then—in imposing a particular interpretation on students and in imagining that I knew what the right one was. I also recognize now that the education of Emma is a theme more often advanced by old-fashioned male critics than by feminist readers and that some of its exponents think that Emma is insufficiently punished at the end of the book. At that point in my life, I think I even agreed with some students that Mr. Knightley was an unsatisfactory romantic partner for the lively Emma once she had completed her education.

But I changed, too. I became more uncomfortable with this reading as I became active in the women's movement and absorbed the new feminist scholarship about literature. Pushed to the limit by a full-time job, a demanding marriage and household, and two young children, I began to read and teach *Emma* as a work of fiction about making mistakes and being wrong—about absorbing and acknowledging one's errors. The book opened up to me and seemed shimmering with wisdom when I read it that way. Stunned that I had missed so much in the novel before, I was deeply moved at the novel's generosity to Emma as a human being (not just as a young woman) who, despite her many faults, is essentially good.

Making my way through the death of my husband and the decisions that took me more into academic administration, I continued to read and teach *Emma*—to find in it an examination of the imperious necessity of change and the health of embracing the necessity. The word *change* appears so often in the novel that I wondered why I had not noticed it before. Mr. Woodhouse, "hating change of every kind" (7; 1: ch. 1), splendidly exemplifies the resistance many people feel. I began to see Highbury, as David Monaghan does, as a world that is too contented (*Jane Austen*). Austen sets the plot in motion by introducing new or returning characters into a society that is a little dormant. Their arrival stirs up the village and makes long overdue change possible for Emma, Mr. Knightley, and even Mr. Woodhouse. Teaching the novel this way, I found that students could recognize their own lives in Emma's world.

More recently, in the company of my Wheelock students, who perceive that this book, like Austen's *Pride and Prejudice*, examines how the mind works, I have recently taught *Emma* as a novel that shows how one's thoughts create the self. Passages in which Austen interweaves the narrator's voice with Emma's reveal that the careful analysis Emma makes of her erroneous perceptions and her mistakes (and the warnings she has ignored) gradually enables her to turn herself into someone she can respect. Such a reading is appealing to students whose struggles as readers, writers, and thinkers gain dignity when they see how hard it is for Emma, too. And by then in my life, Mr. Knightley seemed both vigorously masculine and comfortingly able to make mistakes—a man a woman (like me) could deeply love.

Like many readers, I often read Austen's works with a feeling of awe: How did Austen ever do it? Influenced by Julia Prewitt Brown, I have been struck by the novel's patient presentation of the fabric of everyday life. Brown's essay in this volume, "The Everyday of *Emma*," offers an answer to an old question about Austen's writing: Why did she avoid the larger history of her day? The answer, Brown suggests, is that although historical and political concerns resonate in Austen's fiction, her greatest contribution is "to remind us of the surface and weight of the everyday." Enmeshed, as students and teachers necessarily are, in the realities of our households, our responsibilities both public and private, the small decisions we constantly make, and the surprising relations we experience with people we know well or only slightly, we may find particular satisfaction from reading *Emma* if we focus on its discovery of moral significance in the everyday.

I mention the changes in my own teaching of *Emma* to acknowledge the impossibility of arriving at a final interpretation of the book or of fixing a best way of presenting it. The essays in this volume join a long conversation about *Emma* that takes place in publications and on the Internet and that confirms Trilling's wistful observation about *Emma*: "We never know where to have it." Teachers experience an intense version of that insight. We cannot help changing the way we teach when we reread books we have taught many times. We cannot help changing the way we teach when we observe and think about our students and the experiences they bring into the classroom. Our teaching is influenced by the realities of our own lives, by emerging scholarship and critical interpretation, and by our students—who continue to instruct us as they express disgust, amazement, vigorous objections, or delight about each work we read together. Talking with students about our own shifting understanding of a book we love, like Austen's *Emma*, may open a discussion about the vitality of literature in our lives—as we hope it may be in theirs.

MMF

ACKNOWLEDGMENTS

My first thanks are to my college students, who have given me so much during my years of teaching Austen's novels at Wheelock College. Their faces remain vivid to me, and their words, in essays and in class discussions, have been present to me as I worked on this book. I thank the readers of Austen's novels I have known in the Radcliffe Evening Seminars, in the Teachers as Scholars Project at Harvard, in various book groups, and in the Jane Austen Society of North America. These perceptive readers inspired me to fresh readings of Austen's works every time I taught them.

Four Austen scholars have been exceptionally generous with their time and advice. I thank John Wiltshire of LaTrobe University, Australia, for his encouragement and his wonderful letters to me about Austen's work. My admiration of his work on Austen is evident in many places in this volume, and his admiration of mine has surprised and delighted me. My friends Pamela S. Bromberg, Julia Prewitt Brown, and Ruth Perry have been insightful advisers. Pam read drafts of my essays with acute attention, and she introduced me to the work of Franco Moretti. Ruth, who perceptively reviewed early proposals for this volume, has been a staunch friend of my writing. Julia's enthusiasm about my work on Austen has buoyed my spirit at key moments. All four have contributed essays to this collection, and their scholarship and good judgment are reflected in the book.

I have spent my professional life at a college where a commitment to teaching comes first—in faculty evaluation, in our preparation of students, and in our informal conversations. I especially thank Marjorie Bakken for her steadfast belief in teaching as the heart of our work. My Wheelock colleagues Mary Battenfeld, Laurie Crumpacker, Andrea Hoffman, Jama Lazerow, Theresa Perry, Joyce Hope Scott, Swen Voekel, and Lee Whitfield have helped create an academic institution that combines intellectual energy with humane warmth. The college's explicit dedication to teaching made it logical for me to work on books in the MLA's Approaches to Teaching World Literature series. My friend Michael Downing always helps me see the comedy and the poignancy of the classroom.

I am very grateful to the instructors who wrote essays for this volume and who worked through the stages of revision with remarkable goodwill. I have learned from them all. I appreciate the time and thoughtful responses of the teachers who took part in the MLA survey and of those who proposed essays not included in this volume. Their replies and suggestions helped shape the book. Sonia Kane has been a marvelously perceptive editor. I am also grateful to the consultant readers who went through the manuscript with such care.

My family has been, as always, the source of support and encouragement. My mother, Marcia McClintock Postlewaite, and my mother-in-law, Mary

Elting Folsom, have read sections of this book with their usual attention and enthusiasm. My sisters, Carolyn McClintock Peter and Abbie McClintock Crane, sustain me with sisterly affection, humor, and love. My brilliant and generous sons, Jamie McClintock Folsom and Raphael Brewster Folsom, support each other and me in countless ways, and to them I dedicate this book.

INTRODUCTION:
THE CHALLENGES OF TEACHING *EMMA*

Brilliantly dramatizing the growth of its main character in a richly realized community, *Emma* nevertheless presents numerous challenges to the teacher. The opening page, with its famous first sentence can repel students whose egalitarian values are affronted by Emma's obvious privileges: "Emma Woodhouse, handsome, clever, and rich, with a comfortable home and happy disposition, seemed to unite some of the best blessings of existence; and had lived nearly twenty-one years in the world with very little to distress or vex her" (5; 1: ch. 1).[1] The string of affirmative adjectives in the first sentence—"handsome," "clever," "rich," "comfortable," "happy," "best"—and the hint of divine blessing can make the heroine seem almost too lucky to engage interest. Although the sentence plainly suggests that Emma will soon have experiences that will distress and vex her, some students may feel irritated by the time they reach the end of the first paragraph.

Moreover, in the opening chapters, when Emma plans her "very kind" guidance of Harriet Smith, beginning readers can take offense at Emma's arrogance and self-importance. Student responses to her mistakes in these chapters can confirm Austen's oft-quoted remark: "I am going to take a heroine whom no one but myself will much like" (Austen-Leigh, *Memoir*, Folio ed. 140). The teacher's task is to keep students reading while helping them to understand Emma's errors and to grasp Austen's implicit relish of Emma's energy and attractiveness. In addition, the instructor has to enable students to make sense of Austen's experiment in granting legitimate power to a woman—an experiment so bold that many readers still do not appreciate it.

Another challenge *Emma* presents is the problem posed by other major characters. Even sophisticated readers sometimes respond to Mr. Woodhouse, Miss Bates, or Mrs. Elton as though they were people rather than characters and then express impatience with the trivia of life in Highbury. The teacher must encourage students to read attentively enough to grasp the subtlety of characterization and the brilliance of dialogue that they tend to tune out as boring.

Yet another difficulty is the resistance some readers feel to Mr. Knightley. His role as mature guide to Emma can offend feminist students who feel that Mr. Knightley has authorial approval when he scolds her. These students may regard the ending as disappointing and consider the sixteen-year age difference between Emma and Mr. Knightley as denying erotic power to their marriage. In one of her two essays in this volume, "The Sexual Politics of *Emma*," Ruth Perry strongly corroborates this objection to the resolution of the plot. A teacher who seeks to answer these objections can make sure that class discussions highlight the way Austen sets up Emma and Mr. Knightley as equals from the first chapter onward. Mentioning the ways in which Mr. Knightley's judgment is fallible can also bring out the fact that he too is deeply moved by emotion.

Perhaps a greater challenge to first-time readers is the feeling that, in *Emma*, "nothing happens." Such readers sometimes say, "This book seems really boring to me. I like to read fast books—page-turners like detective novels." Walter Scott was the first published critic to note that the novel has little "story" (357). Following the quiet lives of a few people in a small community, *Emma* chronicles modest outings, conversations in various rooms, occasional dinner parties, a dance at a country inn, and a picnic on a famous hill. Twenty-first-century students may feel that this is tepid stuff, indeed.

For still another example of the difficulties of teaching *Emma*, consider again the implications of Farrer's comment in my preface to the volume. Although the book makes perfect sense as one reads it for the first time, the novel requires rereading to fathom its subtexts of unexpressed motives, implied conversations, and covert feelings. How can teachers construct lectures, discussions, and writing assignments that illuminate these hidden layers?

Perhaps more important, how can we honor students' experience of reading the work for the first time, as we lead them forward without revealing the secret that is explained at the end? Since the first reading of *Emma* is so valuable because of its distinctive limitations, the teacher must try to orchestrate discussions around insights students have when they don't understand the hidden plot. This approach can enable us to illuminate the novel's artistry without spoiling the ending.

One particular challenge in teaching *Emma* has become salient in the last decade or two. Students at my college (like readers in many other schools) are acutely conscious of the issues of race, racism, colonialism, and all manifestations of inequality. Nearly every time I teach *Emma*, a student—reading ahead—discovers Jane Fairfax's mention of the "governess trade" and Mrs. Elton's leap to the "slave trade" (300; 2: ch. 17) even before we get to volume 2. Some students express indignation that Austen is suggesting that the situation of a governess is similar to the incomparably worse oppression of slavery. Other students may express curiosity about what Austen actually knew about the slave trade, or they may ask whether Jane Fairfax's bitter comparison of the "misery of the victims" in the two "trades" reflects Austen's own opinions. Likewise, when I teach *Mansfield Park* or *Persuasion*, students bring up questions about Austen's views on British imperialism, her understanding of the Caribbean colonies, and her attitude toward the slave trade, which was abolished by law in England in 1807.

Teachers who know nothing about the Austen family or about world events in Austen's day may have difficulty answering these questions, yet it is important to discuss them with students. A famous essay by Edward Said, "Jane Austen and Empire," asserts that Austen's novels helped "naturalize" British colonialism and slavery. His essay inspired much debate, and some critics have argued that Austen failed to grasp that slavery was infinitely worse than the servitude women like Jane Fairfax faced.

An essay by Ruth Perry, "Austen and Empire: A Thinking Woman's Guide to British Imperialism," answered Said by placing Austen's attitudes toward slavery and colonialism in the context of her family connections and the realities of the English war with France. This essay is less widely known than it should be, and Perry has revised it for inclusion in this volume. Richly documented with information about the extended Austen family and its connections to both the East Indies and the West Indies, Perry's original essay demonstrates that Austen's views on slavery and colonialism, mentioned in her three last completed novels and in the unfinished final fragment, *Sanditon*, changed as Britain debated abolition and experienced the defeat of Napoleon. Not surprisingly, in her essay on slavery in this volume, Perry discovers that "Austen's relation to colonialism and slavery was . . . conditioned by her gender, her class, and the history of England in her lifetime." Even more important, Perry shows how Austen's allusions to slavery reveal her "powerful commentary on all exploitative human relations." Because of its importance and usefulness, Perry's essay on slavery and imperialism is in the first section of this volume.

Meeting the Challenges

Close Reading

This volume offers many approaches to meeting the challenges I have mentioned: guiding students in understanding the main character and in valuing Emma's energy and her authority; helping them grasp the subtlety of Austen's development of the other characters; illuminating the novel's skillful portrayal of everyday life; and alerting students to apparent gaps in the text as moments that will come into focus when they reread the book.

As many essays in this collection demonstrate, close reading, which was developed in the 1950s by advocates of the New Criticism, is a useful tool in teaching Austen's novels. Participating in classroom discussions based on close reading of specific passages of *Emma* can help students unravel Austen's complex presentation of Emma and of the characters around her and provides opportunities to surmise what has been left unsaid in a passage. With such practice, students can become adept at deducing the hidden events and conversations that lie behind the major scenes in the book.

To illustrate the effectiveness of close reading as a teaching strategy, let us look at the last two paragraphs of the novel's second chapter—a passage that has been analyzed by John Wiltshire in *Body*:

> There was no recovering Miss Taylor—nor much likelihood of ceasing to pity her: but a few weeks brought some alleviation to Mr. Woodhouse. The compliments of his neighbours were over; he was no longer teased

by being wished joy of so sorrowful an event; and the wedding-cake, which had been a great distress to him, was all eat up. His own stomach could bear nothing rich, and he could never believe other people to be different from himself. What was unwholesome to him, he regarded as unfit for any body; and he had, therefore, earnestly tried to dissuade them from having any wedding-cake at all, and when that proved vain, as earnestly tried to prevent any body's eating it. He had been at the pains of consulting Mr. Perry, the apothecary, on the subject. Mr. Perry was an intelligent, gentlemanlike man, whose frequent visits were one of the comforts of Mr. Woodhouse's life; and, upon being applied to, he could not but acknowledge, (though it seemed rather against the bias of incli-nation,) that wedding-cake might certainly disagree with many—perhaps with most people, unless taken moderately. With such an opinion, in con-firmation of his own, Mr. Woodhouse hoped to influence every visitor of the new-married pair; but still the cake was eaten; and there was no rest for his benevolent nerves till it was all gone.

There was a strange rumour in Highbury of all the little Perrys being seen with a slice of Mrs. Weston's wedding-cake in their hands: but Mr. Woodhouse would never believe it.   (19; 1: ch. 2)

Students readily grasp the humor of this account of Mr. Woodhouse's effort to keep the guests from eating wedding cake after the Weston ceremonies. His voice and his habitual concerns are deftly recorded in the first of the two paragraphs, in which the narrator also captures the kind tone of Mr. Perry's response to Mr. Woodhouse's inquiry: Mr. Perry "could not but ac-knowledge, (though it seemed rather against the bias of inclination,) that wedding-cake might certainly disagree with many—perhaps with most peo-ple, unless taken moderately." Distinctive features of Mr. Perry's speech— the hesitating negative ("could not but"), the unemphatic verb ("acknowledge"), the long parenthesis and its temperate tone ("though it *seemed* rather against the bias of *inclination*"), the use of the conditional ("might"), the correction (of "many" to "most"), and the final qualification ("unless taken moderately")—amusingly capture Mr. Perry's effort to be truthful as he de-fers to Mr. Woodhouse.

But, as Wiltshire suggests, the final paragraph seems to step back from the reported conversation to glimpse Mr. Perry's children walking in the town. This sentence implies that other discussions, ones the narrator has not drama-tized even indirectly, must have taken place between the events depicted in the two paragraphs. "There was a strange rumour in Highbury of all the little Perrys being seen with a slice of Mrs. Weston's wedding-cake in their hands: but Mr. Woodhouse would never believe it." Attentively reading these para-graphs, Wiltshire discerns a "sly joke" that "works by suppressing and condens-ing" another scene, the conversation that must have taken place but that Austen has not written. Wiltshire finds the words for it. Emma, he suggests, must have said to the apothecary: "Dear Mr. Perry, as long as this wedding-cake remains in the house, it will make my father miserable. Do take it home to Mrs. Perry, and give a slice to each of your children." How else would the young Perrys have been seen (by talkative but unnamed members of the community) with slices of the cake?

Thus both Emma's and Mr. Perry's resistance to what Wiltshire calls the "mild but stubborn perversity" of Mr. Woodhouse is obliquely rendered—although, as Wiltshire points out, the text explicitly admits no "derision" of Mr. Woodhouse. The festive relish of cake and the wedding celebration itself, both opposed by Mr. Woodhouse, elude his control. But by giving the last word to Mr. Woodhouse, Austen tones down any laughter at him. Wiltshire attributes this softening to the novel's "largesse" and confidence in "its own comic vitality" (126–28).

Beginning readers of this novel—in which the narrator patiently dramatizes so many incidents—tend to feel bogged down by its full disclosure of daily life. Examining this small moment early in the novel, however, can give students experience in deducing events that occur in scenes that are not dramatized. When students realize that appreciation of the novel depends on the constant involvement of their imagination, they begin to fathom Austen's extraordinary invitation to active reading. This is the kind of reading that Farrer characterized in his allusion to the pleasure "squared and squared again." Only through active reading, in fact, can we make sense of the great issues that underlie the plot, the many characters that Austen fully imagined but only partially revealed, and the scenes that must have taken place but that are not dramatized. Before students have finished the book, the class can analyze scenes like this one, because they do not contain clues about the ending.

One of Austen's purposes in not dramatizing certain scenes is to keep the novel's primary vantage point close to Emma's, so that what she cannot know is usually not depicted. Sometimes, however (as in the passage at the end of ch. 2), the novel omits scenes in which Emma must have been an actor. The suppression of implied scenes makes reading the novel resemble our own conscious lives: we often feel that we do not understand what is going on. We experience the novel (as we sometimes experience daily life) as an epistemological problem.

The process of closely reading a passage like the one at the end of chapter 2 helps students identify appropriate language to describe characters they may not like at first. As they read the paragraphs, students of course recognize Mr. Woodhouse's preoccupation with the dangers of rich food, but in discussing the passage, they can see that Austen never uses the hostile language that they may feel inclined to apply to his foibles. To find apt words to describe Mr. Woodhouse, students must first consider the author's attitude toward him, which is implied in her temperate diction. Likewise, "hearing" the indirect rendering of Mr. Perry's voice allows students to discern both his courtesy and his sensible energy. In class discussion, instructors can also elicit from students the fact that Mr. Perry serves as an authority figure in many of the characters' lives while remaining slightly outside the novel's dramatic frame.

Most important, students can observe in the two paragraphs (and in the implied scene that readers themselves must compose) two qualities that anchor our understanding of Emma. One is her concern for her father's feelings, which is frequently depicted quietly, by implication, or buried in sentences in which it is not the main topic. Because the novel rarely emphasizes Emma's steadfast kindness to Mr. Woodhouse, beginning readers habitually underestimate its significance. Yet comprehending this trait is essential to an accurate reading of the novel. The other, equally important attribute in Austen's conception of Emma is revealed in the "offstage" exchange between Emma and Mr. Perry—her vigorous, healthy resistance to Mr. Woodhouse's faulty thinking, which she expresses steadfastly and acts on reliably. With the teacher's guidance, students will see that, here as elsewhere, Emma tactfully corrects her father's errors.

As always, attentive reading of any passage in Austen's novels throws into relief sentences, phrases, or expressions that shed light on the whole work. Buried in this passage, for example, is a comment about Mr. Woodhouse that some students may notice and call a key to the plot: "he could never believe other people to be different from himself." Thus he assumes that everyone finds rich foods as disagreeable as he does. Emma, too, is inclined to project particular feelings—not her dislikes, but certain other attitudes—onto her perceptions of some of the people around her. Emma knows that she is "an imaginist" (335; 3: ch. 3), but she does not recognize that her responses to other people (especially outsiders and newcomers to Highbury) are often based on her conceptions of who they must be. Emma is a kind of plotter—putting real people into stories that she dreams up. In her portrayal of Emma, Austen criticizes a woman who narrates other people's stories—a woman some readers might think resembles Jane Austen herself. Jo Alyson Parker's essay in this volume, "Teaching Emma's Narratives and the Narrative of *Emma*," explores this paradox.

Thus Emma does not accept three other characters as being real and separate from herself. In her thinking, Emma distorts what she perceives about Harriet Smith, Jane Fairfax, and Frank Churchill by creating erroneous scripts in place of their actual stories—stories that are, at the beginning, hidden from Emma and from the reader. Perhaps influenced by literary conventions, Emma imagines Harriet as a princess in disguise (with noble relations who will be discovered later); Frank as an eligible, gallant suitor (possibly for herself); and Jane as a romantic heroine with a secret (and Emma invents the wrong secret to explain the young woman's apparent coldness and reserve). Emma fails to grasp that each of the three has a life as complete as her own, and this lack of understanding resembles her father's. Finding a phrase, like this one from an early chapter, that works as a key to the novel usually occurs only to second-time readers (and a class may include a few of them), but reading closely will bring certain phrases into sharp focus.

This collection includes a number of essays that offer close readings of specific passages, although no book of criticism can include all the passages that repay this kind of attention. In fact, there is scarcely a page in the novel that does not. I sometimes teach a chapter or episode by asking students to choose a single paragraph in that part, which we then read aloud together. From such a random selection, the class glimpses the richness of Austen's writing and the humor, suggestiveness, irony, and haunting phrases that can be found on every page. This classroom exercise also works as a writing assignment. (The danger of this approach, of course, is that we cannot do justice to the whole book by closely reading every single page.)

The writers who have contributed essays to this volume have selected various passages, some familiar and some obscure, to read closely. All their essays illustrate how responsive Austen's prose is to such attentive reading. Patricia Howell Michaelson, in her essay, "Language and Gender in *Emma*," suggests that "few writers' prose invites the kind of close study we practice with verse, but Austen's every sentence can be examined for ironies and ambiguities." In their different ways, essays on teaching *Emma* inevitably suggest that students who learn to slow down and read thoughtfully will be rewarded by the feeling of joyful discovery that Farrer described.

Setting *Emma* in Literary Context

An excellent way to enable students to measure Austen's achievement in *Emma* is to set the book in literary context. Several essays in this volume offer comparisons between *Emma* and works by some of Austen's literary predecessors and contemporaries. Early in her essay, for instance, Lorna J. Clark says, "I try to bring Austen into every course I teach." The best place for an Austen novel, she says, is as the triumphant last work in a course on the eighteenth-century novel. A teacher of imagination and verve, Clark illustrates how *Emma* fits into a course that includes novels by Samuel Richardson, Laurence Sterne, Tobias Smollett, and Henry Fielding in the first half, and *Emma* and women writers in the second half. Clark suggests several sets of novels to teach with three Austen novels, *Pride and Prejudice*, *Northanger Abbey*, and *Emma*. She observes that "what is remarkable about reading *Emma* alongside other novels of its day is the surprise and pleasure it gives, the ways in which the work differs from them. Students come to appreciate Austen's ability to master the conventions of the genre and infuse into them new life and authenticity." Teaching *Emma* in an eighteenth-century-novel course allows students to perceive Austen "not as an isolated genius but as positioned within a female tradition."

The pleasure of seeing Austen's indebtedness to her predecessors as a way of measuring her originality is apparent, as well, in Wiltshire's first essay in this volume, "The Comedy of *Emma*," which compares *Emma* with Frances Burney's *Evelina*. His contrast between Burney's "comedy of discomfort" and Austen's "comedy of cross-purposes" (or even "comedy of comfort") is grounded in astute readings of each novel and analyses of specific scenes from each. Wiltshire's essay rewards the reader with deeper appreciation of how funny Austen is, and he links her humor with the comedy of eighteenth-century playwrights like Richard Brinsley Sheridan and Oliver Goldsmith.

Celia A. Easton, while fully sympathetic to her students' impatience with Richardson, makes wonderful use of a comparison between *Emma* and the first volume of Richardson's giant work *Sir Charles Grandison*. Acknowledging the difficulty of Richardson's "prolix style and tedious narrative" (as Austen's brother Henry said about Richardson in his "Biographical Notice of the Author" [7]), Easton first assigns Austen's short play *Sir Charles Grandison; or, The Happy Man*, a juvenile send-up of the novel that demonstrates the young Austen's familiarity with the long work. The students read one volume of Richardson's novel, which Easton suggests will enable them to discern Austen's playful re-creation, reordering, and reconceiving of characters, plot, and events from *Grandison*, whose characters were Austen's "living friends," as her nephew James Edward Austen-Leigh reported (*Memoir*, Folio ed. 79).

Parker's essay, "Teaching Emma's Narratives and the Narrative of *Emma*," places Austen's novel in a Seminar in Narrative Form, which includes works by Sterne, Marcel Proust, William Faulkner, Italo Calvino, and Shelley Jackson. By reading *Emma* first in the course, students experience the "ostensibly traditional narrative structure of *Emma*—the linear chronological movement, the overt guidance of the savvy omniscient narrator"—as a starting point for examining narrative form. Without treating Austen's novel as a foil to more experimental texts, Parker probes narrative qualities of *Emma* to increase students' confidence as they discuss issues—like causality, ambiguous closure, and authority—in supposedly less-traditional texts (or hypertexts). Parker's imaginative writing assignments offer students the chance to make intriguing intertextual connections.

How Does Austen Make Sure We Love Emma?

Let me return to the question of Emma's privilege and students' resistance to Emma's authority. How does Austen make sure that we feel Emma's endearing qualities as we proceed through so many chapters that chronicle her mistakes? This problem has continually flummoxed critics—let alone first-time readers. How can a teacher help students understand Emma's position as a woman with power and Emma as a person whom readers love even when they behold her arrogantly interfering in other people's lives?

One approach is to begin with a meticulous reading of chapter 1, perhaps with students reading successive paragraphs aloud, to establish the terms of Austen's exploration of Emma's character. The dangers implied by that first sentence are elaborated in the fourth paragraph, where the narrator's language is more severe: "The real evils indeed of Emma's situation were the power of having rather too much her own way, and a disposition to think a little too well of herself" (5). Austen's use of the phrase "real evils" both to describe Emma's "power" to get what she wants and to characterize her tendency to be too self-confident may seem to invite a misogynist reading of the novel—a reading that, unfortunately, some intelligent critics have offered. The qualifications—"*rather* too much" and "*a little* too well"—are sometimes ignored, as is the humor of the paragraph.

The fifth paragraph ends, "Her father composed himself to sleep after dinner, as usual, and she had then only to sit and think of what she had lost" (6). Emma's solitude as he drifts off is gently emphasized by the words "as usual." The narrator alludes to Emma's relation to her father, whom she "dearly loved" but who "could not meet her in conversation, rational or playful," and then reviews, paragraph by paragraph, the other possible companions her world offers her. "Not one among them" would be acceptable for "even half a day" (7). The question "How was she to bear the change?" sets up the problem the novel explores (6). The second half of chapter 1 presents Emma through dialogue rather than narration, first in a conversation between her and her father and then in a three-way conversation when Mr. Knightley joins them. These conversations can be read aloud, with students taking the roles of the characters and the narrator; hearing Emma talk helps students discern her energy and sauciness as well as her warmth and kindness.

As students begin reading volume 1, they easily grasp that Emma is making mistakes, and her errors with Harriet and Mr. Elton are more evident to first-time readers than are the mistakes she makes later. The teacher's task at this point is to support students' indignation at Emma's presumption and yet to keep them wondering how Austen makes her annoying heroine so fascinating and so endearing. Dorice Williams Elliott's essay in this volume, "Teaching about Free Indirect Discourse," offers an excellent way to work out this problem in class discussion. By sorting out the tones of the narrator's voice from the tone and spirit of Emma's speech and thoughts, Elliott develops a lively analysis of Austen's intermingling of the narrator's voice and Emma's own. Austen's achievement in interweaving these ways of "talking" is one of her technical triumphs, and it accounts for her ability to create sympathy for Emma even as the heroine may offend the reader by making mistakes of judgment while asserting that she is right.

Elliott closely reads the opening of chapter 16 in volume 1, in which Emma thinks through her surprise and mortification that Mr. Elton has just proposed to her instead of to Harriet Smith. Teachers can use that passage, as well as others, to give students a vocabulary for distinguishing the narrator's voice from Emma's. Working through such passages in class discussion can help students discover how Austen enables us to love Emma—partly because of her capacity for regret, generosity, remorse, and kindness and her sense of justice and partly because of her warmth and spirit.

In his second essay in this volume, "Health, Comfort, and Creativity: A Reading of *Emma*," Wiltshire, a reader with unusual sensitivity to Austen's distinctive vocabularies, explores her use of the word "comfort." In an earlier work, he noted the persistence with which the word "spirit" or "spirits" appears in the novelist's characterization of Emma (*Body* 128). The word "spirit" especially captures the vitality and creative energy that make Emma charming. Once students are alerted to watch for a word like "spirit," it seems to jump out at them: "dear Emma was of no feeble character . . . and had sense and energy and spirits that might be hoped would bear her well and happily" (18; 1: ch. 2); "With an alacrity beyond the common impulse of a spirit which yet was never indifferent to the credit of doing everything well and attentively" (24; 1: ch. 3); "Does my vain spirit ever tell me I am wrong?," Emma asks, and Mr. Knightley replies, "Not your vain spirit, but your serious spirit.—If one leads you wrong, I am sure the other tells you of it" (330; 3: ch. 2). Tracing the history of the word "spirit," with its mix of physical and psychological suggestions, Wiltshire shows that Austen seems to associate Emma's spirit with health, verve, and well-being.

In fact, Emma's spirit is perceptible in many passages that do not contain the word. In *Jane Austen and the Body*, for example, Wiltshire analyzes the passage in which Emma decides to befriend Harriet Smith and improve her (the whole passage is quoted in this volume by Brown). He notes the way Austen mixes Emma's errors in judgment with her enthusiasm and elan. After citing the long, fascinating paragraph, he says, "The point is *not* that one does not remark the self-deception and snobbery, even arrogance that these manoeuvres manifest, but that one picks up, at the same time, contrapuntally, and as a part of that very same self-deception and arrogance, the warmth, the eagerness, the panache and brio that enable these feats of psychological legerdemain to pass off successfully as if what were taking place were a process of reasonable thought" (131–32; emphasis added). Thus our recognition that Emma deceives herself and ignores her own accurate perceptions mingles, from the beginning, with the delight we feel in Emma's verve. Such passages as this one (in ch. 3) can be discussed in class to examine how Emma's stubborn misinterpretations are mitigated for the reader by her vivacity.

In her essay in this volume, "The Everyday of *Emma*," Brown argues that "Austen lays claim to nothing more (and nothing less) than Emma's irreplaceable individuality." Brown's essay helps make clear how much that "irreplaceable individuality" underlies and defines the greatness of the novel.

Responding to the Charge That "Nothing Happens" in *Emma*

Two essays in this volume, by Brown and by Jonathan Grossman, provide answers to students' comments about the novel's tedium. In "The Everyday of *Emma*," Brown points out that many readers and critics judge this work to be Austen's greatest novel. We usually designate the greatest as a novelist's most characteristic work of fiction—the one that "best achieves what that writer can do," she argues, and *Emma* "delivers best—precisely and to the exclusion of all else—Austen's forte: mastery of the moral landscape of the everyday. The more unremarkable the social situation, the greater Austen's achievement in showing that it does have human importance."

Brown illustrates this argument, perhaps a hard one to sell to undergraduates, by analyzing the narrator's comments during and after the Crown Inn ball. One of those remarks is this: "Of very important, very recordable events, it was not more productive than such meetings usually are" (326; 3: ch. 2). This line, buried in a paragraph that begins, "The ball proceeded pleasantly," suggests how great a task Austen set herself in chronicling events that may not seem at all worthy of narration. The next day, when Harriet encounters the Gypsies and is rescued by Frank Churchill, the narrator offers another interesting remark about the short duration of our memories of everyday life: "last night's ball seemed lost in the gipsies" (336; 3: ch. 3). After examining these comments, Brown explains, "The events of everyday life are either forgotten because superseded by new events that claim human attention or they are passed on orally" and are often distorted in careless retellings. "Only the novelist redeems them," she says, and Brown's essay pays tribute to Austen's astounding achievement in *Emma*—disclosing and redeeming the "moral scale of everyday life." The novel rests on the clarity of Austen's insight into the significance, both human and narrative, of the mundane. She locates in the most commonplace activities, in the smallest and apparently least dramatic moments, details that may be critical to the story as a whole. Of course this attention to minutiae is essential to the comedy of manners in realistic fiction, but its humane effect is to hint at the moral importance of ordinary life. By implication, the lives of students (and teachers, too) may themselves be worthy of recollection by an observant narrator.

Why events of everyday life have moral importance is suggested, as well, in Grossman's essay, "Manners in *Emma*," when he ponders the significance of manners in the lives of Highbury's people. By taking seriously the "labor of the leisure class," Grossman finds a key to the workings of Emma's mind as she comes to understand that she cannot marry Frank. This approach allows Grossman to offer a satisfying analysis of the Box Hill episode and to explain why we feel that Emma's unkind remark to Miss Bates represents a crisis. These two essays, then, explore ways of responding to students who wonder why Austen wrote a novel in which it appears that nothing happens.

Teaching about Patterns across the Novel

Many essays in this volume suggest how useful it is to emphasize close reading in class discussions and in writing assignments. Students need encouragement to slow down and read Austen's sentences as carefully as they would read lines in a Shakespeare play; paying adequate attention to the novel's text can bring surprise, insight, and even a sense of awe. At the same time, students benefit from knowing about narrative patterns underlying this long novel. (Of course, the book may seem longer to first-time readers than to those who have read it before.) There are a number of ways to convey the novel's overall structural design without revealing the plot.

The Three Volumes

Instructors can briefly outline the novel's divisions before students start reading, to provide them with a sense of what lies ahead. If students are reading an edition that retains the three-volume structure, teachers can point out that the volumes have nearly the same number of chapters—eighteen, eighteen, and nineteen— and that the three volumes bear equal weight in the novel's design. Teachers can also mention that Emma experiences three major epiphanies, one in the first volume (ch. 16) and two in the third volume (chs. 7 and 11–12), as well as numerous moments of reflection and new understanding throughout the work.

In the first volume, a character living in Highbury joins Emma's coterie for the first time; in the second volume, three people arrive in Highbury. These developments are responsible for stirring up a busy social world that has become a little static. In volume 1, Emma meets Harriet Smith, a young woman attending Mrs. Goddard's boarding school in Highbury. The introduction of Harriet into Emma's life, in chapter 3, sets the action of volume 1 in motion. But the focus remains on Emma remains, as she vigorously controls Harriet, the new person in her life.

In volume 2, two new people and one long-absent member come into the community. Neither Mrs. Elton nor Mr. Frank Churchill have ever been in Highbury, although they differ in their prior acquaintance with the town. Jane Fairfax, Miss Bates's niece, has a long-standing, important connection with the town, but her return, like the introductions of Mrs. Elton and Frank, constitutes a kind of arrival. These newcomers energize the novel, and they displace Emma from the center of her world. Moreover, Frank and Mrs. Elton challenge Emma's place as a controlling force, for they are just as active and assertive as she is. In fact, as Pamela S. Bromberg points out in her essay in this volume, "Learning to Listen: Teaching about the Talk of Miss Bates," Frank uses Emma as a bit player in his plot. Jane Fairfax, whose beauty, accomplishments, and air of mystery make her more of a romantic heroine than Emma herself, challenges Emma in another way. As the world of Highbury broadens out in the second volume, students often find themselves liking Emma better, partly because there are more people to compare her with and partly because the focus is less exclusively on her. Knowing that in the first two volumes new characters enlarge the community enables students to recognize one of the novel's major patterns, and teachers can alert readers to expect changes in their perceptions of Emma as they go through volume 2.

Chronology

A useful tool for students is a chronology of the novel, such as the one that Chapman provides in an appendix to his edition or the revision of Chapman's that Jo Modert offers in *The Jane Austen Companion* (57–58). I sometimes hand out my own version of the chronology, showing students that the action takes place during a fourteen-month period. Austen carefully figured out the days of the week and the months, seasons, and seasonal weather of the novel, but she indicates the specific days and dates in a very unobtrusive way. Coincidentally, Austen wrote *Emma* in about the same length of time as the novel's action occupies; Austen began it on 21 January 1814 and finished it on 29 March 1815—fourteen months. Using the novel's indication that Christmas Day fell on a Saturday (138; 1: ch. 6), Modert observes that the novel could begin in either 1802 or 1813. Other evidence convinced Modert that Austen placed the action in the fall of 1813 and the winter, spring, summer, and fall of 1814.

Such an outline as the one in this volume (pp. 10–12) or a simplified version of it may help students to see the governing rhythms of the seasons beneath the novel's surface and to understand that Austen conceived of the action as unfolding in time. For the benefit of teachers, I include in the chronology many details from the text. I also note Modert's reasoning, for she finds that Austen carefully plotted the novel around holy days and holidays in both the Old Style, or Julian, calendar and the New Style, or Gregorian, calendar. However, students don't need to figure out how the dates are uncovered and rationalized. In fact, for first-time readers, a shorter version of the chronology of *Emma* is plenty.

Discussing the detailed chronology will bring up important ideas about *Emma*, especially about the novel's realism. Teachers can begin by asking two questions. Why was Austen so precise in placing events accurately on the calendar? And why, apparently, does she reveal the days and dates in chance disclosures by characters? For an example of the way Austen makes such information surface inconspicuously, consider how we find out the time of Emma's dinner party for the Eltons. By overhearing the thoughts of John Knightley, who is indignant that Mr. Weston would walk over to Hartfield after his day in London, we discover that the party took place in April: Knightley is astonished that Mr. Weston decided "to quit the tranquillity and independence of his own fire-side, and on the evening of a cold sleety April day rush out again into the world!" We learn that the dinner took place on a Thursday, because we hear Mr. Weston's description of Mrs. Churchill's decision to go to London: "for *she* is as impatient as the black gentleman when any thing is to be done; most likely they will be there to-morrow or Saturday" (303–04; 2: ch. 17; the "black gentleman" is Mr. Weston's euphemism for the devil).

Students trying to answer the two questions can discuss how we ourselves are aware of the days of the week. Someone may mention the experience of remembering what day it is. "We somehow understand that it is Thursday," a student may say, "but we would never think, 'Well, today is April 14, and it is Thursday, and therefore I will be having a dinner party tonight.'" We are more likely to feel intuitively what day it is and to organize our activities according to specific plans or to our daily or weekly routines. Thus Austen's way of revealing days and dates feels realistic, because the characters are conscious of the markers incidentally, as asides in thoughts about something else that seems more important. Yet because observing time is a part of daily existence, Austen's reliable, well-planned calendar contributes to the novel's sense of everyday reality.

The Eight Major Scenes

Another way to illustrate the novel's patterns across the three volumes is to highlight the series of scenes in which large numbers of the community converge. Volume 1 contains the first two of the eight group events that form a kind of backbone of the novel and that demonstrate Austen's superb management of a large cast, in both interior spaces and exterior landscapes. Teachers use descriptions like "choreographing the dance of many characters" or "cinematic shifts of the frame of focus" to capture the pictorial quality of movement, conversation, and time passing in these memorable panoramas. In *Emma* more than in any of her other novels, Austen portrays large, crowded scenes, with characters engaged in public conversation, private dialogues, listening, overhearing, and observing one another. All eight of the scenes offer lively entertainment on a first reading, but on a second or later encounter, they reveal the writer's masterful command of behavior and motivation.

Austen uses several strategies for shifting focus between characters; she usually narrates from Emma's point of view but skillfully employs dialogue and the voices of other characters to encompass a variety of personalities, relationships, and physical activities. For example, Bromberg's essay shows how Austen uses the talk of Miss Bates to create the rooms, the mood, and the presence of numerous guests at the Crown Inn ball. Bromberg points out that "rather than employ third person description to set the scene of the ball at the Crown Inn, Austen uses Miss Bates as her viewpoint, dramatizing the heightened emotion and activity of this social gathering . . . with her breathless exclamations" and greetings. Miss Bates becomes a "counternarrator," and her "broken sentences and incomplete phrases convey the general air of excitement" of a large party at the town's inn.

Readers familiar with the plot should be able, in rereading these scenes, to discern the subtleties of hidden communication, the errors of interpretation, and the comedy or deep suffering beneath the conversation and physical movement. Teachers can assure students that a second reading of the scenes is likely to reveal the truth of Farrer's comment that our pleasure in the book will be "squared and squared again." It may be useful, however, for first-time readers to have a list of these events, and of the characters who attend them, for a sense of mastery as they proceed through the novel.

Teachers can alert students to anticipate these eight scenes, which together involve the main characters, as the novel unfolds. The following list provides scenes, characters, and locations of the scenes.

1. *The John Knightleys' visit and first dinner at Hartfield* (vol. 1, chs. 11–12): Emma, Mr. Woodhouse, George Knightley, John Knightley, Isabella

Woodhouse Knightley, and, at the beginning, Isabella's baby, Emma, in her aunt's arms

2. *The Woodhouse and Knightley Christmas Eve dinner with the Westons at Randalls* (vol. 1, chs. 14–15): Emma, Mr. Woodhouse, George Knightley, John and Isabella Knightley, Mr. and Mrs. Weston, and Mr. Elton; Harriet Smith is too ill with a cold to attend

3. *The Coles' dinner party* (vol. 2, ch. 8): Emma, Mr. and Mrs. Cole, Mr. and Mrs. Weston, Frank Churchill, George Knightley, "a proper unobjectionable country family," the "male part of Mr. Cox's family," and, later, Miss Bates, Jane Fairfax, and Harriet Smith

4. *Dinner at Hartfield in honor of the new Mrs. Elton* (vol. 2, chs. 16–18): Emma, Mr. Woodhouse, Mr. and Mrs. Elton, George Knightley, Mrs. Weston, John Knightley, Jane Fairfax; later Mr. Weston joins the party; Harriet Smith declines the invitation

5. *The Westons' ball at the Crown Inn* (vol. 3, ch. 2): Emma, Mr. and Mrs. Weston, George Knightley, Harriet Smith, Frank Churchill, Mr. and Mrs. Elton, Miss Bates, Jane Fairfax, Mr. and Mrs. Cole, and many others, including Dr. and Mrs. Hughes, Mr. and Mrs. Otway and Miss Otway and Miss Caroline, Mr. George and Mr. Arthur, Mr. William Cox—all people whom Miss Bates mentions by name

6. *The game with alphabet blocks at Hartfield* (vol. 3, ch. 5): Emma, Harriet Smith, Mr. Woodhouse, George Knightley, Mr. and Mrs. Weston, Frank Churchill, Miss Bates, Jane Fairfax

7. *Strawberry picking at Donwell Abbey* (vol. 3, ch. 6): George Knightley, Emma, Mr. Woodhouse, Mr. and Mrs. Weston, Harriet Smith, Mr. and Mrs. Elton, Miss Bates, Jane Fairfax; Frank Churchill arrives late

8. *The outing to Box Hill* (vol. 3, ch. 7): Emma, Frank Churchill, George Knightley, Mr. Weston, Harriet Smith, Mr. and Mrs. Elton, Miss Bates, Jane Fairfax

There are many ways to consider the connections between the major scenes. An examination of how the guest lists are compiled and of how the characters are transported to the events is one of the concerns of my essay in this volume. Another way to work out the links among the scenes is to follow Monaghan's argument in *Jane Austen: Structure and Social Vision.* Monaghan notes that when Emma is on familiar territory, she is usually responsible and generous. When she ventures forth into places she considers outside her domain, though, she experiments with reckless feelings and conversation. The contrast can be seen as typical of a young person whose sense of decorum and responsibility weakens when she is at a remove from the center of her moral life and upbringing. This argument may provoke discussion among students who recognize the pattern—the way first-semester students behave in residence halls, the way even sophisticated sophomores and juniors may behave at parties off campus, and the way younger siblings behave at the mall.

Thus, during the two dinners at Hartfield and during the Christmas Eve visit to Randalls, Emma behaves with reliable kindness, courtesy, and concern for the feelings of everyone else. But during the dinner at the Coles', a household Emma has never before visited, she betrays her own standard of good behavior and allows herself to speculate that Jane Fairfax may have attracted the romantic interest of her best friend's husband, Mr. Dixon. Even worse, she relays this suspicion to someone else—her new acquaintance, Frank Churchill. The essay by Joseph Wiesenfarth in this volume, "A Likely Story: The Coles' Dinner Party," places this important scene in the context of the novel and offers a fascinating way to teach its complex structure.

Likewise, when she is part of the large group visiting Donwell Abbey, an estate closely connected to her family and its past, Emma is thoughtful, sensitive, and grounded. But the next day, when the exploring party goes farther afield—all the way to Box Hill, where Emma has never been—the ill will among participants and Frank Churchill's defiance of propriety lead her to make a cruel remark to Miss Bates. Neither her father nor Mrs. Weston is present at this outing, and perhaps their absence also makes Emma feel reckless and unfettered; she usually does not permit herself to speak negative thoughts even when she is provoked (as she certainly is in many earlier scenes). Grossman's "Manners in *Emma*" adroitly decodes Frank's disrespectfulness in the Box Hill episode and explains the reason his behavior tempts Emma into forsaking her habitual courtesy.

The one exception to this pattern occurs in the scene in which Frank makes words with alphabet blocks on the new table in Hartfield. There, Emma does not live up to her responsibilities as host to the entire party; she allows Frank to amuse her by spelling out a word that reflects her indiscretion at the Coles'. She protests, "Nonsense! for shame!" but finds it "highly entertaining." She opposes Frank's suggestion to show the word to Jane Fairfax: "No, no, you must not; you shall not, indeed," but does so with such "eager laughing warmth" that Frank ignores her insistence (348; 3: ch. 5). Emma's inappropriate behavior occurs partly because she did not witness the prior scene in which Frank makes the "blunder" regarding Mr. Perry's carriage and about which he is trying to communicate with Jane. And certainly, Emma would never have behaved unkindly at Hartfield to either Miss Bates or Jane if she had not been tempted by Frank's doubly deceptive playfulness.

Parallels in Plot and Character

Another pattern that inspires discussion is Austen's technique of setting up parallel elements that illuminate one another across the novel. Calling students' attention to these similarities, instructors can observe that discovering the parallels between characters or events provides an opportunity for the reader to draw distinctions between them. An obvious parallel, for instance, is the one between the three unmarried young women (with an implied link to Miss Bates, who is unmarried but no longer young). We are invited to compare the personalities and prospects of Emma, Harriet Smith, and Jane Fairfax and to find likenesses as well as contrasts between the young women.

In her feminist essay in this volume, "The Sexual Politics of *Emma*," Perry argues that these three young females must accept the "real condition of women," which is vulnerability and dependence on men, as Miss Bates's situation demonstrates. Perry also examines the novel's multiple representations of women's friendships—between Harriet and Emma, Emma and Miss Taylor / Mrs. Weston, Harriet and Elizabeth Martin, Jane Fairfax and Miss Campbell, and, most of all, the "never-quite-managed" friendship between Emma and Jane Fairfax. All these relationships are frustrated by the necessity that marriages will conclude the novel and thwarted by the realities of women's lives. The hints of Emma's homoerotic feeling for Harriet have been noted by critics who admire it and those who deplore it, but Perry points out that all possibilities of female bonding are foreclosed by the expectations of the genre of the "marriage plot."

We also meet several eligible men who are actually or speculatively paired with unmarried women. The novel scrutinizes Philip Elton, Robert Martin, Frank Churchill, and George Knightley, and it contrasts them in manliness, vigor, and good sense. Claudia Johnson analyzes the novel's exploration of "what a man should be," in her essay by that name (*Equivocal Beings* 191–203).

In a novel about courtship, readers gain insight into marriage by considering how the behavior of the married couples suggests what lies ahead for the to-be-wedded characters. The Westons' marriage, with its joyful relief for "poor Miss Taylor" (vol. 1, ch. 1) may subject Anne Weston to some discomfort, for she is certainly more perceptive than her undiscriminating husband. And every glimpse of Mr. and Mrs. John Knightley indicates that a union based on total wifely devotion has its drawbacks.

The Eltons—who, oddly enough, seem well matched—have taken on each other's worst characteristics. A telling thought about them crosses Emma's mind: "It was not to be doubted that poor Harriet's attachment had been an offering to conjugal unreserve, and her own share in the story, under a colouring the least favourable to her and the most soothing to him, had in all likelihood been given also" (282; 2: ch. 15). The phrase "conjugal unreserve" captures the probability that in the privacy of their home, husband and wife mock their neighbors. The notion of conjugal unreserve offers a sharp contrast to the narrator's observation, "Seldom, very seldom, does complete truth belong to any human disclosure" (431; 3: ch. 13), when Emma and Mr. Knightley become engaged. Emma's silence then (and thereafter) about Harriet's crush on Mr. Knightley suggests that even in marriage, there can sometimes be greater virtue than total candor. Other married couples remain outside the novel's dramatic frame, but from distant glimpses, we suspect that Mr. and Mrs. Churchill exemplify husbandly weakness and wifely tyranny, and the Cole and Perry marriages give us hints of kindness and concern. Thus, without calling attention to the contrasts among marriages, the novel abounds in instances that invite comparison.

Another obvious parallel is the one between Emma's patronage of Harriet and Mrs. Elton's attempt to be "Lady Patroness" to Jane Fairfax. One effect of this pattern is to show the potential gravity and even repulsiveness of one woman's management of another's life; another effect is to make Emma seem less reprehensible in her interference than Mrs. Elton is in her intrusiveness. Devoney Looser's essay in this volume, "'A Very Kind Undertaking': *Emma* and Eighteenth-Century Feminism," provides insights into the relations—both historical and literary—between privileged women and their companions. Her essay suggests that Austen, entering a lively contemporary debate about the injustices done by domineering patronesses, implies in *Emma* that their power should be limited.

Several other parallels exist in the novels. One is in the relation of adult children to elderly parents—Emma to her father, Miss Bates to her mother, perhaps even Frank Churchill to his aunt. A second is between Frank and Jane Fairfax, who were both young when their mothers died and who were both brought up in households other than their own families'. There is a similarity between Anne Taylor, who was the governess in the Woodhouse family before the novel begins, and Jane Fairfax, who might have been the governess to the Smallridge family after it ends. In her essay "The Sexual Politics of *Emma*," Perry highlights the echo of Miss Taylor's situation in Jane Fairfax's.

The novelistic device of pairing characters is one Austen used with remarkable complexity in *Pride and Prejudice* and with fascinating redundancy in *Sense and Sensibility*. In *Emma* her technique of setting up characters as foils for one another is handled more dramatically and perhaps less obviously. As I've noted, Austen does not call attention to the parallels but lets the reader draw conclusions about the contrasts. I have found that when students discover parallels between characters and situations, they are immediately drawn to articulate differences. Discussion of Austen's inventiveness in exploring such patterns heightens students' appreciation of her artistry.

Debates and Duets

Yet another way to note the novel's careful patterning is to call students' attention to the conversations that could be called the book's "debates." Austen frequently constructs scenes in which pairs or groups of characters argue about specific issues. She uses such scenes with philosophical rigor and purposefulness in *Pride and Prejudice*. In *Emma*, too, much of the dialogue consists of disagreements on particular topics. Class discussion on the debates should probably come after students have read most of the first two volumes.

Austen's patient presentation of every speech in such conversations, in which motivated characters who argue not only from conviction but also in response to each other's arguments, makes these scenes among the most brilliant in the novel. The exchanges are so well dramatized that they spring to life when they are read aloud, and classroom discussion can consider which character is right—or which one seems more reasonable—and later, when students have finished the book, whose point of view is vindicated by the unfolding of the plot. Reading these scenes aloud and debating the issues will make them memorable to students and, therefore, heighten students' surprise when they discover that the point of view they favored on their first reading is defeated or at least qualified by the time they have reached the end of the novel.

The first of these debates occurs in chapter 1, when Emma argues with Mr. Knightley (and even argues a little with her father) about her plan to find a worthy partner for Mr. Elton. A few chapters later, Austen dramatizes a scene from which Emma is absent—one of a few instances in which Emma's consciousness is not the center of the narrative. This scene occurs in chapter 5, as George Knightley and Mrs. Weston argue about the meaning of Emma's friendship with Harriet Smith. Johnson observes that in this chapter, "Knightley and Mrs. Weston debate the wisdom of Emma's rule with the maturity and candor of opposition that mark so many of the disagreements in this novel" (*Jane Austen* 128). Mr. Knightley foresees potential dangers in the friendship, while Mrs. Weston expresses her satisfaction that Emma has found a new friend and her confidence that Emma "will make no lasting blunder" (40; 1: ch. 5).

The Mr. Knightley–Mrs. Weston debate in chapter 5 repays close attention, since many first-time readers assume that Mr. Knightley is entirely right in his apprehensions and that Mrs. Weston is misled by her affection for Emma. But one can argue that the novel vindicates the former governess. Johnson concludes that the novel "amply corroborates Mrs. Weston's faith in the fitness of Emma's rule." Her respect for Emma's judgment, Johnson says, is based not on "blind dependence on the infallibility of Emma's authority" but on a belief in its "basic soundness" (128). Mrs. Weston says that "where Emma errs once, she is in the right a hundred times," and "she has qualities which may be trusted" (40; 1: ch. 5). Johnson asserts that the novel abundantly demonstrates those trustworthy qualities.

Still, from the beginning of the novel to the end, the possibility remains that Emma might bring lasting harm to Harriet by her interference. The potential for disaster can make reading certain chapters in the first volume uncomfortable for students even while they recognize that the tone is comic. Beginning readers—and even experienced ones—sometimes cannot bear to watch Emma making mistakes with Harriet, Robert Martin, and Mr. Elton, mistakes that are all too apparent. Annette M. LeClair's essay in this volume, "Exploring Artist and Audience through Austen's 'Opinions of *Emma*,'" provides an excellent way to teach the scenes in which Emma decides to do Harriet's portrait. In addition, instructors can present LeClair's argument that these scenes give us a glimpse of Austen's own thinking about artistic creation and audience response. Finally, her essay may help defuse any discomfort students feel in reading the scenes.

However, students may believe that Emma is, like Frank (in Mr. Knightley's words), "[t]oo much indebted to the event for his acquittal" (445; 3: ch. 15). That is, the fact that things turn out well for Harriet does not mean that "this great intimacy between Emma and Harriet Smith," debated in chapter 5, was not "a bad thing" (36; 1: ch. 5). At the end, in fact, Emma has done no lasting harm to Harriet, and even Mr. Knightley agrees that Harriet has been "improved" by her friendship with Emma. Students themselves can weigh the evidence, brought forward by Mr. Knightley and Mrs. Weston in chapter 5, to decide whether Harriet's experience was, "[v]ery bad—though it might have been worse," as Mr. Knightley argues later about Frank's "most dangerous game" (445; 3: ch. 15). Thus the debate in chapter 5, which echoes throughout the novel, provides terms for pondering Austen's complex presentation of moral behavior in personal relations. Closely examining the debates—grasping the ways in which Austen seems to defeat generalization, easy moralizing, and simple solutions—helps students become the astute and subtle readers that the novel creates.

Students can examine almost any debate in the novel to see how the dilemma it explores evades a simple solution. Another example is Emma and Harriet's conversation in volume 1, chapter 10, about Emma's plan never to marry. The exchange supplies rich material for considering Austen's endorsement of Emma's authority (as Johnson, in *Jane Austen*, argues in her chapter on *Emma*), but it also reveals unconnected strands in Emma's thinking—we discover contradictions in her ideas about the likelihood of poverty narrowing a woman's mind or about the value of a niece. Likewise, some students may detect in Emma's protestations a psychological resistance to her own erotic interests or note that she invests a good deal of energy in her denial.

And although the narrator never invokes the term "an old maid," Harriet introduces it in this scene. Thus, while students can see that only a naive character would use that label, this conversation echoes as the novel unfolds. Class discussion of Emma's and Harriet's contrasting views on the desirability of marriage for women can lead students to understand the possible applications of the phrase to the writer herself. On the one hand, some students may respect Emma's sturdy self-confidence and independence and admire Austen for creating a character who intends to defy the anticipated trajectory for a heroine: Emma has "very little intention of ever marrying at all" (84; 1: ch. 10). Moreover, students may remind the class that Emma's vigorous assertions should counteract a tendency to feel sorry for Austen herself because she did not marry. Perry's essay on sexual politics, in fact, documents Austen's satisfaction in her life at Chawton, surrounded by women and sometimes enjoying the company of a niece. On the other hand, the ending of the novel, with its protracted working out of a compromise between passion and obligation, often makes readers think about the absence of such pleasure in the writer's life.

As the novel unfolds, however, alert readers can perceive that the security of all women, in whatever circumstance of marriage or singleness, is precarious: women who never marry (like Miss Bates), women whose marriages rescue them (like Miss Taylor, who becomes the second Mrs. Weston, or Augusta Hawkins, who is briefly courted and easily won by Mr. Elton), women who might never marry (like Jane Fairfax and Harriet Smith—unless Harriet grows "desperate, and is glad to catch at the old writing master's son" [65; 1: ch. 8]), and women who marry but die young—leaving a child or two behind (like Jane Bates Fairfax, Mrs. Woodhouse, and the first Mrs. Weston). Thus the naive Harriet's protests against Emma's determination not to marry resonate more deeply as we imagine how a woman (like Jane Fairfax, for instance) would live without the security of marriage or how a woman (like Emma herself, for instance) would live without the fulfillment of passionate love and marriage.

Further, the novel's preoccupation with matchmaking, one of Emma's activities that beginning readers might feel expected to deplore, may obscure its profound concern with the choices and circumstances that lead men and women to marry or to stay single. Explicit in Emma's thinking and talk is an interest in seeing unattached people as potential partners for other single people. But it is implicit in Mr. Knightley's speculation about Emma's declaration that she will never marry (41; 1: ch. 5), Mr. Elton's various courtships (real and imagined), Mr. and Mrs. Weston's hopes for his son, Mrs. Weston's and Mr. Cole's thoughts about Mr. Knightley as a suitor for Jane Fairfax, and in the secret plans that Jane Fairfax is induced to make with Frank. As a result, denunciations of Emma for her efforts at matchmaking seem out of touch with the novel's thoughtful treatment of characters struggling to make such decisions or adapt to their circumstances. Consideration of these issues can emerge from classroom analysis of the chapter 10 debate between Emma and Harriet about women and marriage.

Rich possibilities for discussion are present, in fact, in all the debates. Emma's exchange with Mr. Knightley about Harriet's rejection of Robert Martin (vol. 1, ch. 7) offers resonant, complicated material about social status in Highbury. Emma's sprightly voice and her claim that she has a special insight into "female right and refinement" play off Mr. Knightley's impassioned defense of Martin's mind and manners and his vigorous denunciation of Emma's "nonsense, errant nonsense, as ever was talked!" These highly motivated antagonists respond to each other's arguments and assert their own claims, but students—in class discussion or in written assignments—can discern in the disagreement implications about the social world of Highbury. Their debate reveals the contours of certain boundaries, and it suggests a good deal about the connections between members of the community. Figuring out these boundaries and interconnections will richly repay students who do the analysis. The essay by Carol M. Dole in this volume, "Classless, Clueless: *Emma* Onscreen," explains how teachers can pair the two cinematic costume-drama versions of the debate. The British work places the argument indoors as an angry confrontation that emphasizes Emma's and Mr. Knightley's profoundly different assessments of Harriet's class status. The American production, borrowing a trope from the 1940 *Pride and Prejudice* film, sets the argument outdoors in an archery practice, where physical comedy and lush lawns distract the viewer from the seriousness of the disagreement. Dole uses such pairings from the two films to contrast the directors' implicit attitudes toward social class in the novel.

Teachers can instruct students reading the debate about Harriet's rejection of Martin to look for insights on the persistence of feudal relations between landlord and tenant, the importance of a woman's education and birth, the qualities that make a woman attractive as a wife, and the traits that give dignity and respectability to a family that Emma disdains as the "yeomanry." Laura Mooneyham White's essay in this volume, "The Experience of Class, *Emma*, and the American College Student," explores social class in Highbury through analysis of issues implicit in this debate. White offers excellent suggestions for helping egalitarian students in the twenty-first century grasp both the malleable and the durable aspects of English class structure.

A pair of conversations that can be taught together occur when Emma takes opposite sides of the same question: Why has Frank Churchill not visited his father? When Emma argues with Mrs. Weston about Frank's failure, she takes the position that he ought to have come and that he could have come if he had tried (122; 1: ch. 14). When she argues with Mr. Knightley, she takes the opposite position: she "found herself directly involved in a disagreement with Mr. Knightley; and to her great amusement, perceived that she was taking the other side of the question from her real opinion, and making use of Mrs. Weston's arguments against herself" (145; 1: ch. 18).

This funny passage and the well-developed arguments on both sides of the question might lead teachers to ask, Which arguments seem to have greater merit before you meet Frank Churchill? Which ones seem most correct to you when you have finished the novel? Incidentally, why would someone argue opposite sides of a question in two different conversations? Is the ability to argue both sides of an issue the sign of mental vigor? inconsistent thinking? youth? flexibility? uncertainty? Which reason for Emma's inconsistent positions makes most sense to you? What motivates Emma's opponents in these arguments to take the positions they do? Are they disinterested debaters? What hidden reasons do Mrs. Weston and Mr. Knightley have for their opinions?

Johnson, in her essay "'Not at All What a Man Should Be!': Remaking English Manhood in *Emma*," examines the novel's inquiry into proper masculine behavior, arguing that the "novel works . . . to redefine masculinity" (*Equivocal Beings* 199). Language in the two debates about Frank's failure to visit his father supports Johnson's argument: both Emma (with Mrs. Weston) and Mr. Knightley (with Emma) argue that as a *man*, Frank must have freedom to make the visit. Emma says, "He ought to come . . . and one can hardly conceive a young man's not having it in his power to do as much as that. A young *woman*, if she fall into bad hands, may be . . . kept at a distance from those she wants to be with; but one cannot comprehend a young *man's* being under such restraint, as not to be able to spend a week with his father, if he likes it" (122; 1: ch. 14). Likewise, Mr. Knightley argues vigorously that Frank has an obligation as a man to "pay this attention to his father": "There is one thing, Emma, which a man can always do if he chuses, and that is, his duty; not by manœuvring and finessing, but by vigour and resolution." He adds, "Depend upon it,

Emma, a sensible man would find no difficulty in it. He would feel himself in the right; and the declaration—made, of course, as a man of sense would make it, in a proper manner—would do him more good . . . than all that a line of shifts and expedients can ever do" (146, 147; 1: ch. 18).

Looking at these two debates as a pair can lead the class to consider Johnson's argument about the exploration of gender in *Emma*. According to Johnson, the novel "basically accepts as attractive and as legitimate Emma's forcefulness," but what "true" masculinity is like—"what a 'man' is, how a man speaks and behaves, what a man really wants—is the subject of continual debate" (196). Johnson's essay offers a refreshing perspective on Austen's originality in reconceiving virtue in both men and women. "*Emma* disdains not only the effeminacy of men, but also the femininity of women," she says (202). The exchanges about Frank Churchill's failure to visit his father, then, can be placed in the context of Austen's examination of proper masculine behavior, as well as her interest in Emma's authority.

Two other conversations, not really debates but more like duets, make an intriguing contrast to each other and might be considered with the debates. They are the two encounters, at the Hartfield dinner party for the Eltons, between a man and a woman who are not romantic partners but friends (or acquaintances). The first dialogue is the deeply moving conversation between John Knightley and Jane Fairfax (292–94; 2: ch. 16); the second is the comic dueling monologues of Mr. Weston and Mrs. Elton (305–10; 2: ch. 18). These two encounters, taking place at one event, reveal a striking contrast in the level of genuine listening.

In the first, John Knightley begins with the perfunctory kindness of an inquiry to Jane Fairfax about her trip to the post office. Soon, however, his habitual attitude of resistant sociability makes him denigrate letters—either of business or of friendship. Jane Fairfax's carefully worded replies guard her chief secret but reveal her dependence on distant friends: "I can easily believe that letters are very little to you, much less than to me, but it is not your being ten years older than myself which makes the difference, it is not age, but situation. You have every body dearest to you always at hand, I, probably, never shall again." Her distinctive voice—with its mix of restraint, exactitude, resignation, and frankly expressed vulnerability—touches John Knightley enough to make him reach beyond his own point of view and his own grumpy feelings about the value of letters. He corrects the erroneous impression he has created, and rephrases his prediction: "When I talked of your being altered by time, . . . I meant to imply the change of situation which time usually brings. . . . As an old friend, you will allow me to hope, Miss Fairfax, that ten years hence you may have as many concentrated objects as I have." Because he has heard what she says, he makes a comment of such courteous kindness that "a blush, a quivering lip, a tear in the eye, shewed that it was felt beyond a laugh" (294; 2: ch. 16). She discerns the real feeling and sincere wishes for her in the way he explains himself. Far from offending her, his empathy almost makes her cry.

In striking contrast to this genuine communication between two sentient speakers, the conversation between Mr. Weston and Mrs. Elton is a comic glimpse of two self-absorbed speakers seizing on details of each other's speeches to return to their favorite topics and to continue undeterred on their own trains of thought. Mr. Weston doggedly pursues his preoccupation with his son, with Frank's plans for visiting Highbury, and with the obstacles created by Frank's aunt, Mrs. Churchill. Mrs. Elton even more doggedly pursues her determination to trot out her connection to Mr. Suckling and Maple Grove, her sister Selina, her championing of the female sex, and the "resources" that ensure she can be "quite independent of society." Mr. Weston rises to the occasion at one point, when he hears Mrs. Elton's loud bray for a compliment. He responds "with a very good grace" and gives her the desired assurances. But then, he "had done his duty and could return to his son." A few exchanges later, when Mrs. Elton is "stopped by a slight fit of coughing," Mr. Weston "instantly seized on the opportunity of going on" (307, 308; 2: ch. 18). Stimulated by such hilarious moments as this, read aloud to illuminate the subtleties of Austen's comic sense, students can offer lively reminiscences and anecdotes from their own experience.

Both of these conversations proceed with a minimum of intervention by the narrator; character is revealed almost entirely through dialogue. In class, a teacher can set up a trio of readers to take the parts of the two characters and the narrator and read some or all of these exchanges aloud. As with the debates, hearing these dialogues as little dramas can supply students with abundant material for discussion of personality, of the various experiences of conversation, and of Austen's success in fully imagining such distinctive characters.

Emma's Moments of Awakening

A powerful way to indicate the novel's deepening seriousness and its tracing of the heroine's increasing knowledge of herself is to compare the three scenes in which Emma goes through a moment of solitary self-examination. Students can observe differences among the three scenes in the language describing Emma's feelings, in the length of time her anguish continues, and in the effectiveness of the resolutions she makes. In the first of the scenes, after she discovers that Mr. Elton is courting her, not Harriet, Emma ponders her errors and "blunders" (an important word in the book) and is "quite concerned and ashamed, and resolved to do such things no more" (137; 1: ch. 16). The language here is serious but mild.

In an analysis of Emma's mental turmoil, defensiveness, and, finally, self-criticism, Dorice Williams Elliott traces Austen's mastery of free indirect discourse to move into and out of Emma's mind. At night Emma is shocked at her mistake and ashamed of herself; in the morning her spirits improve: "To youth and natural cheerfulness like Emma's, though under temporary gloom at night, the return of day will hardly fail to bring return of spirits" (137; 1: ch. 16). Thus her suffering is real, but its duration here is not long.

The second moment when we follow Emma's thoughts at a time of self-reproach comes after Mr. Knightley's remonstrance at Box Hill, discussed in the essays of Bromberg, Grossman, and Perry ("Sexual Politics"). In this scene, the language is far more severe than in the earlier one. Emma feels "anger against herself, mortification, and deep concern. . . . She was vexed beyond what could have been expressed—almost beyond what she could conceal. Never had she felt so agitated, mortified, grieved, at any circumstance in her life. She was most forcibly struck. . . . Time did not compose her. . . . She never had been so depressed" (375–76; 3: ch. 7). The language echoes and reverses the novel's opening paragraph, which portrays a young woman, almost twenty-one, "with very little to distress or vex her." To the repeated language of mortification—of profound embarrassment—is added the notion of depression, an experience that is accurately associated with an acute loss of self-esteem, and morning brings little dissipation of her anguish. Emma's resolution the next day to make amends to Miss Bates is deeply felt and decisive.

Finally, when Emma discovers that Harriet believes herself to be loved by Mr. Knightley, Emma's shame and self-criticism become intense. Through many paragraphs of examination and anguish, Emma reviews the past and her behavior, and the language of her self-reproach is categorical: "With insufferable vanity had she believed herself in the secret of everybody's feelings; with unpardonable arrogance proposed to arrange everybody's destiny" (412–13; 3: ch. 11). The long day and night of remorse go on for pages of continuing reflection and suffering. The far-reaching resolution with which they conclude is this: "the only source whence any thing like consolation or composure could be drawn, was in the resolution of her own better conduct, and the hope that, however inferior in spirit and gaiety might be the following and every future winter of her life to the past, it would yet find her more rational, more acquainted with herself, and leave her less to regret when it were gone" (423; 3: ch. 12). Fearing she has done irreparable harm to herself and to Mr. Knightley, Emma makes a chastened resolution to conduct herself better in the future, no matter how bleak her situation may be for the rest of her life. Elliott's essay suggests that when students sort out elements of interior monologue, psychonarration, and free indirect discourse in these scenes, they gain understanding of Austen's achievement as a literary artist.

The Structure and Purposes of the Last Chapters

A final discussion of the novel's structure can take place after students have finished the work. The discussion might begin with this question: Why does the novel continue for fifty pages (434–84) after the traditional resolution of the comic novel—the engagement of the main characters? What other issues are resolved in the long coda, and how does Austen's construction of chapters 14–19 of volume 3 undermine, defeat, or fulfill readers' expectations?

One important purpose of the last chapters is, of course, to bring the stories of Harriet Smith and Robert Martin and of Jane Fairfax and Frank Churchill to satisfying conclusions. The continuing anguish Emma feels even in her moments of greatest happiness, after reaching an understanding with Mr. Knightley, is poignantly connected to Harriet. Repeatedly, the discomfort readers may experience at Emma's interference in Harriet's life in volume 1 is played out again in Emma's mind, even more intensely after her engagement (434–35; 3: ch. 14); (451; 3: ch. 16); (470; 3: ch. 18). Emma cannot fully rejoice in her own happiness because she feels such a strong "sense of injustice, of guilt, of something most painful, which had haunted her when remembering how disappointed a heart was near her" (451).

Emma's discovery that Harriet is engaged to Robert Martin occasions the most effusive language of happiness in the book, reflecting the relief Emma feels that she did not, after all, ruin Harriet's life: "She was in dancing, singing, exclaiming spirits; and till she had moved about, and talked to herself, and laughed and reflected, she could be fit for nothing rational. . . . The joy, the gratitude, the exquisite delight of her sensations may be imagined. The sole grievance and alloy thus removed in the prospect of Harriet's welfare, she was really in danger of becoming too happy for security" (475; 3: ch. 18). Readers sometimes incorrectly remember these lines as a description of Emma's happiness at discovering that Mr. Knightley loves her. Rather, they describe Emma's joyous relief that her egregious mistakes with Harriet have not caused irreparable harm.

Frank Churchill's letter and the three meetings with Jane Fairfax (first Mrs. Weston's, then Emma's, and finally the reunion at Randalls of Jane, Frank, and Emma) all provide the satisfying denouements that Austen is so good at—in conversations that review events to reveal how characters whose feelings had been hidden experienced them. The healing of hurt between Emma and Jane is a particular relief, and Jane's explicit apologies to Emma lessen Emma's responsibility in not reaching out in friendship to Jane. Although, as Ruth Perry points out, in "Sexual Politics," Emma and Jane will be separated by their marriages, Austen allows them explicitly to clarify the past, and their look back implicitly appeases the reader's longing for a connection between the characters. The hidden layers of Jane's and Frank's motives, timing, and moods after the Box Hill outing become comprehensible. In retrospect, Mr. Perry's reported words about Jane's suffering seem extremely painful (389; 3: ch. 9): we now know that she had decided in total isolation to break the engagement. But students may detect something ominous for the future of Mr. and Mrs. Frank Churchill in his continuing playfulness and in his epicurean delight in giving Mrs. Churchill's jewels to his beloved. Especially disturbing may be these words: "I am resolved to have some [jewels] in an ornament for the head," he says. "Will it not be beautiful in her dark hair?" (479; 3: ch. 18).

Finally, the solution to the problem for Emma of fulfilling her responsibility to her father while also marrying the man she loves is worked out with fascinating originality in the last chapters. Parker points out that it is Mr. Knightley, the "daring imaginist," who comes up with a solution to Emma's desire for an "unconventional plot that would allow her both to be a dutiful daughter and to gain a loving husband." Here again, Johnson, in *Jane Austen*, offers a way to discuss the novel's design with students who might be tempted to call the ending "conventional" or even "conservative"—the marriage of the most privileged man and woman in Highbury. According to Johnson, Mr. Knightley's offer to solve the problem of Emma's "filial piety" by moving to Hartfield represents an extraordinary concession of his traditional authority. "Emma and Knightley do not have to bend to the yoke of conventions that do not suit them, and neither, within limits of course, does Austen. . . . Emma and Knightley yet have their separate concerns, their separate realms, their separate rule. . . . [E]ccentricity is one of the privileges of the elite, and in this case it permits the hero and heroine to be husband and wife yet live and rule together with the autonomy of friends" (142–43). Johnson argues that Austen confidently endorses Emma's authority even after marriage, and she suggests why the impulse to criticize or humiliate or punish Emma for her mistakes defies the spirit of the novel—a spirit demonstrated in its profoundly unconventional ending.

John Wiltshire's essay "Health, Comfort, and Creativity: A Reading of *Emma*" is placed last in this volume because of its remarkable achievement in discovering patterns of meaning in Austen's complex use of one word—in this instance, "comfort." Wiltshire's essay offers a resounding conclusion to our many approaches to teaching Austen's *Emma*: "There are many different ways in which the humor, the intricacy, the vigor of *Emma* can be brought out to new readers. . . . But there is no way around the fact that *Emma* addresses issues of physical, psychological, even moral health that are vital to life itself."

As I have described ways of teaching about the structure of the novel across the novel, I have inevitably looked at specific scenes and chapters; seeing the big picture always relies on the reading of moments in the text. But examining recurring patterns is a great help to students and teachers who are trying to encompass the entire novel and to appreciate the magnificence of the book as a whole. Even more important, discussions about the overall structure of the narrative should assist instructors in counteracting the fatal tendency to go deeply into every scene as it occurs. Such an approach is impossible because no one—in any course or in any reading—has enough time to do justice to every line, every scene, every speech, every character, and every conversation in this astonishing novel.

NOTE

[1]All page references to passages from *Emma* are to the 1933 Oxford third edition, edited by R. W. Chapman, with revisions by Mary Lascelles (1966), and reprinted in 1987. The numeral before the semicolon is the page number (continuous throughout the book, 5–484). To aid readers using a different edition, the volume number and chapter number from Chapman are also given (the work is in 3 volumes: chs. 1–18, 1–18, and 1–19).

Part One

MATERIALS

Editions

The standard collection of all Jane Austen's novels is the Oxford, edited by R. W. Chapman and originally published by the Clarendon Press, Oxford, in 1923. The third edition (1932–34) of the five-volume set, with revisions by Mary Lascelles (1963–69), has been frequently reprinted. (A sixth volume, Austen's *Minor Works*, was issued in 1954; Brian C. Southam subsequently added revisions, 1963–69.) My set is the 1987 reprinting. The text of *Emma* is in volume 4 of *The Novels of Jane Austen*, along with Chapman's "Introductory Note to *Emma*," nine illustrations, notes to the text, notes on the illustrations, and four appendixes: "Chronology of *Emma*," "The Manners of the Age," "Punctuation," and "Index of Characters, etc." The notes to the text include emendations proposed and explained by Chapman, as well as emendations from Chapman's notes added by Lascelles in 1966. The notes also contain Chapman's identification of some of the text's literary allusions.

As Chapman pointed out, the "sole authority for the text is the edition of 1816" ("Notes" 489), the first published version, and he noted that "the text of *Emma* presents few difficulties to an editor. The edition of 1816 is well printed, and very little correction is necessary" (xi). Modern paperback editions of *Emma* abound—some decidedly inferior in paper and printing, but all indebted to the Chapman edition. For college courses, the three logical choices are the Norton Critical Edition, edited by Stephen Parrish; the Bedford-St. Martin's edition, edited by Alistair Duckworth, in the series Case Studies in Contemporary Criticism; and the Penguin Classics Edition, edited by Fiona Stafford. The Norton Critical and Bedford-St. Martin's editions have valuable appendixes and well-chosen critical materials that offer rich possibilities for classroom discussion and student writing. Because the Penguin Classics *Emma*, first printed in 1996, has a fine introduction and notes by Stafford, is less expensive than the other two, and includes no other critical material, it may be the appropriate choice in some courses. At the beginning of each chapter and at the top of even-numbered pages, the Penguin Classics edition identifies the text's original division into volumes (1–3) and chapters numbered separately by volume. Sequential chapter numbers (1–55) appear at the top of odd-numbered pages.

I have used the Norton Critical Edition for some time, and I chose it because of its retention of the three-volume division, its readable print, and its selection of critical essays. The Bedford-St. Martin's edition (2002) also keeps the three-volume division, and in part 2 offers six approaches to the novel: gender criticism, Marxist criticism, cultural criticism, new-historicist criticism, feminist criticism, and a combined approach. Duckworth provides helpful annotation in the text; his introduction, "Biographical and Historical Contexts," contains a lucid review of Austen's life; and his Critical History of *Emma*, at the end of the text, is an excellent study of approaches to the novel from the time of its publication to the end of the twentieth century.

In addition, the St. Martin's edition contains many materials that I have been accustomed to using in class: the pages from Austen's *Minor Works* called "Opinions of *Emma*" (also in this volume); a sample of Austen's letter writing, in which she "fills a page and crosses half" (157; 2: ch. 1) to show what Miss Bates means about Jane Fairfax's letters (I usually bring *Jane Austen's Manuscript Letters*, a facsimile edition edited by Jo Modert, to class); and a picture of a Broadwood piano (I use a photograph from the *Boston Globe* of a Broadwood on display at the Museum of Fine Arts). Also helpful are several illustrations: pictures of a barouche landau, a painting of Box Hill, and a painting of a Lincolnshire ox (in honor of Emma's naughty remark to Mr. Knightley that Robert Martin had been telling him about the dimensions of some "famous ox" rather than about his engagement to Harriet Smith) (473; 3: ch. 18).

The critical essays that appear after the text in both the third Norton Critical and the Bedford-St. Martin's editions provide ready access to some of the most significant writing about *Emma*. Among the essays are several that teachers might assign or recommend to students. Each of these editions includes an essay by Claudia Johnson ("Woman, Lovely Woman" in the Norton; "Not At All What a Man Should Be" in the Bedford-St. Martin's). The Norton contains important early criticism of Austen, a few of Austen's letters, a selection from the fragment *The Watsons* (an earlier version of the novel), several recent essays of criticism, and a brief chronology. The apparatus for comparing the six critical approaches, each exemplified in a modern essay, make the Bedford-St. Martin's edition especially useful for upper-division English majors and perhaps graduate students. The Bedford-St. Martin's edition will appeal to teachers who use the novel in courses on critical theory; the Norton may be more attractive to teachers who place the book in a history of the novel. I think both editions have much to offer. Probably, because of the length of the novel itself, most teachers of *Emma* in undergraduate courses assign few if any critical readings. For many courses, then, the Penguin Classics edition may be the best choice. Teachers, however, may want to own and use both critical editions.

The Chapman third edition—the definitive set of Austen's works—is the one scholars use; because its pagination doesn't change, it is the one to which references in this book are made. But since many teachers may not have the Chapman edition, citations also include volume and chapter numbers. This mode of citation is somewhat cumbersome, but it should be helpful to teachers introducing students to a novel that exists in many editions.

Criticism

Duckworth's excellent review of the history of *Emma* criticism ("Critical History of *Emma*") follows the divisions in the history of Austen criticism laid out in *The Jane Austen Companion* (Grey, Litz, and Southam). The first period extends from 1813 to 1870, when James Edward Austen-Leigh published *A Memoir of Jane Austen*. During this time, only a few perceptive comments on *Emma* appeared, notably those by Walter Scott, George Henry Lewes (cited in this volume by Elliott), and Richard Whateley, archbishop of Dublin. In general, however, Duckworth notes (as do the editors of the *Companion*), for the fifty years after Austen's death, her novels were given little serious or valuable critical attention.

During the second period, from 1870 to 1940, more commentary on Austen's work appeared, but it was dominated by "genteel appreciations and antiquarian interest" (Litz, "Criticism," *Companion* 110). The two most important notices of Austen's work in those seventy years were the superb essay by Reginald Farrer in 1917 on the hundredth anniversary of her death (mentioned in my preface to this volume) and the publication of Chapman's monumental Clarendon edition of the novels, in 1923. "Only seldom in the period 1870 to 1940 do we encounter criticism of high order" (Duckworth 409).

But with the publication of Mary Lascelles's path-breaking academic study, *Jane Austen and Her Art* (1939), most of the serious criticism of *Emma* began. In mid-century, F. R. Leavis included Austen in *The Great Tradition* (1948), as did Ian Watt in *The Rise of the Novel* (1957). These influential books granted Austen a place in the literary canon by illuminating her technical innovations and examining her works in relation to her predecessors' in the history of the novel. The famous essay by D. W. Harding, "Regulated Hatred" (1940), attacked the "gentle Jane" school of thought, discovering in Austen a subversive writer whose irony was directed at the very people who admired her novels. Harding's view of Austen as socially subversive anticipated the writing of Marvin Mudrick and others.

Marxist critics of Austen, like Raymond Williams (*The Country and the City*, 1973) and James Thompson (*Between Self and World*, 1988), found new ways of looking at Austen's novels and were particularly interested in decoding the social structures implied in *Emma*'s portrayal of village life. Other critics discerned evidence of class mobility and financial struggle beneath the comedy. David Spring's influential essay (with the uncatchy title), "Interpreters of Jane Austen's Social World: Literary Critics and Historians" (1983), introduced the term "pseudo-gentry" to describe the Austen family's social class. Spring's success in identifying a stratum between gentry and professional broadened the considerations of Austen's own social class. In his book *Women Writing about Money* (1995) and in other places, Edward Copeland analyzes Austen's changing views of the consumer and commodity culture emerging in the early nineteenth century. His essay "The Economic Realities of Jane Austen's Day" proposed startling, graphic ways to comprehend the levels of wealth in Austen's novels.

In *Jane Austen and the War of Ideas* (1975), Marilyn Butler argued that Austen stood in opposition to the radical ideas of the revolutionary 1790s and that her novels both implicitly and explicitly endorse conservative values, such as the confinement of women to a limited sphere. Mary Poovey elaborated on that viewpoint in *The Proper Lady and the Woman Writer* (1984), a study of the 1790s, when Austen was in her twenties, Mary Wollstonecraft died, and Mary Shelley was born. Like Butler, Poovey emphasized Austen's conservatism in her celebration of marriage. Feminist criticism of Austen, which really started with Sandra Gilbert and Susan Gubar's *Madwoman in the Attic* (1979), has used a broad range of strategies to contest Butler's view. Stressing Austen's "cover story," Gilbert and Gubar asserted that although Austen seems to endorse the quelling of women's energy, her resentment of the necessity of female compliance appears in disguise in the disruptive power of such women as Lady Catherine in *Pride and Prejudice* and Mrs. Norris in *Mansfield Park*. Interestingly enough, Butler generously reviewed those arguments in a new introduction to her book, in 1987.

Other critics—Margaret Kirkham and Alison Sulloway—find evidence of an affirmative feminist attitude in Austen's novels, in which she celebrates women as morally complex beings, deserving of education, authority, and legal rights. I have written before (in the introduction to *Approaches to Teaching Austen's* Pride and Prejudice 21) about Julia Prewitt Brown's excellent essay "The Feminist Depreciation of Jane Austen." According to Brown, Austen's lack of support among feminist critics "hinges on the question of marriage," which they had found too limited and restrictive a resolution for a great novel. In response, Brown—grounding her argument on the social history of marriage and the family—located Austen's feminism in a philosophical stance like Wollstonecraft's: an emphasis on education, on activity beyond the self, and on society as a whole rather than on the individual and on personal freedom.

The writings of Claudia Johnson have substantially influenced recent criticism of Austen; my introduction and my essay here, "'I Wish We Had a Donkey': Small-Group Work and Writing Assignments for *Emma*," acknowledge my debt to her thinking. Her two groundbreaking essays on *Emma* first appeared as parts of books: "Woman, Lovely Woman" is a chapter in *Jane Austen: Women, Politics, and the Novel* (1988); "Not At All What a Man Should Be" is the afterword to *Equivocal Beings* (1995). In the first essay, Johnson vigorously denounces the criticism of *Emma*—written primarily by men—suggesting that the heroine needs correction and even deserves punishment for her pleasure in exerting power. In the second essay, Johnson presents the surprising notion that in *Emma*, Austen is more concerned with defining appropriate masculine behavior than proper female behavior.

Perry's second essay in this volume is a revision of her early feminist essay, "Interrupted Friendships in Jane Austen's *Emma*" (1986). In the original and revised essays, Perry explores the unsatisfactory relationship between Emma and Jane Fairfax as evidence that the exigences of the "marriage plot" prevented Austen from imagining the full potential of friendship between women. For this volume Looser revised the essay she contributed to the Bedford-

St. Martin's edition of *Emma* on Austen's feminism. Keeping in mind the historical context of Austen's writing, Looser turns her attention to Emma's relations with other women and considers the novel's implications about the appropriate bonds between women and especially between privileged women and their less-privileged companions.

David Monaghan's Emma: *Contemporary Critical Essays* contains ten of the most significant essays on *Emma* written between 1971 and 1988; some were originally published as essays and others as chapters in books. Monaghan's introduction, an intelligent, thoughtful review of Austen scholarship, places the essays clearly in their ideological categories: New Criticism, and historical, structuralist, poststructuralist, Marxist, feminist, and reader-response criticism. In his analysis of the theoretical underpinnings of the essays, Monaghan provides a helpful guide to the sources and nuances of the various approaches, and he does not hesitate to point out inconsistencies or even absurdities in the essays he has anthologized.

In his book *Jane Austen: Structure and Social Vision* (1980), Monaghan includes a chapter on *Emma*—a persuasive argument about the stagnation of the Highbury community at the opening of the novel. Social rituals regenerate the community, he believes, and free up Emma to change. Monaghan's discussion informs my suggestions for teaching the eight major scenes.

John Wiltshire's *Jane Austen and the Body* (1992) takes its subtitle, *The Picture of Health*, from *Emma*. The excellent chapter on *Emma* investigates a topic that has received little scholarly coverage: the attention Austen pays to the body, to physical health, and to emotional wholeness. In his more recent study, *Recreating Jane Austen* (2001), Wiltshire considers *Emma*'s role "in the contemporary cultural imagination." He notes the immense popularity of the Austen films of the 1990s (and the remarkable appearance of three *Emma* movies in 1995 and 1996: Amy Heckerling's endearing send-up of *Emma* in *Clueless*; Douglas McGrath's *Emma*, starring Gwyneth Paltrow; and Diarmuid Lawrence's *Emma*, featuring Kate Beckinsale). Indeed, the phenomenon of Austen films led Wiltshire to ponder the "nature and status of 'Jane Austen' in our culture." Wiltshire's book draws freely on these films and on others that allude to Austen. In its bold use of psychoanalytic theory, vivid personal response, and thoughtful scholarship, the work offers fascinating readings of Austen's novels; it is particularly good on contrasts between *Emma* the text and *Emma* the films. The book suggests how inexhaustible Austen's works are as we teach them at new times in our lives and, inevitably, at new times in the world.

Books of Particular Use to Teachers

Certain books are especially important for teachers of *Emma*, and I would recommend the following for teachers who have time to prepare extensively. *The*

Cambridge Companion to Jane Austen, edited by Edward Copeland and Juliet McMaster, is an excellent reference work. The valuable essay on *Mansfield Park*, *Emma*, and *Persuasion* by Wiltshire places *Emma* in the context of the novels Austen wrote just before and after it. Wiltshire compares the social, physical, and conceptual worlds of Austen's last three novels and captures the distinctive tone of wit, optimism, energy, and warmth of this novel, in contrast to its predecessor and successor. McMaster's essay on class, Copeland's on money, and John F. Burrows's on style are well written and informative.

I still read and value *The Jane Austen Companion* (1986) edited by J. David Grey, A. Walton Litz, and Brian Southam. This older "companion" is a compendium of sixty-five short essays written by outstanding scholars on a wide range of topics. Titles include, for example, "Jane Austen and Bath," "Dancing, Balls, and Assemblies," "Education," "Games," "Houses," "Letters and Correspondence," "Jane Austen and London," "Medicine," "Military," "Pets and Animals," and "Jane Austen's Reading." The book is reliable, well written, and rich.

Indispensable resources for the serious reader and a great help to teachers are two works edited by Deirdre Le Faye. One is *Jane Austen, a Family Record*, Le Faye's completion of *Jane Austen, Her Life and Letters*, compiled and published in 1913 by William Austen-Leigh and Richard Arthur Austen-Leigh. Le Faye painstakingly revised and enlarged their work after consultation with family archives, letters, journals, and memoirs, to produce a definitive source for all Austen biographies. The other recommended Le Faye work is *Jane Austen's Letters* (1995), which she annotated with astounding attention to detail (the volume is entered in the works-cited list under "Austen").

Of all the modern biographies of Austen, I am most convinced by (and grateful to) Claire Tomalin's *Jane Austen: A Life*, a perceptive exploration of the Austen family and its forebears; the worlds of Steventon, Bath, and London; the relation between the juvenilia and later works; and the social dynamics of Austen's childhood friends, kin, and neighborhood. The biography will appeal to students who are curious about Austen's life and world, and specific chapters might be assigned for student presentations. Among critical books on Austen by a single author, I return most often to Johnson's *Jane Austen* and to Wiltshire's *Jane Austen and the Body*. Both are inspired and inspiring books by brilliant scholars. *Jane Austen: A Literary Life*, by Jan Fergus, provides essential background on the conditions for authorship in the late eighteenth century. Fergus places Austen's literary accomplishments in the context of publishing as a *business*, book production, audiences, libraries, apprenticeship, and payments and commissions. A fairly short book, it is packed with information that will make Austen's achievement more understandable to students—and more remarkable than ever to experienced readers.

The *Emma* Films

In most courses instructors do not have time to show complete movies, but in Film and Fiction or in a film studies course, teachers might show parts of the three *Emma* movies released in 1995 and 1996. Books and articles on the cinematic *Emma* are also available. The collection *Jane Austen in Hollywood*, edited by Linda Troost and Sayre Greenfield, contains thirteen essays, many of high quality, employing the language of literary criticism and of film studies. The book is essential reading for teachers who play any of the Austen films in class. Two essays in the collection are specifically about film adaptations of *Emma*, and several others offer insights into the difficulties, successes, and oddities of the many attempts to render *Emma* in the truncated form of a two-hour film. Carol Dole's essay in the Troost and Greenfield work sorts out some of the problems of presenting British social class in Austen films aimed at an American mass market. The collection includes an excellent bibliography, "Selected Reviews, Articles, and Books on the Films, 1995–1997." Among those titles cited is a memorable comment by Louis Menand.

Dole has also contributed an essay to the present volume; she suggests that teachers show excerpts of the two costume-drama versions of *Emma* in class and ask students to compare them with passages from the novel. Dole's succinct summaries of the directors' techniques in filming the scenes can serve as keys to underlying assumptions of each movie. Dole also explains why Heckerling's *Clueless* is truer to the spirit of Austen's project than the other two movies. An assignment that Dole recommends is to have students write screenplays of a scene, as a way to explore the difficulties in making a cinematic version of *Emma*.

Teaching about *Emma*'s Chronology

As I explain in the introduction, the chronology of *Emma* is carefully constructed, although Austen does not call attention to the dates and days that she had figured out so precisely. An extensive chronology like the one that follows would probably not be helpful to first-time readers of *Emma*, because it might imply that they should concentrate on certain details rather than on bigger issues of the novel's structure. Instead, teachers can point out (and students will be intrigued to learn) that Austen conceived of the novel as taking place over fourteen months, during which Emma must have had a birthday, so that she would be twenty-one when she marries. But I include this detailed chronology for the benefit of teachers, and students who are rereading the book, because it suggests so much about Austen's way of conceiving the connection between the passage of time and Emma's growth into adulthood.

The Chronology of *Emma*

September

The action begins late in September (details in the novel fit the years 1813–14). Miss Taylor and Mr. Weston get married (6; 1: ch. 1). Emma will have "many a long October and November evening" to be "struggled through" until the John Knightleys come at Christmas (7; 1: ch. 1). Frank Churchill's letter on Mr. Weston's marriage is dated 28 September (96; 1: ch. 11).

October and November

Unfolding friendship of Harriet and Emma, involvement of Mr. Elton (vol. 1, chs. 4–15).

December

Emma's stratagem at the vicarage was the "middle of December" (83; 1: ch. 10). Dinner at Randalls is Friday, Christmas Eve (108; 1: ch. 13); Saturday is Christmas (138; 1: ch. 16); Sunday (138) is 26 December. The John Knightleys' Christmas visit is to last ten days, and since John Knightley must be back in town on 28 December (79; 1: ch. 9), the family is to leave on Monday, 27 December. Mr. Elton sends a note on the "evening of the very day on which they went," saying that he would leave "the following morning" (140; 1: ch. 17), so he departs on 28 December.

January

George Knightley argues that Frank Churchill might have found a time to visit his father "between September and January" (145; 1: ch. 18). On Wednesday, 26 January, Emma hears of Mr. Elton's engagement (173; 2: ch. 3), after, as Miss Bates says, "he has been gone just four weeks . . . four weeks yesterday" (176; 2: ch. 3).

February

Mr. Elton returns to Highbury the first week of February (181; 2: ch. 4). Emma hears that Frank Churchill is to arrive the next day and will stay a "fortnight" (two weeks) (188; 2: ch. 5). Mr. Elton goes back to Bath on the same day Frank arrives (186, 190; 2: ch. 5), a Wednesday (221; 2: ch. 8), making it 9 February. After two days in Highbury, Frank goes to London on Saturday for a haircut (205; 2: ch. 7). Jane receives a pianoforte on Monday—14 February, Valentine's Day, although the narrator does not mention the date (214–15; 2: ch. 8). The Coles' dinner party is Tuesday, 15 February. At the party, Frank tells Emma that he has already stayed "a week to-morrow—half my time" (221). Frank leaves Highbury the following Tuesday (22 Feb.), which Modert points out is Shrove Tuesday. The date of the holy day would explain why the Eltons marry so hurriedly, since weddings were not performed during Lent. Later, Mr. Weston mentions to Mrs. Elton that Frank "was here before," in February (309; 2: ch. 18).

March

Emma remembers (with embarrassment) being in the vicarage "three months ago, to lace up her boot" (270; 2: ch. 14).

April

Mrs. Elton says to Jane Fairfax, "Here is April come!" Emma's dinner for the Eltons is on a "cold sleety April" Thursday (299, 303, 304; 2: ch. 17). Subsequent events mark this as the second week in April, so it was on 14 April, Easter Thursday.

May

The Churchills take a house in Richmond "for May and June." Mr. Woodhouse thinks, "May was better for every thing than February." At the Crown Inn ball, the "whole party" observes that "though *May*, a fire in the evening was still very pleasant" (317, 318, 320; 3: ch. 2). Modert suggests that although no weekday is given, the Crown Inn ball takes place on Thursday the 12th, which would be "Old May Day Eve," and Harriet's encounter with the Gypsies would occur on "Old May Day," Friday the 13th.

June

By inference, we can discover that the exploring party at Donwell takes place on 23 June, at "almost Midsummer" (357; 3: ch. 6), Midsummer Eve. This date is also Harriet's birthday (30; 1: ch. 4). The Box Hill party is on 24 June, and that night Frank goes back to Richmond (377, 383; 3: ch. 8), and the holiday on 24 June is "Midsummer." Thirty-six hours later, Mrs. Churchill dies, on 26 June (387; 3: ch. 9; 440; 3: ch. 14).

July

"One morning, about ten days after Mrs. Churchill's decease, Emma was called down stairs to Mr. Weston" (392; 3: ch. 10). We later learn that this was a

Monday. Modert interprets "about" as meaning "nearly" or "almost." By counting 26 June and the Monday as full days, Modert suggests that Frank returns on 4 July, nine days after Mrs. Churchill's death. On this day, Frank had visited Randalls (392, 394; 3: ch. 10). On the same day, Harriet tells Emma whom she loves (405–09; 3: ch. 11). Mrs. Weston visits Emma on 5 July (Modert) after calling on Jane Fairfax (417–20; 3: ch. 12). In the afternoon, a "cold stormy rain set in, and nothing of July appeared" (421). Chapman notes, "We find out later . . . that the day of the storm was a *Tuesday*" (436; 3: ch. 14). Modert points out that Tuesday, 5 July, the day of the cold July storm, is "*Old* Midsummer Eve." Mr. Knightley returns from London the next day, by implication, Wednesday, 6 July (424; 3: ch. 13), the date of "*Old* Midsummer." Emma writes her letter to Harriet on 7 July. Frank's letter is dated only "July—Windsor" (436; 3: ch. 14). The date when Emma reads the letter must be 7 July, two days after Mrs. Weston's visit (436). She reads it in the morning; Mr. Knightley reads it in the afternoon (444; 3: ch. 15). Harriet is invited to London "for at least a fortnight," and goes there (451; 3: ch. 16). The next day, Emma visits Jane Fairfax (452). That would be Friday, 8 July, as we learn that the planned meeting at the Crown Inn will be "to-morrow," which is also clearly named as "Saturday" (456). Mrs. Weston has a baby girl in July, nine months after the wedding in September (461; 3: ch. 17).

July, August

Harriet stays in London where "her fortnight was likely to be a month at least." The John Knightleys "were to come down in August, and she was invited to remain till they could bring her back" (464; 3: ch. 17). Before Harriet returns, Emma is relieved to hear news about Harriet so different from her "doleful disappointment of five weeks back" (475; 3: ch. 18); therefore, Harriet probably returns after 15 August (481; 3: ch. 19).

September, October, November

Weddings take place (482–83; 3: ch. 19).

See also Chapman's "Appendixes"; Modert 57.

One Idea for Initiating Class Discussion: "Opinions of *Emma*"

It is a fascinating fact that Austen copied down into a notebook, probably in 1816, every comment that she read or heard from *Emma*'s readers in that first year of publication. These remarks—inadequate or lukewarm as they sound to those of us who know the novel well and love it—were evidently important enough to Austen that she preserved them. This short section from her *Minor Works* is reprinted in this volume as an appendix (179–82), because teachers may find in the evocative comments a way to start a conversation in class, to frame a discussion, or to suggest a writing assignment. The essay in this volume by LeClair explains a little of the identity of the readers whose comments Austen recorded, and LeClair offers insight into the way the "opinions" may shed light on the scenes in *Emma* in which the heroine works on her portrait of Harriet Smith.

LeClair points out that most of the comments begin with "personal preoccupations." The various readers express highly divergent views, mention (as first-time readers usually do) whether they "liked" the book or not, and then proceed to criticize it on idiosyncratic criteria: whether the book is "moral," whether it is "natural" (and whether it is desirable for a book to be "natural"), whether it is "interesting," and whether the reader likes the treatment of characters who share the reader's age, profession, or point of view. Students of mine sometimes sound exactly like those original readers as we start *Emma*: "I don't like it." "I don't like it as much as *Pride and Prejudice*." "It's really boring." "My sister says it's good, but I like mysteries better." "These men never do anything." "The characters all talk about trivia."

In the face of such daunting initial responses (occasionally stated outright in class), a teacher might give voice to some of Austen's audience—for example, Mrs. Dickson, who "did not like" the novel because there are a "Mr. and Mrs. Dixon in it," or Mrs. Digweed, who, "if she had not known the Author, could hardly have got through it." But then the class might turn to the second comment from Austen's friend Alethea Bigg, who "on reading it a second time, liked Miss Bates much better than at first," and to the comment by Austen's seafaring brother, Captain Charles Austen. Captain Austen, attentively rereading *Emma* while at sea, might inspire a student: "Emma arrived in time to a moment. I am delighted with her, more so I think than even with my favourite Pride & Prejudice, & have read it three times in the Passage." For initially resistant readers of *Emma*, this promise and the teacher's conviction, goodwill, and enthusiasm may help lure them through a second or third reading, either "in the Passage"—or later in life.

Part Two

APPROACHES

The Everyday of *Emma*

Julia Prewitt Brown

Teaching *Emma* in a course on Jane Austen is a different experience from teaching it in a course on nineteenth-century literature alongside Carlyle's *The French Revolution* or in a course on the development of the novel alongside Thackeray's *Vanity Fair*. When I teach a course on Austen, almost all the students who sign up for it are women who already love her fiction; teaching them can be a little like preaching to the converted. They do not have much difficulty recognizing the importance of Austen's subject, domestic life and the life of the "everyday." These students often take longer to get to the question that plagues students in the other courses from the start—why did Austen choose to neglect the significant historical events of her day?

I am always grateful when this question arises, because it provides the beginnings of a necessary distance on the subject of ordinary life. Rehearsing the psychological, romantic, and social tensions of the novel is essential, but doing so becomes repetitive, even gossipy, if students are not occasionally pressed to ask, Who cares if John Knightley has bad manners, if Mrs. Weston is available to sit with Mr. Woodhouse, or if Frank Churchill goes to London for a haircut? Why might a novelist want to interest us in such things?

In comparison with Austen's other novels, *Emma* is curiously unassuming. It has less story than the others, as Walter Scott was the first to observe; it offers little more, he writes, than "a train of mistakes and embarrassing situations, and dialogues at balls and parties of pleasure" (357). The potentially tragic drama of life that must attend those "born to struggle and endure" in *Mansfield Park* is nowhere to be found in *Emma*, except perhaps in the sense of suffering that attends Jane Fairfax.

Nor is the intellectual intensity of opposing views of life, vividly dramatized in *Pride and Prejudice*, present in dialogue between Emma and Mr. Knightley. In order that all important action be internalized in Emma's consciousness, Mr. Knightley is not viewed critically, nor does he undergo any significant change. The closest we come to an active collision between them occurs at Box Hill, which—in comparison to the proposal scene and its aftermath in *Pride and Prejudice*—appears one-sided. (In *Emma* only the heroine has something to learn.) With less story and outward moral conflict than the previous Austen novels, *Emma* also does not pretend to the historical resonance of the writer's last novel, *Persuasion*. Although *Emma* gives us a memorable portrait of English village life at the beginning of the nineteenth century, the action does not evoke, as it does in *Persuasion*, real and distinctive locales (Bath, Lyme) at a particular moment in history (shortly before Waterloo).

Yet despite—or is it because of?—the relative modesty of its aims, *Emma* is most frequently cited as Austen's greatest work. (Reginald Farrer, Lionel Trilling, Harold Bloom [Emma], and Marilyn Butler are a few of the distinguished critics who have made this judgment.) When I teach *Emma*, I address this conundrum: Why should the novel most careful not to make large claims for itself be considered the author's greatest work?

Critics usually judge as "greatest" a novelist's most characteristic work of fiction—the one that best achieves what that writer can do. *Little Dorrit* is not as finely constructed as *Great Expectations*, but it is often judged Dickens's "greatest" novel because, in its re-creation of the world of institutionally engendered suffering, readers immediately recognize Dickens's accomplishment at its most representative. Likewise *Emma* delivers best—precisely and to the exclusion of all else—Austen's forte: mastery of the moral landscape of the everyday. The more unremarkable the social situation, the greater Austen's achievement in showing that it does have human importance. The climax of *Emma* is an insulting remark spoken at a picnic. To explain the significance of this moment, one must review countless minor details leading up to it, particularly those relating to the target of the insult, Miss Bates. One may show, for example, how Miss Bates's characterization makes her a symbol of Highbury itself. All classes come together in her, just as all neighborhood gossip passes through her mind and appears in her speech. Her small dwelling serves as a link between the older gentry (the Woodhouses and the Knightleys), the new rich (the Coles), and the lower-middle- to lower-class townspeople and clerks. She represents Highbury's fluidity and mobility—she has herself dropped in status in the course of her life—and so Emma's insult is an affront to the democratic character of the community itself. After her disagreement with Mr. Knightley on the subject of her self-centered conduct, Emma visits Miss Bates as though humbly paying deference to Highbury itself.

Early on in the discussion of *Emma*, then, I ask a student to present an explication to the class of a paragraph involving Miss Bates. The explications are two-page close analyses of short passages. (Five sentences of Austen's prose is more than enough.) The student distributes copies of the explication to the class, allows time for class members to read it in silence, then reads it aloud and leads a discussion lasting about fifteen minutes. This is a useful assignment in drawing out shy students, I might add. Because they arrive in class armed with their presentation, they are less nervous; and, in hearing their own voice read the explication, they seem to relax and often surprise themselves with their ease in leading the discussion. I always assign a strong student for the first explication, to set a standard that the rest of the class tries to meet.

Often students select part of the paragraph in chapter 3 that introduces Mrs. Bates and "her single daughter," Miss Bates:

> Her daughter enjoyed a most uncommon degree of popularity for a woman neither young, handsome, rich, nor married. Miss Bates stood in the very worst predicament in the world for having much of the public favour; and she had no intellectual superiority to make atonement to herself, or frighten those who might hate her, into outward respect.   (21; 1: ch. 3)

In alluding to the opening sentence of the novel, the first sentence in this passage places Miss Bates firmly in relation to Emma, a suggestion that continues in the passage but is never made explicit. In what sense is having "the public favour" ever a disadvantage? Perhaps it makes those who themselves love to be admired—namely Emma—slightly envious. The rest of the paragraph shows that there is little else to envy in Miss Bates's situation—a point that Mr. Knightley stresses in his lecture to Emma at Box Hill. In these few sentences, Austen lays the groundwork for the later scene. The word "hate" seems to jar in the gentle, vulnerable world of Miss Bates and her aged mother ("almost past every thing but tea and quadrille") and in that sense foreshadows Emma's jarring insult at Box Hill.

In class we review other key passages involving Miss Bates and Emma, taking note of how much is implied, how little directly stated. One of the purposes of this activity is to recognize that in the climactic scene at Box Hill, no narrator does the work of explaining its significance for us. No voice intrudes to announce in utterances of unsurpassed moral intelligence that this event leads the heroine to emerge from the "moral stupidity" in which she had taken "the world as an udder" to feed her supreme self (Eliot, *Middlemarch* 156). When Emma's tears flow at the end of the Box Hill chapter, Austen does not remind us of "that element of tragedy" that infuses "all ordinary human life," as does the narrator of *Middlemarch* when describing Dorothea Brooke sobbing in her hotel room in Rome (144).

For unlike George Eliot in the portrait of Dorothea, Austen never insists that Emma is more than what she is. The heroine of *Middlemarch* is nothing less than a "latter-day St. Teresa" whose life is thrown into relief against a grand historical background that encompasses the ancient, medieval, and Renaissance worlds as well as the particular historical moment in which she lives:

"When George the Fourth was still reigning over the privacies of Windsor, when the Duke of Wellington was Prime Minister, and Mr Vincy was mayor of the old corporation in Middlemarch, Mrs Casaubon, born Dorothea Brooke, had taken her wedding journey to Rome" (139). No such rhetorical claims are made for Emma. Most readers will not remember that she takes her wedding journey to the seaside.

During the Crown Inn ball scene in volume 3, Austen alludes to the forgettability of her subject when she writes, "Of very important, very recordable events, it was not more productive than such meetings usually are. There was one, however, which Emma thought something of" (326; 3: ch. 2)—referring to the event in which Mr. Elton snubs Harriet and Mr. Knightley rescues her on the dance floor, which Austen then describes. Crucial to both the moral and the romantic structures of the novel because it brings Emma and Mr. Knightley into agreement over a moral act, Harriet's rescue is one of those "very important, very recordable events" observed only by a novelist. In the next chapter, Austen parodies it when Frank Churchill rescues Harriet from the Gypsies in a far cruder moment of chivalry, as if to suggest that significant acts can be overshadowed by lesser ones.

When news of the Gypsies spreads through Highbury, Austen writes: "last night's ball seemed lost in the gipsies," but even the later happening "dwindled soon into a matter of little importance" to everyone except Emma's nephews, who insist that she repeat the story of the Gypsies again and again, "tenaciously setting her right if she varied in the slightest particular from the original recital" (336; 3: ch. 3). These three brief passages—the first about the "recordable events" at the ball, the second about the way the ball is replaced as a topic of conversation by the Gypsies incident, and the third about the passing of that incident, mostly unnoticed, into oral legend—together capture exactly the kind of history neglected by traditional historians. The events of everyday life are either forgotten because superseded by new events that claim human attention or passed on orally. Only the novelist redeems them.

Austen was not the only writer of the early nineteenth century to meditate on the forgettability of recordable experience. In "On History," an essay published fourteen years after *Emma*, her contemporary Thomas Carlyle writes of how much the historical narrative traditionally leaves out: "Well may we say that of our History the most important part is lost without recovery." To Carlyle, it is above all "the inward condition of Life" that is lost—the customs, traditions, and daily habits that "support our existence" and from the first have taught us "how to think and how to act." Compared with this "essential furniture," outside factors such as laws and constitutions "are not our Life, but only the House wherein our Life is led." Because "the inward condition of Life . . . is the same in no two ages," we need the novelist's record of it (53–54). The life of the everyday evolves. Or, as Milan Kundera puts it, "the world is part of man, it is his dimension, and as the world changes, existence (*in-der-Welt-sein*) changes as well" (35). Looking carefully at selections from Carlyle's essay pro-

vides class discussion of Austen's vision of the everyday with a conceptual background that students often lack. Unlike their European counterparts, American students do not generally study philosophy in high school and are sometimes
ill at ease with questions that take them beyond the practical. As one of the
more literary philosophers of history, however, Carlyle is quite accessible to
students of literature.

In her most psychologically concentrated novel, a work in which so much action is internalized, Austen repeatedly shows how outward forces such as social
class are inseparable from the way Emma thinks and acts. Here are Emma's
first impressions of Harriet Smith:

> She was not struck by any thing remarkably clever in Miss Smith's con-
> versation, but she found her altogether very engaging—not inconve-
> niently shy, not unwilling to talk—and yet so far from pushing, shewing
> so proper and becoming a deference, seeming so pleasantly grateful for
> being admitted to Hartfield, and so artlessly impressed by the appear-
> ance of every thing in so superior a style to what she had been used to,
> that she must have good sense and deserve encouragement. Encourage-
> ment should be given. Those soft blue eyes and all those natural graces
> should not be wasted on the inferior society of Highbury and its connec-
> tions. The acquaintance she had already formed were unworthy of her.
>
> (23; 1: ch. 3)

In analyzing this passage in class, I ask students to paraphrase Emma's logic so
that they see how closely Emma's perceptions are tied to her judgments or
how empirical observation is realized in social judgment: Harriet's manners are
deferential. Ergo, the "inferior society" of Highbury is "unworthy of her."
When Emma has little evidence to prompt her, she relies wholly on an abstract
conception of the social hierarchy. Although she is unacquainted with Robert
Martin, she immediately assumes that he is of a class with which she "can have
nothing to do" (29; 1: ch. 4).

In being given Emma's inner life, then, we are given her outer life as well.
The properties of her mind are those of the society in which she lives. One of
her deepest mental tendencies is precisely that manipulative urge "to adapt
means to ends" that Carlyle, in "Signs of the Times" (1829), recognized as the
cardinal trait of the mechanical age: "Not the external and physical alone is
now managed by machinery, but the internal and spiritual also. Here too nothing follows its spontaneous course" (65). To Emma, falling in love does not
occur naturally; doing so is a matter of planning and strategy. (Emma even
adopts an inner division of labor by which she supervises what Harriet experiences.) Becoming educated is not a tentative, deepening process but a matter
of composing long lists of books to be read. Both the romantic and the intellectual projects fail—Harriet does not marry Mr. Elton and Emma does not become the accomplished person she could become—because they are based on

mechanical principles alone. What Carlyle calls "the inward" is in danger of being abandoned altogether by Emma because "cultivated on such principles, it is found to yield no result" (70). Much of the suspense of *Emma* comes not from our desire to know whom the heroine will marry but from our fear that her inner life will be wasted. Using Carlyle's ideas enables teachers to move class discussion beyond an analysis of Emma's psychological and romantic life to pose the question What is Emma's life worth? Would marriage to Mr. Knightley be a satisfactory destiny for her unaccompanied by her self-realization?

Emma embodies yet another of Carlyle's descriptions of the mental habits of the day in her tendency to "indulge in anticipation" (61) or to engage in utopian plans for the future rather than to recognize the realistic possibilities of the present. The Gypsies are not the only fortune-tellers that threaten Highbury. Yet there is hope for Emma as there is not for the character who parodies her, Mrs. Elton. Whereas Mrs. Elton's schemes are purely self-aggrandizing— for example, in her patronage of Jane Fairfax she seeks to augment her own importance to her wealthy relations—those of Emma possess a communal character. Highbury is to be her aesthetic creation; her love of home is just as strong as her love of self. Perhaps because of the love of home (a subtle and persistent theme in *Emma*), Emma—unlike a later Emma in the history of the novel, Madame Bovary—is capable of seeing beyond her fantasies.

In the telling description of Emma's thoughts as she stands at the door of Ford's and looks out into the village street, Austen hints that Emma has within her the ability both to imagine and to return (contentedly) to reality:

> Emma went to the door for amusement.—Much could not be hoped from the traffic of even the busiest part of Highbury;—Mr. Perry walking hastily by, Mr. William Cox letting himself in at the office door, Mr. Cole's carriage horses returning from exercise, or a stray letter-boy on an obstinate mule, were the liveliest objects she could presume to expect; and when her eyes fell only on the butcher with his tray, a tidy old woman travelling homewards from shop with her full basket, two curs quarrelling over a dirty bone, and a string of dawdling children round the baker's little bow-window eyeing the gingerbread, she knew she had no reason to complain, and was amused enough; quite enough still to stand at the door. (233; 2: ch. 9)

Although her tendency is to anticipate and imagine, she is able to engage the truth when it comes. When Emma hears about Robert Martin's behavior at Ford's, she discerns that the "young man's conduct . . . seemed the result of real feeling," Austen writes decisively: "She was obliged to stop and think. She was not thoroughly comfortable herself" (179; 2: ch. 3).

As a result of her concrete interactions with others, deeper forces are unleashed in Emma. One of the forces, what Austen calls "the origin of change," is the drive to mate or marry (7; 1: ch. 1); another, just as deep, is the pedagogic basis of human relations. Emma is interested in matchmaking because she herself is ready for marriage, although she doesn't know it. Since Mr. Woodhouse and Miss Taylor are gentle but deficient educators—*Emma* is full of good and bad mentors, as Juliet McMaster has pointed out—she must rely on Mr. Knightley to prepare her ("Love" 413). He repeatedly intervenes to remind her of what she has chosen to ignore or forget: that young men like to select their wives themselves, that Harriet is not what she wants her to be, that the Martins are worthy people, that Miss Bates has a history in Highbury that should be respected—that, in short, the world is not at her feet, waiting to be moved and manipulated. Highbury's moral historian, Mr. Knightley helps to develop in the child Emma the conscience and memory of an adult.

By the conclusion of the story, Emma has gone beyond herself: "Her own conduct, as well as her own heart, was before her" (408; 3: ch. 11). "Development of self" and "inward suffering" occur simultaneously, and Emma is at last able to see herself, to recognize a self "before her." Although marriage to Mr. Knightley follows this recognition, it is secondary. The hyperbolic description of an Emma "in dancing, singing, exclaiming spirits," experiencing joy, gratitude, and "exquisite delight of her sensations" (475; 3: ch. 18) alludes not to her experience of love but to the relief that comes to her newfound self-awareness when she learns that her bad mentoring of Harriet has not led to the destruction of Harriet's hopes for happiness. As many as seven chapters follow Emma's moment of self-realization—a fact that I emphasize in class, together with the content of the chapters themselves—because the inner implications of that realization are complex. The novel doesn't "just end in marriage," as traditional as well as feminist critics have wrongly complained.

Austen insists on little beyond the achievement of self-awareness. Emma is not made to pay an exorbitant price for her mistakes, as is Dorothea Brooke, and the reader is not invited to pause before her "unvisited tomb" at the end of the novel to shed a tear over lost opportunity (Eliot 613). We mourn Dorothea Brooke because of her obscurity, because of what she might have been, whereas Austen lays claim to nothing more (and nothing less) than Emma's irreplaceable individuality. Her individuality is all the more striking when placed in the context of the passing world of the neighborhood. For when we read *Emma* and become immersed in the concerns of Highbury, wondering if Mr. Woodhouse will find the rooms at the Crown too drafty for a ball, worrying about how Miss Bates will receive the insult at Box Hill, we are acutely aware of the transitory nature of life—although our awareness takes a more bemused form than that which other writers, from the Cavalier poets to George Eliot, may have provoked in us. Not everything that passes need be mourned—by no means the least bit of wisdom students may take away from a reading of *Emma*.

Generations of Austen critics have felt compelled to tackle the question of why Austen avoids the larger history of her day. From the publication of Marilyn Butler's *Jane Austen and the War of Ideas* (1975) to more recent studies of Austen's political consciousness, critics justify the novels by arguing for the existence of continual allusions to the larger world. Yet even if we agree that these allusions are important or that the novels would suffer from their exclusion, we still have not settled the question of why Austen chose to foreground the everyday. The answer is probably found in a less political, more philosophical approach to fiction.

In *The Art of the Novel*, Kundera writes that, because in the modern era human beings have become mere pawns of the forces of technology, politics, and history, our "concrete being or 'world of life'" has been lost to memory. From its origins, the novel undertakes to investigate this "forgotten being," discovering "various dimensions of existence one by one." With Cervantes, it investigates the nature of adventure; with Richardson, the life of feelings, and so on. Austen's place in this "sequence of discoveries" (5–6), we may say, is to have revealed the moral scale of everyday life—and I use the word *scale* in the fullest sense of the word. Although much can be made of the historical and political resonances of Austen's fiction, the greatest contribution of her works—and, above all, that of *Emma*—may be to remind us of the surface and weight of the everyday. This emphasis is in itself historically significant, but its relation to what we call history has yet to be fully appreciated.

More judgment is required of the reader of *Emma* than of any other Austen novel. The conduct of each character, major and minor, is scrutinized in such a way that the reader is brought to the threshold of a judgment that is suggested but left unstated. For this reason, students may usefully be asked to write an analysis of a secondary character. In doing so, they recognize for themselves how the behavior of even the lesser characters, not just Emma, is weighed on the moral scale of communal life: Mr. Weston is indiscriminating and overly accepting; John Knightley, too reactive; Mrs. Weston may be faulted for her disinclination to pass judgment, and so on. Because of the unrelieved attention not to personal relations but to conduct (a distinction made some years ago by Raymond Williams), the reader is inclined to place faith in the best judge of conduct in the novel, Mr. Knightley, only to discover that his vision is also limited.

For example, when Mr. Knightley notices the secret communicativeness between Jane Fairfax and Frank Churchill—proof of his remarkable perspicacity—he relates his suspicions to Emma and completely misreads her response. Taking her steadfast resistance to his suggestion of a secret romance as a sign that she is hopelessly in love with Frank Churchill herself, he is "staggered" by her confident denials and walks home to the "solitude of Donwell Abbey" (351; 3: ch. 5). Students need to be reminded that Austen qualifies her idealization of Mr. Knightley in unobtrusive ways. He is just as human as Emma, merely older and wiser. We cannot place absolute faith in his judgment any more than we can place absolute faith in the judgment of people we have come to respect and admire (as students themselves are likely becoming aware).

When I teach *Emma*, I like to suggest that students try, for one day, to see their own lives through Austen's eyes. Those with the curiosity to attempt this experiment may notice that "very seldom, does complete truth belong to any human disclosure; seldom can it happen that something is not a little disguised, or a little mistaken" (431; 3: ch. 13). The moral attention Austen gives to the life of the everyday in *Emma* is more than most of us can tolerate for very long, and not only because, as George Eliot writes, "the quickest of us walk about well wadded with stupidity" (144). "The world is part of man," the quick and the dull alike; it is our "dimension," as Kundera writes, and is therefore as impossible to see clearly as the nose on our face, unless (like Emma) we look in the mirror—or study works of art.

On the last day of teaching *Emma*, I take about half an hour to focus on other works of art that engage the surface and weight of the everyday: a painting by Vermeer, say, or a photograph by the contemporary Cuban photographer Abelardo Morrell. Whereas a novel may take days to read and therefore submerges us in its world over time, we are less likely to get lost in a painting or a photograph, simply because it can be grasped instantaneously, making us see the world of everyday time and space in a flash. In Vermeer's *The Soldier and the Young Girl Smiling* (c. 1658–60), a man and a woman are seated at a table in a room. Light enters from an open window to the left and a map of Holland and Friesland hangs above, both suggesting a more public world. The erotic equilibrium of anticipation and restraint in which the man and the woman are poised adds a note of intimacy to the scene (Snow 81–82). As in *Emma*, the domain of the home is foregrounded amid allusions to both public and intimate experience. The world beyond Highbury is repeatedly suggested in arrivals of characters and letters from afar, just as private histories vibrate beneath the surface of the everyday. Austen was neither the first nor the last artist to evoke the world through the quotidian and the personal, but she is the greatest novelist before Proust and Joyce to do so.

Jane Austen, Slavery, and British Imperialism

Ruth Perry

Ever since Edward Said published his essay "Jane Austen and Empire," in which he declared that Austen's novels helped naturalize British colonialism, scholars have been debating the political meanings of her references to imperialism. By now we know a great deal about her family's personal connections to slavery and more generally about English attitudes, during her lifetime, toward slavery and colonialism. Austen's views on imperialism were not static but changed in response to shifts in power politics, for her attitudes were affected by the tidal wave of nationalism that swept her country during the struggle with Napoleon; her judgments about British exploration and expansion changed with the vicissitudes of her country's standing in the world. By the end of her life, Austen was ready to glorify the British navy, in which her brothers made their fortunes, and to believe them brave and noble sailors, although she had, in her earlier novels, represented military men as shallow, flashy, or opportunistic. There are references to the English slave trade and to the English colonial presence abroad in all three late novels, but only in *Persuasion* does she endorse the country's imperial reach rather than question it. By the time she drafted that novel, Napoleon had been defeated at Waterloo and the national pleasure and relief in that victory overwhelmed any scruples the public had.

One could start with 1797, the year the fiancé of Jane Austen's beloved sister, Cassandra, the Reverend Thomas Fowle, died of yellow fever off Santo Domingo and was buried at sea, to the "great Affliction" of all those at Steventon (Austen, *Letters* [Le Faye] 94).[1] Like Edward Ferrars, whose disappearance from Elinor Dashwood's life in *Sense and Sensibility* offered Austen an opportunity to demonstrate her heroine's heroic strength of character in suffering—or Bingley, who provides the same exquisite opportunity for Jane Bennet in *Pride and Prejudice*—the ghost of Thomas Fowle peers through Austen's novels, the original of all the disappearing suitors.

Fowle was traveling with Lord Craven on a military mission to the West Indies as his personal chaplain when he contracted yellow fever. Although the expedition that Fowle accompanied was an attempt to reenslave Santo Domingo after the successful slave revolt led by Toussaint L'Ouverture, the English posed in subsequent years as defenders of the independent, newly named Hayti, patrolling the Caribbean to prevent the French from retaking their former colony. In the colonial wars in the Caribbean theater, yellow fever killed three times as many Europeans as muskets or cutlasses did, and by the time Fowle died, some eighty thousand British soldiers had perished in three and a half years of fighting with France. In October 1796, "it was said in Parliament that every person in the country had lost an acquaintance in the Caribbean campaigns"; "the obituary columns of the *Gentleman's Magazine* were strewn with the names of the officers who had died of yellow fever" (Geggus 123–49, esp. 128).[2] The war became as scandalously unpopular in England as the Vietnam War was in the United States in the early 1970s. The degree to which the West Indian theater of operations sapped England's strength in her contest with France, the extraordinary casualties from tropical disease, and the growing opposition of the English public to the slave trade, on which this colonial economy depended—these circumstances led to a cease-fire and the withdrawing of troops from Santo Domingo the year after Fowle died.

Austen had many other family connections to the planter class in the West Indies. Her father's older half brother, William-Hampson Walter, had two sons, William and George, who settled in Jamaica. A letter from Jane's mother to her niece Philadelphia Walter at Christmastime 1786, wishing she were with them and describing the happy family circle at Steventon, declared, "You might as well be in Jamaica keeping your Brother's House, for anything that we see of you or are like to see" (Austen-Leigh and Austen-Leigh 54). Mrs. Austen's brother, James Leigh-Perrot, married Jane Cholmeley, heiress to an estate in Barbados. James Langford Nibbs, an Antiguan planter whom Jane's father probably tutored at Saint John's College, Oxford, was godfather to the Austens' firstborn son, James, and a close family friend whose portrait hung at Steventon. In his marriage contract, Nibbs designated George Austen as the trustee responsible for arranging a jointure of £500 per year to be paid to his wife from his Antiguan property if he predeceased her. Had Nibbs died early, Jane's father would have been expected to manage the plantation in Antigua to fulfill his legal obligation (Gibbon 300). Anne Mathew, the first wife of Jane's brother James, was the daughter of General Mathew, commander in chief of the Windward and Leeward Islands and governor of Grenada. And Jane's younger brother Charles married Fanny Palmer, daughter of the former attorney general of Bermuda, whom he met on duty there.

The Austens also had colonial connections in the East Indies. George Austen's sister Philadelphia had gone to India to find a husband in 1752; there she succeeded in meeting and marrying a Mr. Hancock, twenty years her senior, a surgeon for the East India Company. Jane Austen recorded this family fact in her early fragment "Catharine; or, The Bower," in which the elder Miss Wynne goes to India to make her fortune. There she marries a wealthy man "double her own age, whose disposition was not amiable, and whose Manners were unpleasing, though his Character was respectable" ("Catharine" 194). Mr. Hancock, whom there is no reason to think unamiable or unmannerly, was a friend of Warren Hastings, who stood godfather to the Hancocks' daughter Elizabeth, born in Calcutta (Le Faye, "Jane Austen and Her Hancock Relatives"). This was cousin Eliza, who was visiting the Austens in Hampshire when the French Revolution broke out. Her first husband, M. de Feuillide, was subsequently guillotined by the revolutionaries in 1794; she married Jane's brother Henry in 1797.

Although family connections are easy to trace, the attitudes of Austen's class toward slavery and abolition are less obvious. To begin with, what was at issue was never manumission, or the freeing of existing slaves, but only the outlawing of the "commerce of the human species" as the abolitionist Thomas Clarkson put it (1: 378). Jane Austen's brother Francis opposed slavery, having seen the system firsthand on a number of West Indian islands, including Antigua. On the East India Company's island of St. Helena, he noted in his journal, slaves were not "treated with that harshness and despotism which has been so justly attributed to the conduct of the land-holders or their managers in the West India Islands." The laws of St. Helena's gave masters the right only to their slaves' labor—enforceable with civil and not private power. "This is a wholesome regulation as far as it goes," wrote Francis Austen, "but slavery however it may be modified is still slavery, and it is much to be regretted that any trace of it should be found to exist in countries dependent on England, or colonised by her subjects" (Hubback and Hubback 192). Austen herself read and admired Clarkson's work *An Essay on the Slavery and Commerce of the Human Species* (1786).

Austen refers to the slave trade and England's colonial wars in her three late novels with some significant shifts in attitude and emphasis. A number of critics have convincingly argued that *Mansfield Park* is predominantly about slavery. Both Moira Ferguson and Joseph Lew, following Margaret Kirkham, have pointed out that its title is associated with a landmark legal decision of 1772, in which Lord Mansfield declared that all persons, of whatever race or personal history, were free so long as they were on English soil and could not be compelled to return to servitude in the slaveholding colonies (Kirkham 117–18). In *Mansfield Park* Thomas Bertram, baronet, member of Parliament, and part of the West Indian planter interest, arranges to have Fanny Price brought from Portsmouth to live as a second-class citizen within his household and to serve his wife. Ignorant of the symbolism of global location when she first comes to Mansfield Park, Fanny "cannot put the map of Europe together." Her cousins mock her for referring to the Isle of Wight as *"the Island,* as if there were no other island in the world"* (18; 1: ch. 2). She learns about her uncle's plantation in Antigua as she learns about her own place in the scheme of things, subject to the tyrannies of Mrs. Norris, whose name, as Frank Gibbon and Moira Ferguson point out, was shared by a particularly duplicitous proslavery advocate described in Clarkson's *History of Abolition*, which Austen also read.

Norris, a slave captain responsible for transporting boatloads of captives (as, in a domestic register, Mrs. Norris is responsible for transporting Fanny to her new servitude in *Mansfield Park*), represented himself to Clarkson at first as a humane opponent of the slave trade, interested in its amendment and even its abolition. But he evaded Clarkson's efforts to bring him before the king's privy council in March 1788 as a witness to the corruptions and brutalities of the slave trade and appeared unexpectedly, instead, as a Liverpool delegate in support of the trade. He argued that the Africans were so barbaric, cruel, and murderous to one another that bringing them away and introducing them to European culture was actually a blessing (Clarkson 1: 378, 477). Moreover, Norris said, many slaves were prisoners of war and would have been put to death had they remained in Africa, "whereas now they were saved" (1: 481). This astonishing testimony carried the day, Clarkson reported; the privy council returned the verdict that "the major part of the complaints against this Trade are ill-founded" (1: 482–83).

Refracting Mrs. Norris's treatment of Fanny through Clarkson's anecdote is chilling, particularly her self-justifying explanations, her duplicity, and the extent to which she exploits Fanny all the while exclaiming on Fanny's luck in enjoying the advantages of Mansfield Park. Readers who do not believe that the daily exploitation of dependent women could possibly figure racialized slavery—because their evils are incommensurate—will see in Austen's appropriation of Clarkson's materials the alchemy of a mind transforming the genuinely political into the merely personal. At the same time, readers who see continuities between tyranny in the home and tyranny in the political colonies will find the superimposition of the slave captain's treachery on Aunt Norris's self-aggrandizement a powerful commentary on all exploitative human relations. Jane Fairfax, in *Emma*, makes just such a commentary when she likens her prospects as a dependent woman seeking a governess position at "Offices for the sale—not quite of human flesh—but of human intellect." Commenting on her implied comparison, she adds that the "governess-trade" and the slave trade may be "widely different certainly as to the guilt of those who carry it on; but as to the greater misery of the victims, I do not know where it lies" (300–01; 2: ch. 17).

Mansfield Park, *Emma*, and *Persuasion* all contain references to the slave trade, an issue about which fierce national debates had taken place in the preceding decade. The bill to abolish the slave trade had been ratified in both houses in 1806 and passed into law in 1807; from that date, all slave traffic to the Caribbean ceased. Thus, when Captain Wentworth ships out to the British West Indies after his broken engagement with Anne Elliot, in *Persuasion*, he is patrolling the waters to enforce compliance with the Abolition Bill. When Fanny asks Thomas Bertram, on his return from Antigua, about the slave trade, she is inquiring about the consequences of the bill for his plantation.

In addition to ending the trade in slaves, the Abolition Bill presaged a more humane environment for existing slaves in the West Indies. If slaves could no longer be brought to the islands from Africa, the human property already in the colonies would have to be treated more decently. They could not be abused or worked to death but would have to be handled in a way that would promote their health and reproduction. Fanny's question about the slave trade thus also figures a change in her own status at Mansfield Park insofar as she is a creature of the Bertrams. Despite Mrs. Norris's indignation, she is to have a fire in the East room and the use of the carriage when she is invited out to dine. Fanny's seemingly innocent question is a prelude, moreover, to her passive rebellion against Henry Crawford's suit and Thomas's masterful pressure on her to marry Crawford. She will not mate and breed as they direct her.

When Said accused Austen of unconsciously accepting slavery and British colonialism, thus exemplifying how "humanistic ideas coexisted so comfortably with imperialism," he claimed that her obliviousness to the privileges of class was evident in her "uninflected, unreflective citations of Antigua (or the Mediterranean, or India, which is where Lady Bertram, in a fit of distracted impatience, requires that William should go 'that I may have a shawl')." Said charged that because Austen, among others, took for granted that English colonies supported the Thomas Bertrams of the world—who, from time to time, had to take long and dangerous voyages to supervise and regulate their overseas property—she and her ilk created the "broad expanse of domestic imperialist culture without which the subsequent acquisition of territory would not have been possible" (93, 95). In other words, Said accused Austen of referring to Antigua and to the slave trade casually, merely by way of adding decor to her story of domestic rearrangements in the upper classes, and thus contributing to the naturalizing, or public assimilation, of those unnatural elements, slavery and colonialism.

But, of course, nothing in Austen's novels is ever "uninflected" or "unreflective," and Said is wrong to imagine the references to the slave trade in *Mansfield Park* as morally neutral—any more than are the references in *Emma*. Said does not take into account the inflections of gender in the passages he cites, or Austen's hypersensitivity to the dependent status of women. He does not notice that colonialism in all three of the late novels is associated with women's subordination and dependence. Not only is Fanny torn from her family, transported to Mansfield Park, and put at the disposal of Lady Bertram and Mrs. Norris—all for the price of her maintenance—but she is treated like recalcitrant property when she refuses to marry as Sir Thomas commands. That it is she, rather than her entitled cousins, who wants to know about the slave trade is hardly "uninflected." And when she raises the question with her master in the context of its recent abolition and is met with "dead silence," while her cousins sit "without speaking a word, or seeming at all interested in the subject," that too means something (198; 2: ch. 3).

In *Emma* it is the dependent Jane Fairfax, about to hire out as a governess, who refers to "Offices for the sale . . . of human flesh." The officious Augusta Hawkins from Bristol, England's premier slave-trading port, who has just bought Mr. Elton for "so many thousands as would always be called ten" (181; 2: ch. 4), understands Jane Fairfax's reference but not the more immediate context or personal implication. "You quite shock me," she retorts; "if you mean a fling at the slave-trade, I assure you Mr. Suckling was always rather a friend to the abolition" (300; 2: ch. 17). Despite her protestations, it is she who presses Jane Fairfax the hardest to concede her servitude and to take a position as a governess in a family. As elaborated elsewhere in this volume, the Jane Fairfax subplot underscores the dependent status of women, their reliance on heterosexual marriage, a theme explored further in *Emma* in the situations of Miss Bates, Mrs. Weston, and Harriet Smith.

The manifest inequality between Emma and Harriet, while not slavery, is a relation of patronage, like that Mrs. Elton seeks to force on Jane Fairfax. As in the overt reference to the slave trade and its abolition, the novel is explicit about the moral corruption that follows from the exercise of power over others. Class and gender substitute for race but without more benign effect. The exchange between Mrs. Elton and Jane Fairfax, with its two levels of meaning and consciousness, is calculated to call attention to the economics of the marriage market and to women's uncertain and dependent status. As Mary Astell summarized the problem a century earlier: "If *all Men are born free*, how is it that all Women are born Slaves?" (11).

One has to read Austen's fictional references to slavery and colonialism structurally—that is, to observe where and how these references are used—because whenever these references are introduced, context and position speak eloquently about oppressive and unequal relations closer to home. In *Mansfield Park* the juxtaposition of Fanny's question about the slave trade and Thomas Bertram's reassertion of control over his property—human as well as horticultural—reinforces the reader's sense of Fanny's subordination. In *Emma* the remarks about the slave trade bubble up at the point of crisis in Jane Fairfax's dealings with her secret fiancé, Frank Churchill, underscoring her utter reliance on a "good" marriage to save her from a worse servitude. Slavery in these novels figures the status of women without money of their own. The "slave trade" is a trope for the marriage market and for the tyranny of marriage, a displacement of the subject position of captive Africans onto women.

In *Persuasion*, too, colonial possessions are associated with the weakest and most dependent woman in the novel, Mrs. Smith, Anne Elliot's former schoolfellow who rents a few rooms in the unfashionable Westgate buildings in Bath. Left penniless by the death of her husband, unable to collect the money owed him by the false and faithless aristocrat Mr. Elliot, she cannot claim her inherited property in the West Indies without a male agent. This alienated property, presumably a sugar plantation operating with slave labor, represents at once a literary convention—a standard eighteenth-century novelist's device for restoring lost fortunes—and a reminder that without a man, a woman's authority even over her own colonial plantations was null and void.

Austen was still working on these issues—the gendered terms of colonialism—in her last novel fragment. However she intended to work out the plot of *Sanditon*, she fused gender and race in the character of Miss Lambe, an overprotected, privileged mixed-race West Indian heiress, whom Austen seems to have set up as a target both for money-making schemes and for seduction. The town leaders, the commercially minded Mr. Parker and the shrewd, eccentric matriarch Lady Denham, have joined forces to turn their sleepy village into a tourist attraction, a resort for taking wholesome waters, a new Bath. Among their earliest longed-for customers are the headmistress of a finishing school and three of her charges.

> Of these three, & indeed of all, Miss Lambe was beyond comparison the most important & precious, as she paid in proportion to her fortune.— She was about 17, half Mulatto, chilly & tender, had a maid of her own, was to have the best room in the Lodgings, & was always of the first con-sequence in every plan of Mrs.G.   ("Sanditon" 421)

Lady Denham sees in Miss Lambe the very type of a seaside invalid for their new resort: rich and sickly, a steady customer for her medicinal milch asses' milk, and a woman of means for her nephew by marriage, Sir Edward, to marry. Sir Edward, for his part, aspires to be a rake, handsome and dangerous, a nouveau Lovelace, and this wealthy innocent appears heaven-sent as his sac-rificial lamb. Thus the heiress, because she is a woman, is cast as the victim of colonialism as well as its beneficiary. I imagine that in the moral and spiritual calibrations of this "chilly & tender" character, one of whose grandparents was brought to the island in chains, Austen was planning to chart the relations be-tween the traffic in women and the slave trade, with their corresponding moral corruptions.

Austen's sense of class, like her gender and her patriotic sense of English-ness, was affected by the wars with France and by British imperialism. It was *because* of her class—which was lesser gentry without unearned income—that she revised her estimation of English militarism and imperialism in the last years of her life. As she watched the wars of colonialism over territory enable her brothers' upward mobility, she became something of a British chauvinist in the end—a change of heart recorded in *Persuasion*. The last novel reveals a new attitude about England's global destiny, informed by nationalistic pride over the triumphal defeat of Napoleon, and about her brothers' successful ca-reers in the naval establishment. The years that Austen replays in *Persuasion*, between 1806 and 1808—the very period that Thomas Bertram is absent from his English plantations in *Mansfield Park*—become in the last novel a time not of moral anarchy but of idealized personal history for the new self-made man and his mate.

Austen's relation to colonialism and slavery was thus conditioned by her gen-der, her class, and the history of England in her lifetime. Opposed to enslaving anyone, she used the discourse of abolition to comment on the dependent position of women without means or the possibility of advancement in their so-ciety. She seems to have been refining those perceptions about the commodifi-cation of persons—and the gendering of that commodification—in *Sanditon*. At the same time, because of her class status, she knew that the navy provided upward mobility for men without fortune, family, or connections. Her last complete novel, written after Waterloo, has an appreciative sense of the na-tional destiny that made this mobility possible. Thus she registered the democ-ratizing of power across class for men, seemingly oblivious of the colonial domination that it entailed elsewhere, but always acutely aware of the personal limitations that confined Englishwomen.

Austen represented the hypocrisy of the enterprising Bristol slave traders in Augusta Elton and in Mrs. Norris, and the responsible authoritarianism of the West Indian plantocracy in Thomas Bertram. In the equivocal lineaments of these characters, she traced the meanings of British imperialism in all their ironies. Augusta Elton may be shocked by the mention of the slave trade, protesting that Mr. Suckling, her brother-in-law, was "*rather* a friend to the abolition" (emphasis added), but she basks happily in the reflected prosperity that slavery brought to her native Bristol and, as noted earlier, is the character most invested in delivering Jane Fairfax over to captivity as a governess. Cheerful Mrs. Smith in *Persuasion*, confined to her room while eking out a charitable mite for the poorer families in town by selling homemade thread cases and pincushions, owns a plantation halfway around the world. The slavery that Jane Fairfax invokes is not merely a literary metaphor but a reality to members of Austen's own family. Men of her generation went to India to retrieve their fortunes; women went there to find husbands. Colonialism and slavery had very different meanings for men and women of England's ruling class. Jane Fairfax's characterization of governess agencies as "Offices for the sale . . . of human intellect" stems from her bitter observation of what an educated gentlewoman could expect to do with her learning. Thus Austen's colonial references reveal the deep contradictions of the Enlightenment itself—it was simultaneously an age of slavery and imperialist expansion; of wealth and poverty; of widening class division at home; of ancient lineages, great estates, and itinerant Gypsies; of expanding opportunities for educated men and continued dependence for educated women. Austen represented the ideological pressures of her age even as she was susceptible to them—in her attitudes toward Robert Martin, the Sucklings of Maple Grove, or the deserving poor of Highbury. She reveals her own class-and-gender location in her sympathetic portrayal of the plight of single gentlewomen—Miss Bates, who is grateful for gifts of food (apples and pork); Jane Fairfax, who is about to sell her elegant self to the Smallridge family with their three daughters; and even Emma, who, despite her money and adoring father, must in the end submit to the authority of a husband.

NOTES

This essay is a revised version of my essay "Austen and Empire: A Thinking Woman's Guide to British Imperialism," *Persuasions: Journal of the Jane Austen Society of North America* 16 (1994): 95–106.

[1]Eliza de Feuillide wrote this to Philadelphia Walter on 3 May 1797.

[2]For the history of Haiti, see the classic work by C. L. R. James, *The Black Jacobins*.

The Experience of Class, *Emma*, and the American College Student

Laura Mooneyham White

Of all Austen's novels, *Emma* most conspicuously brings the language of rank and status to the fore. In the first three chapters alone, readers will come under a barrage of class markers, many inevitably opaque to the modern American undergraduate or high school student. "The yeomanry," Emma declares, "are precisely the order of people with whom I feel I can have nothing to do" (29; 1: ch. 4). The Martins, "though very good sort of people," "must be coarse and unpolished" (23; 1: ch. 3). Emma herself, the narrator tells us, is "so great a personage in Highbury" that Harriet is overwhelmed by Emma's willingness to shake hands with her at the end of their first evening together. The recipient of Emma's surprising "affability" (25; 1: ch. 3), Harriet, is but the "natural daughter of somebody" (22; 1: ch. 3). Besides Harriet, Emma populates her first evening party of the novel with the "come-at-able," a "second set," rather than with the missing Westons or Mr. Knightley, "the chosen and the best" (20; 1: ch. 3). Miss Bates, one of the second set, lives in "untoward circumstances" (21; 1: ch. 3). Mr. Weston belongs to a family that "had been rising into gentility and property" (15; 1: ch. 2); his "easy competence" makes it possible for him to marry a woman "as portionless even as Miss Taylor" (16; 1: ch. 2).

We can guess at some of the baffling questions that arise in readers unfamiliar with late-eighteenth- and early-nineteenth-century English class orderings.[1] Are Miss Bates's untoward circumstances worse than Miss Taylor's lack of portion? (Yes.) Why is Mr. Weston, "always acceptable wherever he went" (12; 1: ch. 1), the social superior of Mr. Perry, an "intelligent, gentlemanlike man" (19; 1: ch. 2)? (Because although Mr. Weston was once a military officer and involved in trade, he is now a nonworking landed gentleman; Mr. Perry, a professional man, a working physician, remains on the fringe of gentility.) Is Frank Churchill, "tacitly brought up as his uncle's heir" (17; 1: ch. 2), superior in social status to his own father? (Yes, presuming the heirship becomes more than tacit.) What is the status of Mr. Knightley, who initially is presented with a remarkable absence of status markers—all we learn, at his introduction, is that he is "a sensible man about seven or eight-and-thirty, . . . a very old and intimate friend of the family [who] . . . lived about a mile from Highbury" (9; 1: ch. 1)? (He is the largest landowner in the district, the squire and magistrate.) And last, resisting any relatively easy answers, what is Harriet's status—what can being the "natural daughter of somebody" possibly mean? How is the reader to decode these utterances and comprehend the complex social relations and hierarchies depicted in the novel? And, further, what is at stake in grasping the minutiae of class affiliation?

The difficulties for undergraduates do not arise from historical ignorance alone, for this audience brings to Austen's novels, and to *Emma* in particular, a powerful understanding of class. The ordinary middle-class undergraduate's experience of class structure and class markers writes over, as it were, his or her perception of the operations of social strata in *Emma*. Johanna M. Smith has pointed out that students reflexively understand class in terms of the tripartite lower, middle, and upper structure commonly invoked in American society (67)—a model woefully inadequate for the nuances of class in *Emma*. Further, American students are strongly predisposed to believe that individuals can move up in class; they are as sure of their ability to transcend class boundaries as were any of the Americans Alexis de Toqueville met almost two hundred years ago. Projecting the myth of class permeability onto Austen's canvas, students expect a world in which the substantial social barriers between Emma and Harriet, for example, can be overcome with a little goodwill and tolerance.

Moreover, most students in my experience will aver that they have no particular experience with class as a social reality—that there is no class in America, that the whole point of a democracy such as the United States is to do away with class distinctions. Americans tend to be embarrassed by the very idea of class; as the sociologist Paul Blumberg has claimed, class stands as "America's forbidden thought" (qtd. in Fussell 15). On examination, of course, students reveal themselves as highly acute observers of social distinctions, especially in such class-inflected subcultures as junior and senior high schools, where social relations are governed by hierarchies both internal to the subculture and external (e.g., the status of parents, the status of the school). In denying class while skillfully dissecting class relations, my students reflect the larger patterns of American behavior. Paul Fussell has noted, "Being told there are no social classes in the place where the interviewee lives is an old experience for sociologists" (17). And as Leonard Reissman reports, once this disclaimer is out of the way, "the class divisions . . . can be recorded with what seems to be an amazing degree of agreement among the good citizens of the community" (30).

Nonetheless, the idea that there are no classes in the United States dies hard, partly because where middle-class life predominates, as on college campuses, the middle class itself seems more pervasive than it is. Even television narratives that purport to tell of upper-class life often re-create middle-class dilemmas and diction tricked out with jewels, Armani suits, and Jaguars, and the spectacles middle-class people see of wealth (e.g., Donald Trump's real estate holdings or the weddings of film stars) are firmly middle class, dressed up with luxuries but unembarrassed by upper-class sensibilities or proclivities. We should not be surprised that students have difficulty separating Hollywood and television representations of upper-class life from the real, but unseen, phenomenon.

The middle-class identity of most college students adds a further complication, for this social stratum is the most class-anxious.[2] Fussell explains:

> You reveal a great deal about your social class by the amount of annoy-
> ance or fury you feel when the subject is brought up. A tendency to get
> very anxious suggests that you are middle-class and nervous about slip-
> ping down a rung or two. On the other hand, upper-class people love the
> topic to come up: the more attention paid to the matter the better off
> they seem to be. [The working class] generally [does not] mind discus-
> sions of the subject because they know they can do little to alter their
> class identity. . . . It is the middle class that is highly class-sensitive, and
> sometimes class-scared to death.   (16)

Since Austen's day, middle-class traits have included a strong desire to belong,
an emphasis on correctness and on doing the right thing, earnestness, and optimism about the chances of moving up socially. Then and now, the middle class
tends to be suspicious of the upper-class characteristics of idiosyncrasy, intro-
version, and love of privacy. For instance, "among the [middle class] there's a
convention that erecting a fence or even a tall hedge is an affront" (Fussell 42).

It can't be too flattering to middle-class students and middle-class professor
alike (including this middle-class author) that of all the characters in *Emma*,
the one who most closely fits these middle-class markers is Mrs. Elton, that
great social climber. It is she, we remember, who is most dismayed by Emma
and Mr. Knightley's unconventional plan to live at Hartfield after their wedding: "Shocking plan, living together. It would never do. She knew a family
near Maple Grove who had tried it, and had been obliged to separate before
the end of the first quarter" (469; 3: ch. 17). Eccentricity is the elite's prerogative, and is in consequence to be distrusted. In truth, Mrs. Elton is unrepresentative in Highbury because of her uncloaked class anxiety.

Further, because students are themselves middle class, they tend to see
Emma's elite as belonging more to the middle class than it does; again, in train
with Mrs. Elton, students expect more "finery or parade" from those near the
top of the social ladder (484; 3: ch. 19) than they see in Mr. Knightley, Emma,
or the Westons and thus misconstrue (downward) the status of these characters. Students may need to be shown that even though *Emma*'s world includes
no kings or queens (not even a baronet or viscountess, as are on display in
other Austen novels), the gentry—as represented principally by Mr. Knightley,
the Woodhouses, and the Westons—was still a very small set of the population,
far above the middling, or middle, social and economic reality. As Julia Prewitt
Brown reminds us in "The 'Social History' of *Pride and Prejudice*":

> In Austen's day England was still to a large extent an "aristocracy," or hi-
> erarchy based on property and patronage in which people took their
> places in a pyramidlike structure extending down from a minority of the
> rich and powerful at the top to ever wider and larger layers of lesser
> wealth to the great mass of the poor and powerless at the bottom.   (58)

Rather than represent a middle slice of English society, then, Emma and the other ladies and gentlemen of Highbury—even the distressed Mrs. and Miss Bates—occupy a position far elevated above the farm laborers, industrial workers, tradespeople, military rank and file, and other members of the working classes who made up most of the population. Even further removed from the gentry are the servants—James and Serle at Hartfield; Hannah at Randalls; Mrs. Hodges and William Larkins at Donwell Abbey; Mrs. Elton's housekeeper, Wright; and Patty at the Bateses'. But our view of the servants is skimpy at best; instead of learning their thoughts or feelings, we observe the servants chiefly as they are perceived by their gentry employers (of Hannah, for instance, we know that Mr. Woodhouse approves of the soft way she closes doors).

Given the reality of hierarchical social relations in *Emma*, students may, at first, attempt to understand the relations as a ladder, to be descended from the top (Mr. Knightley in Highbury, Mrs. Churchill in the world of the novel as a whole) to the bottom (the servants, the poor family visited by Emma and Harriet, the Gypsies, and, last, the poultry thieves who serve as dei ex machina at the novel's end). A useful class exercise is to write out on the board—with the students' help—where each character seems to stand in the implied hierarchy.[3] The exercise is particularly helpful if it includes the larger social realm of the unseen characters who help set the main characters more firmly in their places by comparison. For instance, we see Jane Fairfax's economic plight all the more clearly by comparing her temporary "adoption" by the Campbells with the permanent, legal adoption of Frank by the Churchills, who are, in any case, wealthier and have no other heir with whom to compete.[4] What is especially instructive about this exercise is that it allows students to sort out for themselves the criteria for social distinctions. Students tend to assume that wealth will suffice—the richest characters go at the top and the poorest go at the bottom. But complications quickly arise. Why does Emma willingly consort with Miss Bates, whose income is meager in the extreme, but shun the well-to-do Mr. Martin, or the wealthy Coles, whose style of living is "second only to the family at Hartfield" (207; 2: ch. 7)? And why do Emma and Mr. Knightley quarrel so over Harriet's status?

The first helpful complication is that of gentry status: who is and is not a lady or a gentleman. In some sense, all of Austen's works present this factor as pretty much unchanging, determined by birth and upbringing. But her novels also render, quite accurately, the beginning of the dismantling of the term as a simple descriptor in the real world of nineteenth-century social relations. Already in Austen's work we see that a man born a gentleman can lose his gentlemanly status if his *behavior* is ungentlemanly. In the nineteenth century, the term was ambiguous—both a straightforward acknowledgment of birth (as late as 1844, an English dictionary stated that the term denoted a man "born of or descended from good family" [Letwin 16]) and a morally and behaviorally determined assignation. According to the former view, the gentry are those with land who do not work for a living and who occupy the rank between the barons, knights, and baronets (the bottom of the aristocracy), on the one hand, and the yeomanry and merchants, on the other. Thus the Coles, while very rich, have only just entered the gentry; they have bought property and given up their work in the unnamed trade that made them prosperous. Thus, too, the Martins: although they have been tenants of Mr. Knightley's for a long time, renting a large farm, they are not gentry because they do not own the land and because they themselves labor on it; they are indeed the "yeomanry" Emma terms them. According to the latter—and later—view of gentility, however, gentlemen and ladies show themselves as such by their behavior. By 1890, for instance, Samuel Smiles, in *Life and Labour*, can proclaim what is by his day an established, more democratic view: "He is the true gentleman, whatever be his station in life, who possesses and displays the gentler graces" (35).

Emma enters into this debate with a vengeance. At times, Austen shows her agreement with the older and simpler class boundary (for example, Robert Martin, no matter how "gentlemanlike," retreats to his yeoman status at the novel's close, with Austen's evident approval). At other times, and more commonly, Austen suggests how contested the category of gentility can be. For example, is it possible that Frank Churchill can be a true gentleman if he neglects to make his father a wedding visit, or, later, fatigues Jane Fairfax at the piano? Is he amiable, or merely the less gentlemanly (and French) "*aimable*," as Mr. Knightley terms him (149; 1: ch. 18)? Why, further, is Emma so incensed when Mrs. Elton discovers that Mr. Knightley is "quite the gentleman"? Emma fumes, "Actually to discover that Mr. Knightley is a gentleman! I doubt whether he will return the compliment, and discover her to be a lady!" (278–79; 2: ch. 14). As such moments in the novel demonstrate, gentility works both ways, both as a supple, malleable marker for acceptable behavior and as a stable indicator of wealth, birth, and property.

Stability is itself valued as a marker of class. Students often find it hard to see why Frank Churchill's gadabout habits are so damning—why, for instance, a quick excursus to London for a haircut undermines Frank's status as a gentleman. But *Emma*, like the rest of Austen's novels, mirrors the social code of the time that placed a premium on the length of time an individual or a family resided in one place. For this reason, the poor family in the hovel, although more impoverished than the healthier, robust Gypsies, are clearly the Gypsies' social superiors. The Gypsies have no home—they have been nowhere long. In contrast, the reach of years behind the Knightley family's ownership of Donwell Abbey serves as yet one more guarantor of Mr. Knightley's unselfconscious claim to social preeminence. Among the points on which Emma congratulates herself in her regard of Donwell Abbey (on the ostensible grounds that her complacency arises from her sister's connection by marriage with the Knightleys) loom the signs of long-standing occupancy: "its ample gardens stretching down to the meadows . . . of which the Abbey, with all the *old neglect of prospect*, had scarcely a sight—and its *abundance of timber* in rows and avenues, which neither fashion nor extravagance had rooted up." To belong to an old family living in one place for a long time, owned and overseen with stewardship for future generations: here is much of what Austen's world recognized as "true gentility" (358; 3: ch. 6; my emphasis).

"True gentility" such as Mr. Knightley's also requires the exercise of noblesse oblige (literally, "nobility obliges"), the feudal doctrine that the upper classes have a duty to take care of the lower, by doing charitable deeds and by setting a good example of manners and morally unblemished behavior. One of the key ways Austen reinforces our sympathy for Emma in the midst of her outrageous behavior toward Harriet and Mr. Elton is to show her exercising noblesse oblige for the poor of Hartfield.[5] Austen's description of Emma as ministering lady is notable for its lack of irony:

> Emma was very compassionate; and the distresses of the poor were as sure of relief from her personal attention and kindness, her counsel and her patience, as from her purse. She understood their ways, could allow for their ignorance and their temptations, had no romantic expectations of extraordinary virtue from those for whom education had done so little; entered into their troubles with ready sympathy, and always gave her assistance with as much intelligence as good-will.   (86; 1: ch. 10)

Irony reenters after Emma and Harriet depart the hovel, as Emma acknowledges that she may not long remember the scenes of misery that so forcefully strike her now. And, indeed, forget she does when Mr. Elton comes into view. But we are meant to contrast Emma's genuine if sporadic charity with Mr. Elton's total lack of it. Although he maintains that he was about to visit the poor family, he is easily turned away by the prospect of a walk with Miss Woodhouse: "His visit he would now defer" (87; 1: ch. 10). Worse, he spends the next few minutes of conversation dilating on the epicurean delights of the Coles' last banquet—"the Stilton cheese, the north Wiltshire, the butter, the cellery, the beet-root and all the dessert"—a feast that cannot but painfully contrast with the cottagers' meager foodstuffs. By the end of the chapter, the reader learns that even the putative visit to the hovel was a sham; Mr. Elton shamelessly admits that he had headed in the direction of the hovel only because "he had seen them go by, and had purposely followed them" (88–89, 90; 1: ch. 10). That Emma's sense of noblesse oblige is genuine but flawed sets her above the clergyman whose charity is a masquerade.

An understanding of noblesse oblige and its social importance also helps render more intelligible the weight of Emma's insult to Miss Bates. Some students find it puzzling as to why this incident seems to serve as the climax of Emma's education. But Mr. Knightley's rebuke can be as instructive to readers about mores in Austen's day as it is to Emma herself. Tellingly, as Mary Poovey has argued, he focuses on the issue of dependence and . . . appeals to the responsibilities that accrue to Emma's social position. . . . [He] reminds Emma not only of her current place in the social hierarchy but also of that moment when the notice of any—even Miss Bates—was an "honour" for a child. This reminder [positions] Emma . . . first as chronological inferior, then as social superior. . . . Because some are dependent (whether as children or as the unprotected poor), one must assume responsibility; to assume responsibility is to voluntarily limit one's childlike desires, to think of others before or in relation to oneself.   ("True English Style" 398)

Emma's duties to Miss Bates are in keeping with her other social obligations, especially to the single women, like Miss Bates, who are not in her enviable state of independence. As Marilyn Butler explains, "The hurt to Miss Bates is not . . . a single instance, for there is a pattern in the novel of vulnerable single women, whom it is the social duty of the strong and rich to protect" (270). Emma owes Harriet Smith and Jane Fairfax similar consideration; that she treats both women properly by the end of the novel is one vital sign of her moral education.

If Emma's adventures offer examples of both noblesse oblige appropriately exercised and noblesse oblige forgotten, we turn to Mr. Knightley as an example of noblesse oblige at its best. He is continually on the move in the novel behind the scenes, arranging for apples and carriages and other aids to those less fortunate than he, most notably the Bateses. Even in very minor details, Mr. Knightley's consideration for his neighbors shows through, as when he points out to his brother that a path had better not be moved if "it were to be the means of inconvenience to the Highbury people" (106–07; 1: ch. 7). As Butler puts it, Mr. Knightley is a "fantastically wishful creation of benign authority, in whom the benefits and attractions of power are preserved and the abuses and encroachments expelled" (141). In implicit acknowledgment of the obligations of benign authority stand Emma's efforts to make amends for her bad behavior; she begins a campaign of charity of her own to the Bateses. Visits, arrowroot, notes, offers of a carriage: all are given as propitiation, and Emma reflects, "could Mr. Knightley have been privy to all her attempts of assisting Jane Fairfax, could he even have seen into her heart, he would not, on this occasion, have found any thing to reprove" (391; 3: ch. 9). Emma's sense of charity now mirrors Mr. Knightley's even in his absence. This harmony of purpose and motive is a signal of their more far-reaching accord of values.

Once students have sorted out the criteria for gentility, they inevitably notice that setting out a hierarchy of social relations is made trickier by the fact, in the novel, of social mobility. For instance, before the book starts, Miss Taylor is no better off than Jane Fairfax; at the novel's close, Miss Taylor, now Mrs. Weston, has risen by marriage into secure gentility. But Jane Fairfax has gone even further, for she will soon be the wife of the heir of an immense fortune held by a "great Yorkshire family" (15; 1: ch. 2). Students are often surprised to reflect, further, that the current poverty of Mrs. and Miss Bates was not their lot while Mr. Bates, the former vicar, was alive; before his death and the advent of Mr. Elton, these two women must have had the benefit of a clergyman's comfortable living, and resided, indeed, in the comfortable vicarage that now houses Mr. Elton. But a "living," like the current institution of academic tenure, is only for life and leaves no provision for surviving relatives, and thus the Bateses are in a sad situation, having moved to rented and cramped quarters. Their circumstances, in fact, bear some relation to that of the Austen family's descent in fortune when the Reverend George Austen, Jane's father, gave up his living.

In this way and in others, the social mobility in *Emma* reflects the world Austen knew. The social realities of her own family were marked conspicuously by mobility, both up and down:[6]

> Her great-grandfather was a scion of wealthy clothiers and had five sons. The eldest inherited the estate, and the others were apprenticed to an attorney, a haberdasher, a surgeon, and a stationer. The attorney, who grew rich, paid for the education of the surgeon's orphan son, who became the Rev. George Austen, who [in turn] married the great-niece of a duke, and was [Jane Austen's] father. Of his sons, one became a clergyman, one a [very wealthy] country gentleman, and two were admirals. Among their descendants, there are academics, members of the professions, a royal spouse, . . . and a bricklayer's apprentice.   (Letwin 8)

Austen's family was not unrepresentative, moreover. The system's flexibility was noted memorably by Mme de Staël (like de Toqueville, a foreigner who saw social relations perhaps more clearly than did those in the society she examined):

> If a son of a common shopkeeper . . . displays superior talents at the bar, he may rise without obstacle to the rank of lord chancellor; enter the house of peers with an hereditary title. . . . One of his sisters may marry a descendant of the Howards or the Percies, and become related to all the great nobility celebrated in the history of England. . . . Another [brother], less fortunate, may continue in the shop of his father, or in the office of an attorney, without this great difference between the members of the same family exciting astonishment in anyone.
> (Staël-Holstein 130–31)

This world of social flux is accurately rendered, then, in *Emma*, where almost every character is rising or falling or at least trying to rise or trying not to fall.[7] The upwardly mobile characters include the Coles, Mrs. Elton, Jane Fairfax, Frank Churchill, Miss Taylor, Harriet, and Emma herself. The only downward-moving characters are Mrs. and Miss Bates, but the novel offers the possibility that other vulnerable women might fall, too—Harriet and Jane, who are both saved by marriage.

The social mobility of women, in particular, is correlated with the degree of their education. Jane Fairfax's expensive and careful schooling makes her otherwise improbable marriage to Frank Churchill possible. Harriet's spotty education (she praises Elizabeth Martin by saying she is "quite as well-educated as me" [31; 1: ch. 4], a touching grammatical error that may imply that it is Elizabeth Martin who is the better educated) provides but one reason to justify her eventual alliance with Robert Martin rather than with Mr. Elton, Frank Churchill, or Mr. Knightley. It is a mark against Emma that her own education has been so erratic—her wealth and independence, Austen shows, have insulated her from the need to become as accomplished or as well-read as Jane Fairfax. Austen, the largely self-taught daughter of a country rector, knew full well that education for women was potentially liberating.

As students come to terms with the many complicating factors regarding class, such as level of education or social mobility, they observe the drawbacks in taking a simplistic view of social demarcations, as Emma herself does on occasion. As G. Armour Craig has pointed out, "Tiny as it is, the society of Highbury contains more exceptions and more recalcitrant differences [relative to problems of rank] than the most active imagination [such as Emma's] or the most comfortable ambition [such as Mrs. Elton's] can foresee" (241–42). Even Emma's marriage to Mr. Knightley brings up the issue of social position, for Mr. Knightley must temporarily lose some of the status of Donwell Abbey by moving into Hartfield after his marriage. The confusions and complexities regarding class are themselves part of the world Austen knew and the world she creates.

One last criterion bears on students' categorization, by social strata, of the characters in the novel: Who judges? One cannot consider Harriet, especially, without determining whose perception of rank is to prevail. In Emma's eyes, Harriet deserves far better than Mr. Martin. Mr. Knightley demurs, violently: "he is as much her superior in sense as in situation. . . . What are Harriet Smith's claims, either of birth, nature or education, to any connection higher than Robert Martin? She is the natural daughter of nobody knows whom, with probably no settled provision at all, and certainly no respectable relations" (61; 1: ch. 8). Emma and Mr. Knightley also battle over Mr. Elton, about whom Emma's first words in the novel are "There is nobody in Highbury to deserve him" (13; 1: ch. 1). By the end of the novel, however, Emma has come to Mr. Knightley's understanding of proper social relations—she confesses, for example, that she now sees the "littleness" in Mr. Elton's character that had shown itself far earlier to Mr. Knightley (330; 3: ch. 2). But what most propels Emma's readjustment of her notions regarding Harriet is the latter's presumption in wanting Mr. Knightley for herself: "How she could dare to fancy herself the chosen of such a man till actually assured of it!—But Harriet was less humble, had fewer scruples than formerly.—Her inferiority, whether of mind or situation, seemed little felt." These reflections, in turn, generate the most cutting observation of all: "Who but herself had taught her, that she was to elevate herself if possible, and that her claims were great to a high worldly establishment?—If Harriet, from being humble, were grown vain, it was her doing too." When class-driven "presumption" threatens Emma's union with Mr. Knightley, her illusions about class fall away (414; 3: ch. 11).

No discussion of social relations and class hierarchies in *Emma* would be complete without the Marxist critique of Austen's position. Arnold Kettle was the first to enunciate this critique at any length, in his *Introduction to the English Novel*. He posits that "the truth is that in so far as *Emma* does reveal [Austen] as a conventional member of her class, blindly accepting its position and ideology, the value of *Emma* is indeed limited, not just relatively, but objectively and always." Dispensing with the more generous view that we must "approach the novels with sympathy in their historical context" (101), he argues instead that "the values and standards of the Hartfield world are based on the assumption that it is right and proper for a minority of the community to live at the expense of the majority" (397). More recent critics of Austen, such as Claudia Johnson, Mark Parker, James Thompson, and Mary Poovey, have acceded to the proposition that *Emma* fundamentally accepts English class structure.[8] But many critics question the premise Kettle set out a half century ago, that "the question at issue is not Jane Austen's failure to suggest a *solution* to the problem of class division but her apparent failure to notice the *existence* of the problem" (99). After students have worked through the various intricacies of class in *Emma*—its flexibility, its competing definitive boundaries, its reliance on subjective analysis—they may be in a strong position to weigh the merits of Kettle's claim and to decide for themselves to what degree it is true that Austen does not "notice the *existence* of the problem." In so doing, students may move even further, uncovering for themselves something of what "class" means in contemporary American experience. They will learn that class considerations are remarkably persistent, pervasive, and complex, both in Austen's day and in our own.

NOTES

[1]The confusion is not abated by Austen's frequent recourse to introducing characters with their incomes attached, like price tags around their necks. Mrs. Elton, for instance, is described as having an "independent fortune, of so many thousands as would always be called ten" (181; 2: ch. 4). Students can of course be taught how to convert these amounts of capital into yearly income by calculating 4 or 5%, the two most widely employed rates of interest in the first two decades of the nineteenth century. This calculation yields, for example, the £400 or £500 Mrs. Elton brings to her *caro sposo* each year. But converting annual income into a modern-day standard of living, given the radical differences in types of expense—food, clothing, housing, servants—is a far more complex matter. For a helpful analysis of the variables, see Copeland, "Economic Realities."

[2]Nearly 70% of Americans think of themselves as middle class, regardless of their income, according to a Gallup-CNN-USA Today poll taken in September 2000. Only 6%

call themselves either lower or upper class; most of the remaining respondents (24%) identify themselves as "working class." See Zeller.

[3]Any such categorization is nuanced by several considerations, such as when in the novel we make the ordering, where we set the level separating the "genteel" from the nongenteel, whose perspective we use (e.g., employing the narrator's point of view rather than Emma's would change the placement of Harriet and of several other characters). Such a list would look something like the following (in the right-hand column are characters who are away from Highbury but who impinge on the plot). Students should realize that arrows will need to be added to suggest the many changes in social status that occur as the novel proceeds. What follows is my best sense of the hierarchy as each character is introduced in the novel, from the narrator's point of view:

In Highbury	*Away from Highbury*
Mr. George Knightley	The Churchills
Emma and Mr. Woodhouse	The Sucklings
Frank Churchill	
The Westons	The Campbells
The Eltons	The Dixons
The Coles	The John Knightleys
Mrs. and Miss Bates, Jane Fairfax	

————(Beginning of problematic line of gentility)————

Mrs. Goddard
Mr. Perry
Harriet Smith

————(End of problematic line of gentility)————

The Martins
William Larkins (Mr. Knightley's agent)
Mrs. Hodges (Mr. Knightley's housekeeper)
Miss Nash and other teachers
James, Hannah, and other servants
Poor family in hovel
Gypsies
Poultry thieves (may be the same people as the Gypsies, at the same social level)

[4]Craik has noted that *Emma* is graced by a rich array of characters we hear of but never meet, from Mrs. Churchill, at the top of the social scale, through the Sucklings of Maple Grove, the Campbells off in Ireland, with their newly married daughter and son-in-law in tow, down further to Mr. Perry the apothecary and doctor, and to Miss Nash the teacher. Descending firmly beneath the gentry we find Mr. Martin's mother and sister, William Larkins, Mrs. Hodges, the parlor boarder Miss Bickerton, and Patty, among many others, who help readers determine the social stratum of the major characters more accurately in relation to them. For example, the Sucklings "make [Mrs. Elton's] true social standing quite plainly a good deal lower than her social pretensions" (443). These many unseen characters also enhance *Emma*'s formal realism by tricking the reader into believing that the novel's social field is more densely populated than it is.

[5]Mrs. Elton provides an instructive contrast, as well as another way in which Austen maintains sympathy for Emma by making her foil, Mrs. Elton, seem so much worse. Mrs. Elton's arrogance toward both Harriet Smith and Jane Fairfax reveals how short she falls from her self-proclaimed status of "Lady Patroness." Considering the marked difference between Emma and Mrs. Elton, as Johnson explains, offers a further means for readers to "distinguish the use of social position from the abuse of it, a proper sense of office from a repulsive officiousness" (*Jane Austen* 129).

[6]Spring argues that Austen's own class is not the gentry but the "pseudogentry" (53). Copeland expands on Spring's category: "[They were] rural, nonlanded professionals— the Anglican clergy, lawyers, preferably barristers living in the country, officers in the fighting services, . . . people in respectable lines of great trade—who [had] strong country connections with the gentry through kinship and personal loyalties" ("Economic Realities" 42). Briggs, in his magisterial *Social History of England*, however, disputes the idea that many of the higher professionals—doctors, lawyers, clergymen, and army officers—could not lay claim to gentry status: "there were extremely large numbers of 'middling folk,' who increased in numbers and income . . . and growing groups of professional people [including] lawyers. . . . There was no doubt that they, like physicians (if not apothecaries) and army officers, were gentlemen [as were clergymen] even if they were very poorly paid" (194).

[7]Craig well summarizes the social movement in Highbury, a "small community that is responding to some strange pressures from a strange outside world": "Outside Highbury is a mysteriously powerful institution called 'trade' from which rich men like Mr. Cole retire to a life of anxious respectability. . . . Enscombe, the seat of the proud Churchill family, is in a northern county [Yorkshire] where feudal haughtiness still flourishes. In Weymouth and Bristol conventional social relations are queerly scrambled, and illicit flirtations have their proper habitation. . . . London [is a] much larger social distance away. Highbury may be small and serene, but like The Crown, its principal inn, it is just a little seedy. The quality of its neighborhood is declining; there are no longer enough county families even to provide a homogenous guest list for a ball. Emma's father, the first citizen, is a comic valetudinarian who rarely leaves his house. . . . Highbury, in short, is no longer an eighteenth century county town nor is it yet a fashionable suburb like Richmond. It is precisely the place where an 'imaginist,' as Emma is called, can make mistakes about 'rank,' about the social position of any stranger who comes within her acquaintance" (238–39).

[8]Johnson cleverly points out that there is only one point in *Emma* in which the language of radical assaults on class rises to the surface—when we hear a "hue and cry about an 'infamous fraud upon the rights of men and women'" (254; 2: ch. 11). However, this imputed attack on the rights of humankind is no more than hyperbole employed by some of the characters planning the ball, who complain about the prospect of a dance without a dinner attached. Johnson readily acknowledges, as well, that Austen's conservatism is far from the "anarchistic and egalitarian novels of Godwin, Holcroft, and Wollstonecraft" (*Jane Austen* 126). One of the most impressive analyses of class in *Emma* can be found in Parker's "The End of *Emma*," in which Parker argues that Austen can be more properly understood less through the idea of a political unconscious (the term, of course, is Fredric R. Jameson's) than as a "conscious ideologue": "While her novels may, as Poovey and Thompson suggest, work on the level of a 'political unconscious' when she speaks of romantic love or when she defines her relation to

material objects, Austen speaks of class with a startling clarity and at times an unexpected irony. Her historical moment, in which the boundaries of class seemed less fixed, enforced a kind of consciousness upon her presentation of class relations. . . . The clarity with which [she] examines class relations might, to a modern reader, suggest a progressive attitude. . . . But Austen operated in another political context, one which she was able to lay bare, in a remarkably perceptive way, the relational structure of class while fully accepting it" (345–46). For a further discussion of Austen's "political unconscious," see Poovey, *Proper Lady*; Thompson, esp. 3–8.

Emma, the Eighteenth-Century Novel, and the Female Tradition

Lorna J. Clark

What is immediately striking about teaching Jane Austen now, as opposed to twenty years ago, is the spectacular increase in the level of awareness of her work; most students have heard of her, and some are enthusiasts. "I love Jane Austen," someone will exclaim on the first day of class. "I've read all her novels—over and over."

The recognition factor is not limited to the movies alone—although clearly the many film and television adaptations (of *Sense and Sensibility*, *Pride and Prejudice*, and *Emma*, for instance) have played their part in giving Austen visibility and acceptance. The films seem to have inspired an appreciation of the novels. Whereas Henry Fielding, Samuel Richardson, Frances Burney, and Maria Edgeworth are unfamiliar names to most students, even to those specializing in literature, Austen stands out. Austen's brand-name recognition and ready-made following are invaluable assets to anyone trying to make early fiction come alive for the post–generation X student.

I try to bring Austen into every course I teach. An introductory course on English literature can usefully include an Austen novel. She can be seen as a pivotal figure bridging the gap between eighteenth- and nineteenth-century novels. Building on, improving, and refining the work of her predecessors, she explored the potentialities of the new form and discovered solutions to technical difficulties that were adopted by those who followed her. After Austen, I tell my students, the novel would never be the same again.

Even when teaching the Victorian novel, I begin by discussing Austen—at the end of an introductory lecture on the origin and development of the novel as an emerging literary genre. But my favorite course to teach is on the eighteenth-century novel, which leads up to and ends, triumphantly, with Austen. Before my students graduate, I want them to know a writer they can take with them, as a guide, companion, and friend. I urge them to read and reread her often. I tell them how, like Shakespeare, Austen offers fresh insights with every reading; the riches of her novels are never exhausted but can be mined again and again. To read her at twenty, at thirty, at forty, is to see new perspectives, to learn lessons about life each time. Few writers, as any instructor knows, stand up to multiple rereadings. I advise my students to return to her periodically throughout their lives, to try her again in five years' time, and then in ten. Judging from the attentive faces, I think that some may follow my suggestion.

A course in the eighteenth-century novel will attract a bright and motivated group of students (who else would even attempt to read eight long novels in thirteen weeks?). Keen to fill gaps in their knowledge, they are eager to learn about a period that is unfamiliar to them. I give them a mixture of conventional and less conventional texts. In the first half of the course, up to the midterm break, we cover the classics, the dead white males who have traditionally dominated courses on the eighteenth-century novel. After discussing the socio-economic conditions that predisposed the public toward this new literary genre, we look at Daniel Defoe, the journalist-cum-novelist, and consider the realism of his settings and the embedding of concrete particularity in his narratives. A novel by Richardson follows, probably *Pamela* (the story of the servant girl making good), whose brilliance lies in the telling of the tale. We see how the epistolary method concentrates on emotional subjectivity, imposing restrictions on time and point of view that remained influential in the development of narrative. Fielding's *Joseph Andrews* or *Tom Jones* comes next; either one is a breezy on-the-road novel that provides a good contrast to Richardson's hot-house atmosphere. We discuss neoclassical aesthetics, Fielding's use of general types for satiric purposes, the revelation of character through external mannerisms, and the realism of objective assessment.

Laurence Sterne and Tobias Smollett are also included and serve to reinforce some of these patterns and trends. *A Sentimental Journey* is desirable for its length. I find my students slow to finish very long novels, perhaps because of the inflation of expectations (from one term paper, the norm twenty years ago, to two or three for each course) that forces them to focus, early in the term, on those assignments that are worth the greatest number of marks. In this driven environment, there is less tolerance for the leisurely pace of a slow-moving story (a complaint, ironically enough, made by Victorian readers). Assigning shorter novels whenever possible is a good strategy for reducing stress; these works spark the most discussion, since everyone in the class should at least have read to the end and be able to contribute.

Sterne's fragmentary narrative, with its erotic suggestiveness, goes down well with students, as does Smollett's more virulent prose in *Humphry Clinker*, which provides a variety of epistolary voices. Students in the postmodern age feel at ease with the multifaceted presentation, which emphasizes the partial and subjective nature of perception, and the self-conscious construction of a narrative from conflicting points of view.

Although emphasis on the female tradition of the novel comes in the last half of the course, I always include a work by a woman writer early on. I may glance at Aphra Behn, Delarivière Manley (1663–1724), or Eliza Haywood (1693–1756), but I have had the most success with Charlotte Lennox's *The Female Quixote*, whose publication date (1752) puts it in the first half of our reading list, which proceeds in chronological order. This novel serves to introduce romance conventions, and our approach appeals to the feminist readers in the class. The rigid conventions governing the role of women and Arabella's obtuseness can irritate some, until we consider that the world of romance grants women an imaginative power not otherwise available to them. The heroine's stubborn clinging to her fantasies succeeds in prolonging artificially the period of courtship, during which she can dominate, demanding her lover's subjection. With method in her madness, she somehow manages to stave off the moment when she must undertake the submissive role of wife, with its consequent loss of autonomy. The end can be seen either as a diminishment of her role or as a successful adjustment to reality, in the form of a female bildungsroman, a pattern that underlies so many women's novels. The ironic undercutting, subversion of values, and reversal of expectations appeals to students and can spark some interesting essays.

In the second half of the course, we hit the glory days, the later eighteenth century, when so many novels were written of women, by women, and for women; these works were dismissed lightly at the time and subsequently neglected. I tell my class that until recently, the works we purchase in paperback could be read only under controlled conditions in rare-book libraries. I share with my students the excitement of doing the groundwork of such research and tell them that there is still much to do in uncovering the lives and works of these forgotten women writers. Novels by this "injured body," so passionately defended by Jane Austen, are now being rediscovered, reedited, and reread. "Let us not desert one another," she wrote:

> Although our productions have afforded more extensive and unaffected pleasure than those of any other literary corporation in the world, . . . there seems almost a general wish of decrying the capacity and undervaluing the labour of the novelist, and of slighting the performances which have only genius, wit, and taste to recommend them. "I am no novel reader—I seldom look into novels—Do not imagine that *I* often read novels—It is really very well for a novel."—Such is the common cant.—"And what are you reading, Miss———?" "Oh! it is only a novel!" replies the young lady; while she lays down her book with affected indifference, or momentary shame.—"It is only *Cecilia*, or *Camilla*, or *Belinda*;" or, in short, only some work in which the greatest powers of the

mind are displayed, in which the most thorough knowledge of human nature, the happiest delineation of its varieties, the liveliest effusions of wit
and humour, are conveyed to the world in the best chosen language.

(Austen, *Northanger Abbey* 37–38; 1: ch. 5)

As a corollary to Austen's defense of the novel, and to demonstrate the large
numbers of women who took to the pen, I direct students to pages from Dale
Spender's *Mothers of the Novel: One Hundred Good Women Writers before
Jane Austen*, first published in 1986 but still a useful list. I point out that many
of these writers produced just one or two novels, and we place their work in
the context of what writing as a "career" could mean during the period. We
glance at conditions in the publishing trade to see how many literary genres
these professional writers, intent on earning money, were willing to try; surprisingly, many of the women were quite as versatile as the men. The novel can
be seen as simply the latest way to play the game, a sure way to earn a few
pounds, and we consider why this genre might have appealed to women in particular. A relatively undemanding form (in that it did not require a classical education), the novel could be written conveniently in the home, as the natural
extension (particularly in the case of epistolary novels) of a woman's habitual
occupations. The subject matter, love and marriage, was congenial to women,
and the action could take place in the private domestic sphere, the feminine
domain. The vast majority of readers were women, benefiting from improve-
ments in education and newfound leisure, who formed an eager market for a
genre that placed their experience at the forefront.

I try to help my students see the evolution of the novel in practical terms,
embedded in the life of the time. The imaginative re-creation of the historical
past comes as a liberation for students, who realize that the "masterpieces" analyzed and theorized so earnestly in an academic setting centuries later, as self-
conscious literary constructs, may actually have been written quickly and
geared to a specific market. Grounding the novel in the period helps bring
both alive for the students.

This approach seems particularly apt for Austen, whose novels are imbued
with the life and literature of her day. Her work is much better understood
when placed in the context of the female tradition from which she drew. Situ-
ating her in the living tradition of women writers helps clarify her achievement
and highlight the astonishing originality and quality of her writing.

As for which novels to choose from among those written by women before
Austen, there are many possibilities, and I have never taught the same work
two years in a row. An obvious lead-in is Frances Burney, long identified as a
precursor. We first note the traditional view, which sees her combining the best
of Fielding and Richardson, the satiric social commentary and boisterous
humor with didactic and sentimental elements. *Evelina* offers realistic scenes
set in London and Bristol Hotwells, with a focus on the domestic sphere. We
also look at recent feminist readings, which find in Burney an undercurrent of
protest and suppressed violence.

Burney's first novel is epistolary; a motherless child, brought up in the country by an unworldly clergyman, is seen nervously "coming out" in fashionable society, far from her mentor, to whom she writes breathlessly of her adventures. Beautiful and virtuous but unpracticed in social forms and customs, she commits errors and gaffes, and finds her character liable to misconstruction. Her social position is equivocal because she is denied the protection of her aristocratic father, who repudiates the connection; she is exposed to predatory men who exploit her vulnerability; she is placed in a dangerous position until she can win an effective male protector (father or husband). In the course of running this gauntlet, she must learn to conduct herself with decorum, to exercise good judgment, to evaluate correctly the moral character and social merits of potential suitors, and to avoid serious mistakes.

A useful way to teach *Evelina* is to bring out the pattern of the adolescent novel, or the novel of education, with its underlying theme of a quest for financial and emotional security. Launched on the stage of the world, the heroine faces a series of tests that will establish her character and prove her integrity and self-worth. When she succeeds, she is rewarded with an appropriate mate and a place in the community; she makes the rite of passage from one patriarchal household to another. Female identity involves a loss of autonomy, which the heroine learns to accept as she is socialized into the patriarchal world.

Many women's novels were written in the form of the coming-of-age story, a construct that underlies Austen's works as well. A recognition of the pattern shows where Austen varies the conventions and invigorates them with her original genius. The presence of orphans, for example—heroines who have lost one or both parents or whose guardians are either absent or inadequate—occurs often in fiction. Suspense and conflict are increased when the heroine is forced to act alone, to make choices and forge her destiny; her isolation heightens her vulnerability and offers a contrast to her eventual happiness. The plight of "a Female Alone" and unprotected (Burney, *Journals* 10: 701) haunts Burney's works as well as Austen's and afflicts all their heroines, although much less melodramatically in the latter.

Reading Burney's *Evelina*, Maria Edgeworth's *Belinda*, and Austen's *Pride and Prejudice* as a trilogy offers variations on the reformed heroine. Instructors can point out the courtesy-book elements and the self-consciously didactic role of the novel in reforming manners and reinforcing lessons of acceptable social behavior. Placed in this context, amid rigid and prescriptive codes of feminine decorum, the forthright qualities of Austen's heroine are the more striking, as she pleads to be considered "a rational creature speaking the truth from her heart" (*Pride and Prejudice* 109; 1: ch. 19).

Another pattern might be formed by pairing a Gothic novel, perhaps one by Ann Radcliffe (other possibilities are shorter, lesser-known works, such as Clara Reeve's *The Old English Baron*), with Austen's *Northanger Abbey*. Catherine's sturdy common sense appears funnier when Austen's protagonist is placed in relief against Radcliffe's exquisitely tormented heroine (recalling Richardson's Pamela), and the abbey passages come into their own. Moreover, the vogue for the Gothic, at its height in the 1790s—the decade in which Austen first tried to get published—is a useful lead-in to other novels as well. Students can experience firsthand, as did Austen's contemporaries, the quietness of her effects, in contrast to the thrills provided by the novels of sensation. At the same time, these novels suggest the sexual repression underlying women's imprisonment in the domestic sphere and hint at a darker subtext beneath the surface, which may reflect on Emma's situation.

One novel from the 1790s, Elizabeth Inchbald's *A Simple Story*, is a favorite with students. The first attempt at fiction by a prolific playwright, the book met the same fate as Austen's early work, in being rejected initially, and then, after a lapse of several years, finding a publisher. *A Simple Story* shows clearly the theatrical talents and practical experience of its creator; the action is fast-paced and dramatic, almost cinematic, in its presentation. Like many other works published in that decade, it is revolutionary in its presentation of female experience.

The novel is divided into two parts; the first portrays a surprisingly modern situation—love as a battlefield, a contest of wills—that resonates today. The heroine, Miss Milner, a warm-hearted coquette, falls in love with her guardian, Dorriforth, an austere Catholic priest. Her forbidden passion figures the illicit nature of female desire. When her love is acknowledged and returned (the vows of priesthood are dissolved when he inherits a title and an estate), the impediment becomes internal—a struggle for mastery and power as, during the courtship, she rebels against his efforts to control and dominate her. The question of female education is raised in that her acquisition of frivolous accomplishments has left her ill prepared to meet life's challenges. Although, as a result of incompatibility of temper, the lovers decide to part, the second volume closes with their hasty marriage after an eleventh-hour reconciliation.

In the second part, beginning some twenty years later, the consequences of the marriage of such an ill-assorted pair are all too evident: the volatile Miss Milner has fallen into adultery; the self-controlled Dorriforth has evolved into a monster of stern authoritarianism, whose will must not be crossed. He banishes his daughter, Matilda, in revenge for her mother's sins, and is persuaded to revoke this decree only when another man challenges his rights to her, which puts him on his mettle to defend his female property. Lady Matilda remains passive throughout, worshipping somewhat fetishistically her unknown father's belongings, in scenes with oedipal undertones.

The monstrous figure of the patriarchal tyrant, the archetypal Gothic villain, provides an amusing contrast to Mr. Woodhouse in *Emma*. With a comic reversal of situation, Austen's novel features a feeble hypochondriac at the heart of the paternal mansion. His selfishness is real and the household revolves around his needs, but laughably, his blind egotism lays him open to being managed by his masterful daughter. A characteristic element of parody is seen as Austen stands the conventions on their heads. The heroine "whom no one but myself will much like" (Austen-Leigh [ed. Chapman] 157)—clever, self-assertive, and outspoken—is the complete opposite of the insipid, passive maiden featured in so many novels. Rather than refrain from action until rescued by the hero, Emma takes command from the start; her vitality, intelligence, and wit are remarkable, as are her confident efforts to dominate those around her. Frank Churchill, the ostensible hero introduced partway through, who seems intended to marry Emma, is by no means her match, and the story develops in an unusual way. The plot works out how these two do *not* come together, an ironic result, which is made to seem the most plausible and natural outcome, though with an atmosphere of intrigue and secrecy underneath.

Conventional feminine characteristics—the elegance and reserve of Jane Fairfax, Harriet's good nature and blushing beauty, and Mrs. Elton's superior accomplishments—all appear in a negative light, even as somewhat sinister. Typically, however, Austen does not go too far in challenging social mores—the chivalrous Mr. Knightley is certainly an upholder of patriarchy and privilege. Emma's fate is not unusual, in falling in love with a mentor-guardian figure and marrying a much older man. At the same time, the content of the match is unconventional, in the emphasis on the intellectual equality of the couple and on the plain speaking and respect that Mr. Knightley offers her. Austen's success in creating vital, attractive women is notable, especially when we compare her characters with earlier heroines, on whom she drew.

There are many ways to teach *Emma*, many lessons, patterns, and analogies to be drawn. As a female bildungsroman, in which the heroine comes to terms with reality and dispels her illusions of power, *Emma* harks back to *The Female Quixote* and looks forward to Dorothea Brooke in *Middlemarch*. As a mystery or a puzzle to be solved, with clues planted throughout, *Emma* could be read as an early detective novel. It is, in addition, an excellent work for teaching point of view; the element of surprise in the first reading can never be repeated, but students can be asked to reread key scenes, in the light of their knowledge, to appreciate various viewpoints and to create alternative versions of events. This activity may lead to a discussion on the construction of narratives and the fracturing of simple plot lines. *Emma* also illustrates one of Austen's technical achievements—restriction of the third person point of view primarily to one consciousness—that would be influential in the development of the novel. Finally, students enjoy the humor, the tale of matchmaking schemes gone awry, although few students initially notice the added irony that it is Mr. Knightley's initiative that makes all right in the end. With a first, successful attempt at matchmaking, Mr. Knightley sends Robert Martin on an errand to London when Harriet is there, effecting quickly what Emma has failed to accomplish, a happy match for Harriet. The novel can then end conventionally, with a marriage—three of them, in fact.

What is remarkable about reading *Emma* alongside other novels of its day is the surprise and pleasure it gives, the ways in which the work differs from them. Students come to appreciate Austen's ability to master the conventions of the genre and infuse into them new life and authenticity. Austen is best understood not as an isolated genius but as positioned within a female tradition.

The course emphasizes that she was writing within a rich cultural and literary context, of which she was well aware. Linking Austen to other women authors helps students place her innovations, discoveries, and achievements in better perspective. What stands out is her refreshing quality, the transformation of conventional elements, infused with her genius and insight. I am astonished every time I teach her, simply by how good she is. The students come to realize why she was hailed by discerning contemporaries, although I remind them that, while moderately successful in their day, her novels by no means created the sensation of *Pamela* or *Evelina*. Her reputation increased steadily in succeeding generations and stands at an unprecedented height today. What has happened, I ask them to consider, to create conditions that allow Austen's art to triumph?

At the end of the course, several students write their papers on Austen, and in the final class, when I ask them to vote for their favorite author, even more will profess themselves to be enthusiastic fans of Austen. I feel that the time I spend has been worthwhile, if I send students out into the world enlightened and entertained, with a capacity for rational amusement that I hope will stand them in good stead for the rest of their lives.

The Comedy of *Emma*

John Wiltshire

One of the best ways to begin a course on Jane Austen's novels, or to introduce *Emma*, is to set Austen's work within the context of contemporary female authors, as the narrator indeed invites us to do in the fifth chapter of *Northanger Abbey*.[1] The most commonly taught, and the most useful of these, is Frances Burney, and the novel usually chosen is *Evelina*—for the good reason that young readers still find it enjoyable. Another is that Burney is the novelist whose works are most frequently alluded to in Austen's; she seems to have remained a lifelong favorite, since there are references to *Cecilia* in *Persuasion* and to *Camilla* in the late, unfinished *Sanditon*.

The teacher can readily bring out the general relevance to Austen of Burney's first novel. Its subtitle, *The History of a Young Lady's Entrance into the World*, sums up the narrative of *Northanger Abbey*; the plot of a young woman from the country, who must find her way in a more sophisticated society, negotiating its unexpected challenges and steering clear of predatory males, surviving to marry, handsomely, into the patrimony, is echoed in almost all of Austen's novels. Even more important, perhaps, was the attitude that Burney (at least intermittently) took toward her heroine. Good-hearted as she is, Evelina simultaneously makes a series of silly mistakes. The reader is encouraged to feel warmly toward this innocent and naive young woman, but at the same time to find her youthful presumptions and errors amusing. (Letter 8, for example, shows Evelina trying to persuade herself she doesn't want to go to London, while every second line reveals how intensely she does—students can be asked which Austen heroines are treated the same way.)

The recent criticism of Burney, however, depicts a novelist who is strikingly unlike Austen. It has emphasized "the dynamics of fear," the "chronicle of assault," the "trauma of growing up female," the "fictions of violation" in *Evelina* and in Burney's later novels.[2] Much less has been said about those aspects of the novel that endeared it to, and entertained, Burney's contemporaries: the range of its comedy from affectionate irony to satire, slapstick, and burlesque, and its gallery of vividly depicted characters. For, although in *Evelina* there are certainly passages of terror (and melodrama), the frame and design of the novel is comic. And it is as a female comic novelist that Burney was probably most useful and most instructive to Austen—and is surely most useful to the instructor who wants to describe the comedic mode of *Emma*. The would-be genteel Branghton girls and their beaus, Mr. Brown and Mr. Smith (whom Dr. Johnson and Mrs. Thrale especially enjoyed), are obviously a template for Austen's later handling of such figures as the Steele sisters in *Sense and Sensibility*, as well as Mr. and Mrs. Elton in *Emma*. The Branghtons' vulgarity is less important than the fact that their "ill-breeding" is aligned with "brutality," most markedly in their treatment of their poverty-stricken lodger, the poet Mr. Mc-Cartney, just as the Eltons' is with their cruel treatment of Harriet Smith at the ball. Not coincidentally, Emma accuses herself of being "brutal" to poor Miss Bates (376; 3: ch. 7).

The lines of social class, then, underscore the comedy of *Evelina*, just as they do that of *Emma*. Primarily, however, although Burney and Austen are both comic novelists, the comedy of Burney's novel offers a clear and instructive contrast with the comedy of Austen. Thomas Macaulay long ago pointed out that Burney excelled in eccentrics, while Austen's figures were much more delicately and subtly differentiated from each other—that is, individualized (Southam 122). But this point is not what is perhaps most striking when one teaches the two novelists together. For, varied as it is, the comedy of Burney's novel can be summed up as the comedy of discomfort. Laughter in Burney's novel is habitually in the enjoyment of another's discomposure—whether the overturning of Madame Duval's carriage, toppling her into the mud, or Mr. Brown's being caught arm in arm with prostitutes or Mrs. Selwyn's witty assaults on the vanity of Lovel and Lord Merton. When Madame Duval relates the episode of the carriage ambush to the Branghtons, expecting their sympathy, the men burst into laughter, and the young ladies, at first straight-faced, stuff their handkerchiefs into their mouths. We share their laughter while laughing at them for laughing. Here, as with the notorious later episode of Lovel's attack by a monkey dressed as a fop, the novelist is playing the scene for a derisive laughter that, at the same time, she condemns (those who stand aloof, like Evelina and Lord Orville, are commended for their benevolence). The simultaneous participation in a character's amusement and comic irony toward it is found also in *Emma*, although to quite different effect.

An instructor whose class has read *Mansfield Park* might recall the scene at the beginning of the second volume in which Sir Thomas Bertram, newly returned from Antigua, comes on Mr. Yates in full theatrical flight on the improvised stage. This is a scene of comic discomfort—both Mr. Yates's and Sir Thomas's—"a ranting young man, who appeared likely to knock him down backwards" (182; 2: ch. 1). The encounter is viewed (and enjoyed), though, from the point of view of Tom Bertram, who here resembles the more rascally and irresponsible males who figure in Burney's novels. His enjoyment of the scene, shared with the reader (as the instructor might suggest), is a revisiting of the kind of comedy associated with Burney.

Apart from the crude comedy exemplified in the attack on Lovel in Burney's *Evelina*, social discomfort is the motif of all the amusement to be had from the Branghtons' misunderstanding of genteel arrangements, as it is from Evelina's own slips, mistakes, and social embarrassments. The comedy of *Emma*, or rather the kind of response elicited by the comedy of *Emma*, is quite different. A tiny incident, deeply embedded in the text, could usefully serve a teacher in bringing out the salient characteristics of Austen's distinct comic sense. This is the moment when Miss Bates confides to Jane, in the midst of a long speech, itself in the midst of the ball at the Crown Inn, that Mrs. Bates has been a bit disappointed at her outing to Mr. Woodhouse's because, after "a delicate fricassee" of sweetbread and asparagus was offered, the treat has been withdrawn because Mr. Woodhouse fears that the asparagus is a trifle underdone (329; 3: ch. 2). The reader is amused at both these old people: at Mrs. Bates's expectation of a delicacy (we can perhaps imagine the look on her face as the dish is sent away) and at Mr. Woodhouse's fussiness, once again carried to an absurd extreme. Both dismay and amusement might be the appropriate response to the frustration of Emma's kindly endeavors to cater to their guest. But only an insensitive reader, I think, would mock either of the characters, Emma or Miss Bates.

This tiny episode might suggest to a class the comic form of *Emma* in embryo. This is not the comedy of discomfort but of mutual good intentions gone awry (the comedy of comfort, perhaps?). It is a miniature comedy of cross-purposes. We enjoy this moment the more because it forms an item in the running joke about food at Hartfield. Mr. Woodhouse's executive action is a successful move in that submerged domestic battle that began in the novel with Emma's successful sabotage of her father's wishes about Mrs. Weston's wedding cake, at the end of chapter 2. Every time dietary preferences are in question at Hartfield, the comic motif is repeated. In fact, a comedy of cross-purposes often gathers around the figure of Mr. Woodhouse—for example, in those scenes in which he and his daughter Isabella comfortably converse but are always in danger of veering off the broad road of their apparent obsession with health and illness and crashing into each other. The reader watches with growing amusement each time Isabella brings up the advice of her doctor, Mr. Wingfield, and Mr. Woodhouse brings up the advice of his doctor, Mr. Perry, knowing that sooner or later, and despite Emma's efforts to take the reins, they will meet headlong (vol. 1, ch. 12). A teacher who is focusing on the novel's comedy might well find it helpful to give a class extracts from the "Opinions" of the novel collected by Jane Austen (see appendix to this volume), as well as Walter Scott's review, since Austen was especially pleased by Scott's commendation of these two figures. Another example to which a class might be directed is the "duet" between Mrs. Elton and Mr. Weston in the last chapter of volume 2, which is commented on by Marcia Folsom in her introduction to this volume.

The comedy of cross-purposes necessarily involves two or more participants, and sets the reader apart from both. Since it inheres in the total situation, it is not often a cruel comedy, one that pokes fun at bodily indignity (Madame Duval in the mud; Sancho Panza tossed in the blanket); rather, it savors, ruefully, the spectacle of human misunderstanding wrought to its acutest pitch. For this comedy to yield its greatest delight, the participants must not just misunderstand; they must interpret the same thing in completely different ways, or attribute to the same sign opposite meanings. Such a comedy depends, too, on the creation of individuals as agents, as characters with definable intentions and schemes, so that, as a teacher might point out, Emma is a better target than the demure, self-conscious Evelina (or the retiring Fanny Price). In the first volume of *Emma*, her scheme to marry Harriet to Mr. Elton is productive of much comedy of this kind. Emma sees the portrait she has created of Harriet as signifying that Harriet is attractive, and Mr. Elton's praise of it as overtures of courtship. For Mr. Elton, in contrast, the portrait signifies Emma's genteel accomplishments, and his flattery is meant to further his courtship of her. Once given the hint, students will be able to find many other examples of comic cross-purposes in these chapters, for here they reach a near-farcical pitch. They come to a head in the carriage scene in which Mr. Elton—turned by "Mr. Weston's good wine" into a hometown impersonation of Sir Clement Willoughby leaping into the carriage with Evelina and "actually" grasping her hand in his—is found "actually making violent love" to Emma (129; 1: ch. 15). (Students will need to be told that this expression does not mean what they think it means.) The adverb catches, as in Burney, not only the immediacy of the scene but Emma's astonishment, and—to the reader, who has long seen what is coming—her comical indignation.

The comedy of *Emma*, then, is the comedy of cross-purposes. But the teacher might guide the class to see how Austen varies the formula. Later in the novel the pattern is merged or cohabits with something subtler. Again at the ball at the Crown, when Miss Bates tells Jane Fairfax about her grandmother, a little window, or vista, opens on another mode of life. The moment is an aperture within an incursion, for Miss Bates's speech itself appears to trespass on Emma's consciousness. (Instructors can demonstate to students how Austen contrives to bring depth to her created world.) Mrs. Elton and Mrs. Weston, we gather, have vied for the privilege of offering their carriage to bring Miss Bates and Jane to the ball, and Miss Bates is full of gratitude: "Never were such neighbours," she enthuses (322; 3: ch. 2). But in this long speech, again overheard unwillingly by Emma, we learn that this woman, for whom a shabby village inn decorated and lit by candles has become a "fairyland," has had to slip out, in the midst of the festivities, to put her elderly mother to bed. No one has offered a carriage for this errand, and, as she says, "nobody missed me" (329; 3: ch. 2). Thus, although Emma may be unaware of them, the realities of class in Highbury are communicated to the reader: Miss Bates's unobserved dutifulness toward her mother differs remarkably from the demonstrative forms of charity that Emma extends to the Bateses. And the understanding of charity this implies is nested in a speech that the reader is invited to find, in its garrulous inconsequence, typically amusing.

Miss Bates's chatter here exemplifies a variation on the notion of cross-purposes—what one might call, pushing the idea a little further, comic self-contradiction, a variation of the kind of speech Austen often uses to expose her characters. In *Pride and Prejudice*, for example, Mrs. Bennet complains "that those who never complain are never pitied" (113); Mrs. Norris, in *Mansfield Park*, boasts of her charitable nature, in passages which reveal just how mean-spirited she is (7). In *Emma*, for example, Mr. Weston tells Emma that he never allows himself "to speak ill" of Mrs. Churchill on his son's account, but such discretion doesn't prevent him from ending his confidences with "she has no more heart than a stone to people in general; and the devil of a temper" (120–21; 1: ch. 4). At the Crown Ball, Miss Bates first protests that she doesn't want to preempt Jane's telling her grandmother about her dance partners, and then blurts out a gentleman's name; she soon protests that she doesn't want the disappointment over the sweetbread and asparagus to reach Miss Woodhouse's ears, at the same time as she is broadcasting it all over the room (329–30; 3: ch. 2). Wrapping around the self-contradiction, of course, is yet another form of amusement for the reader: if Emma were really able to attend to what Miss Bates is saying, she would certainly understand the older woman's world better, and might even notice Frank Churchill's particular attentions to Jane.

The comedy of cross-purposes reaches its apotheosis in the scene of Mr. Knightley's proposal. The cross-purposes of farce have been kept up—perhaps stretched too far?—in the mix-up between Frank Churchill's chivalrous rescue of Harriet from the Gypsies and Mr. Knightley's chivalrous rescue of her from the Eltons (vol. 3, chs. 3 and 4). Now Emma, believing that Harriet might be right about Mr. Knightley's feelings for her, dreads to hear the news. Walking in the garden at Hartfield, Emma and Mr. Knightley are each uneasy about the other's emotional investments, and each fears that the other is in love with someone else. They are equal in their misapprehension. Emma interprets Mr. Knightley's demeanor as a signal that he has encountered his brother's displeasure at his prospective match with Harriet; he interprets her hesitancy as disappointment at Frank Churchill's engagement to Jane. Thus their conversation resumes the many comic misunderstandings (including those between the two of them) with which the novel has familiarized the reader. The dialogue seems to be moving toward final clarification when Emma, thinking that Mr. Knightley is on the point of telling her about Harriet, stops him: "'Oh! then, don't speak it, don't speak it,' she eagerly cried. . . . 'Thank you,' said he, in an accent of deep mortification, and not another syllable followed" (429; 3: ch. 8). At this moment their being at cross-purposes becomes potentially tragic.

Farcical misunderstanding requires that two characters read the same signal or sign in ways that contradict each other. Here the confusion is in fact resolved by the very words that seem to deepen it. Emma, unable to let Mr. Knightley suffer, offers to listen to him "as a friend." There is something wonderfully complementary in this gesture, since it is because he is "satisfied with proving myself your friend" that Mr. Knightley has spoken to Emma most earnestly at their most intense previous encounter, at Box Hill (375; 3: ch. 7). On that occasion Mr. Knightley has set himself, and his own desires and prospects, aside in order to put himself at what he believes is the other's service. Here, Emma does the same. Neither of them quite realizes that "as a friend" now means, if not "as a lover," then "as one who truly loves." "As a friend!" repeats Mr. Knightley, "that I fear is a word—." Then he sees. "Emma, I accept your offer—Extraordinary as it may seem, I accept it, and refer myself to you as a friend. —Tell me, then, have I no chance of ever succeeding?" (429–30; 3: ch. 13). Thus the comedy of cross-purposes reaches its consummation.

Much recent criticism of Austen has embedded her work in the context of her contemporary female novelists. We can now read her novels as dialogically engaged with those writers, Burney among them; and, as I've suggested, *Evelina* offers some useful entry points for a class to think about the specific achievement of *Emma*. But this feminist-historicist criticism, valuable as it is, has obscured an important aspect of Austen's literary inheritance. Her indebtedness to the eighteenth-century theater was probably as important (see the books by Byrne and Gay, both titled *Jane Austen and the Theatre*). Even more useful might be a comparison of the novel with *The School for Scandal* or *She Stoops to Conquer*. *Emma* owes a good deal to the "laughing comedies" that succeeded sentimental comedy on the eighteenth-century stage and to the plays that Austen herself saw and alludes to, as familiarly as our students do to the TV series *Friends* or *Sex in the City*. Austen takes the character foibles, the overhearings, the vanities, and the misunderstandings that are the staple of these plays and, reimagining them in a precisely rendered domestic setting, makes a comedy that is both more subtle and more moving. Critics might well claim, then, that Shakespeare, David Garrick and George Colman, Richard Brinsley Sheridan, and Oliver Goldsmith provide the models for the entanglement of cross-purposes that is the dominant comic mode of *Emma*.

NOTES

[1] Austen's famous defense of the novel, from *Northanger Abbey*, is quoted in Clark's essay in this volume.

[2] The first three quotations in the sentence are from the titles of essays by Patricia Meyer Spacks, Judith Lowder Newton, and Mary Poovey, respectively. All are reprinted in Bloom. The phrase "fictions of violation" is used by Epstein (85).

Emma and Richardson's *Sir Charles Grandison*

Celia A. Easton

In his 1817 "Biographical Notice of the Author," published with *Northanger Abbey* and *Persuasion*, Henry Austen cites his sister's early acquaintance with significant English essays and novels. Among the many novelists she read, Jane Austen appreciated Samuel Richardson for his creativity and for the consistency of his characters. Henry Austen apparently had less tolerance for the enormous length of Richardson's novels, about which he offers restrained criticism in complimenting his sister's superior narrative technique. *Sir Charles Grandison*, he observes, "gratified the natural discrimination of her mind, whilst her taste secured her from the errors of his prolix style and tedious narrative" ("Notice" 7). This line is popular with my undergraduate students, who read one volume of *Grandison* along with Austen's novels. "Surely if her taste secured her from Richardson's excesses," they ask, "why can't it secure us as well?"

When they read Brian Southam's edition of Austen's short play *Sir Charles Grandison; or, The Happy Man*, my students are pleased with Austen and irritated at Richardson. The farcical five acts of the play, focusing on Harriet Byron's kidnapping and rescue with a few allusions to the Italian characters and Charlotte Grandison's love interests, reduce the events of Richardson's novel to mad comic dialogue. Happy to burn their bridges behind them, my students declare that the English novel, having arrived at Austen, should dispense with Richardson forever. By holding on to *Grandison* through our readings of Austen's novels, however, I have managed to get many of them to appreciate the dialogue Austen maintains with the author who created characters James Edward Austen-Leigh said his aunt knew as well as "living friends" (*Memoir*, Folio ed. 79).

In her discussion of Austen's "mining" of *Grandison* for *Mansfield Park*, Jocelyn Harris describes the novelist's attitude toward Richardson as "creatively critical . . . affectionate but never reverential" ("'As If'" 361). Harris's observation is even more apt in regard to *Emma*, in which Austen both invokes and parodies Richardson's characters and plots. While she develops an economically privileged heroine who shares Charlotte Grandison's wit and Harriet Byron's independence, Austen rejects the powerlessness of Richardson's women. When we read *Emma* and volume 1 of *Grandison* together, my students and I focus on the construction of female characters, Richardson's abduction plot, father figures, and sibling affection. Austen's novel is, of course, an original creation, not a revision of *Sir Charles Grandison*. Nevertheless, *Grandison* resounds in *Emma*, as Austen demonstrates her ability to thin out Richardson's didacticism, discovering rich moments worthy of satirical critique beneath his "prolix style."

Female Characters

Richardson focuses on Harriet Byron and Charlotte Grandison in the first volume of his novel. Both are well-spoken, educated, and financially independent. Before Harriet's masquerade adventure and kidnapping, Richardson involves her in many conversations about the marriage market and women's right to choose to be married or remain single. Not wanting to appear too anxious to be a wife, Charlotte ruminates on whether to wed Lord G. She is the model of the woman Mr. Collins, in *Pride and Prejudice*, erroneously takes Elizabeth Bennet to be—to assuage his vanity, he decides that she has rejected his marriage proposal out of mere punctilio. In contrast, although Emma keeps her desire for George Knightley in an erogenous blind spot for most of the novel, when he finally declares his love, she unhesitatingly says "[j]ust what she ought" (431; 3: ch. 13). Austen's heroine wants to postpone marriage for practical, responsible reasons, not out of concern for her reputation. Emma values her father's health and security above her own immediate happiness. Charlotte Grandison, for her part, "makes free" with Lord G. to keep him at a distance (1: 341).

Grandison, like *Emma*, takes up the question of women's education. Harriet received a private education from her grandfather in modern languages, literature, and the Bible. Against the pedant Mr. Walden, who argues women's inferiority on the basis of their lack of university education, Harriet defends the practical knowledge women obtain through the university of the "world" (1: 66). Unimpressed, Mr. Walden proclaims he "should rather choose to marry a woman whom I could teach something, than one who would think herself qualified to teach me" (1: 67).

Although no more a scholar of ancient languages than Harriet is, Emma epitomizes the clever woman who is more likely to teach than to be taught. Mr. Knightley observes to Mrs. Weston that Emma at ten "had the misfortune of being able to answer questions which puzzled her sister at seventeen" (37; 1: ch. 5). Rejecting Mrs. Weston's suggestion that Emma's friendship with Harriet Smith will induce her to read more, Mr. Knightley complains that Emma has made plans for self-improvement since age twelve. Yet he reveals himself to have had a long-standing affection for the teenager, as well as a willingness to be taught by a woman, when he admits admiring a reading list Emma drew up at age fourteen: "I remember thinking it did her judgment so much credit, that I preserved it some time" (37; 1: ch. 5). In *Emma* Austen not only extols intelligent women, she also replaces their misogynistic critics with sensitive, sharing partners.

His sensitivity, however, does not stop Mr. Knightley from believing he has a responsibility to correct Emma's behavior. He is most explicitly corrective in the Box Hill episode, when Emma—allowing her wit to overcome her politeness—insults Miss Bates by joking that in their picnic game she could easily contribute three dull thoughts—but she must restrict herself to "only three at once" (370; 3: ch. 7). The question of Emma's wit again recalls *Grandison*.

Harriet Byron writes to her cousin that Charlotte Grandison "has a vein of raillery, that, were she *not* polite, would give one too much apprehension for one's ease" (1: 265). It is Charlotte's wit that makes her an attractive character. While Harriet worries that her savior, Sir Charles, will face death in a duel with Sir Hargrave Pollexfen, Charlotte attempts to cheer her up with shocking jokes: "What a deuse ails the girl then? Take care I don't have cause to beat you?—Have any of your fellows hanged themselves?—and are you concerned that they did not sooner find the rope?" (1: 300). Charlotte's wit almost scandalizes Harriet, but Austen obviously preferred her levity to Harriet's self-condemning angst. "[P]ictures of perfection as you know make me sick & wicked," Austen wrote to her niece Fanny Knight in 1817, anticipating the publication of *Persuasion* but also reflecting on her less-than-perfect character Emma Woodhouse. "You may *perhaps* like the Heroine [Anne Elliot], as she is almost too good for me" (Austen, *Letters* [Le Faye] 335).

Austen's strongest heroines follow the model of Charlotte: brilliant and beautiful, but also clever and critical, hardly pictures of perfection. Harris finds a great deal of Charlotte in the witty but immoral Mary Crawford, in *Mansfield Park* ("'As If'" 375). Charlotte's taunting relationship with Lord G., Harris also suggests, is the model for Elizabeth Bennet's teasing repartee with Darcy both before and after they admit their love for each other ("Influence of Richardson" 96). Emma's comment to Miss Bates is unkind, but, like Charlotte's remarks, it *is* funny. In constructing Mr. Knightley's reaction, however, Austen defers to Richardson. Charlotte, too, must have her wit "managed" by a man, not the man who will marry her but a better friend, her brother Sir Charles (1: 300). In following Richardson, Austen acknowledges—as she does in *Mansfield Park*—that the witty woman must learn restraint or lose the respect of the world and the affection of the nobleman (Harris, "'As If'" 375–76).

Abduction Plots

Although it occurs halfway through the first volume of Richardson's seven-volume novel, Harriet Byron's abduction is the pivotal scene in *Grandison's* plot. It is the source of her guilt and remorse—for attending a masquerade dressed in the gaudy, silvery outfit of an Arcadian princess—and it is the foundation of her love, for she is rescued from Sir Hargrave by the brave and dashing man of feeling, Sir Charles Grandison. In *Emma* Austen rewrites the classic scene of the heroine confined in a coach with a villain. Austen's heroine maintains her dignity, feels embarrassment rather than fear, and observes quite belatedly the sexual tension of her plight. Mr. Elton is an emasculated Sir Hargrave, a pretentious rather than a vengeful suitor.

Harriet Byron is trapped in Sir Hargrave's chariot in the final stage of her kidnapping, having been carried away by corrupted chairmen and imprisoned in the home of a woman who is too fearful of Sir Hargrave to defy him. Emma, in contrast, is left alone by chance in a carriage with Mr. Elton when John

Knightley, with his wife and his father-in-law, drives ahead of Emma's carriage after a winter dinner party at Randalls. Sir Hargrave gags Harriet to muffle her screams. Inversely, Emma wants to "restrain" Mr. Elton "by her own manners," to prevent his "talking nonsense" in his inebriated state (129; 1: ch. 15). Harriet is constantly aware that her tormentor means to dominate her sexually. "What, my sweet Byron, I don't hit your *fancy*!" says Sir Hargrave. "*You don't like my morals*! laughing again. My lovely fly, said the insulting wretch, hugging me round in the cloak, how prettily I have wrapt you about in my web!" (1: 243). When Richardson's villain has "wrapt" Harriet about in his "web," the students sneer and twist sinister air-mustaches.

Before Emma knows what is happening, the discourse of her coach ride also turns sexual. When Mr. Elton passionately announces his adoration for her, seizing her hand and demanding her attention, Austen's prose imitates the emotional agitation of Emma's "tête-à-tête drive" with the vicar. The rhythm of Mr. Elton's sexual excitement can be felt in even a small portion of the half-paragraph-long sentence: "she found her subject cut up—her hand seized—her attention demanded, and Mr. Elton actually making violent love to her: availing himself of the precious opportunity, declaring sentiments which must be already well known, hoping—fearing—adoring—ready to die if she refused him" (129; 1: ch. 15). Mr. Elton seems to collapse after climaxing as the sentence concludes in the resolve that Emma will immediately be his. Students are as prepared as Emma is to dismiss Mr. Elton's rhetorical excess ("hoping—fearing—adoring—ready to die") as the harmless ranting of a man who naively thinks he has mastered the language of love.

Harriet Byron is spared the fate of Richardson's earlier abducted heroine Clarissa Harlowe by the bold intercession of Sir Charles. Emma extricates herself simply by expressing her astonishment at Mr. Elton. When Sir Charles hears Harriet's cries and stops Sir Hargrave's horses, Harriet's captor tries to "muffle [her] up again" with the handkerchief to keep her silent (1: 245). For Emma, silence is not dangerous, but it contributes to misinformation and increases her discomfort. She is dumbfounded by Mr. Elton's insistence that she has been leading him on for weeks; he interprets this as an "interesting silence [that] confesses that you have long understood me" (131; 1: ch. 15). Harriet must be carried, nearly unconscious, to Sir Charles's coach. Emma emerges by herself from the coach at Hartfield, met by her father's welcome and the comfort of her sister and brother-in-law. Once Harriet is nursed back to health, the story of her abduction—both her version and Sir Charles's—dominates the novel. But Emma puts on a cheerful appearance and keeps her mental perturbation to herself.

Austen drains the coach-entrapment scene of its danger and its romance. In doing so, she reveals the structure of her novel, making that scene as pivotal as Harriet Byron's abduction. In the novel, Emma is satirically introduced in the hyperbolic rhetoric of "evil" and "danger": the *evil* of "having rather too much her own way" and the *danger* of losing "her many enjoyments" through an inflated sense of herself (5; 1: ch. 1). A distorted belief in romance narratives has motivated Emma's adoption of Harriet Smith. Since Harriet's parentage is uncertain, Emma erroneously presumes that her quest to identify her friend's father will uncover a source of riches and status. She must ultimately face the reality of hurt feelings and embarrassment rather than "evil," as she discovers unremarkable illegitimacy and meager talents rather than a hidden, miraculous prize. By transforming the dangerous and romantic villain into a presumptuous but harmless vicar, Austen foreshadows Emma's own deflated fantasy and reassessed sense of self.

Father Figures

Despite her illusions, Emma is a loyal daughter. Emma Woodhouse insults Miss Bates, snubs Jane Fairfax, misleads Mr. Elton, and manipulates Harriet Smith, but she never shirks her duty toward her father. Students at first find Mr. Woodhouse to be a self-centered, opinionated, hypochondriacal, gruel-eating, nervous, and depressed old man. "[T]hough everywhere beloved for the friendliness of his heart and his amiable temper," we are told, Mr. Woodhouse had no talents that could "have recommended him at any time" (7; 1: ch. 1). All of Emma's talents recommend her: she is gracious, charming, and naturally gifted, even in arts she doesn't practice. Because of her devotion to Mr. Woodhouse, however, Emma consciously chooses to restrict her life, gently humoring her father when he resists change and adjusting her early married life to suit his needs rather than hers or her husband's.

In Richardson's novel, Harriet Byron clearly misses having a father. Orphaned and raised by relatives, Harriet voices an extraordinarily generous view of parental authority. Although Harriet seems to have read Richardson's second novel, *Clarissa* (she accuses Charlotte of being a "very Miss Howe"), she sympathizes with the tyrannical Harlowes over their daughter. The most restrictive parents, she writes to her cousin Lucy, are less of a threat to women's liberty than the presumptive suitors who insist on "dangling after" her: "parents, if ever so despotic (if not unnatural ones indeed,) mean *solely our good*, though headstrong girls do not always think so" (1: 13).

Emma, a "headstrong girl," treats Mr. Woodhouse indulgently and patronizingly, not with awe-filled respect. Yet that relationship bears a resemblance to Harriet's connection to her "adopted" father, the silly knight Sir Rowland Meredith. Harriet refuses Sir Rowland's proposal that she marry his nephew, the laconic Mr. Fowler, but she endearingly begs the uncle, "let me look upon you as my father" (1: 129). Harriet modifies her theory of parental good by carefully declining Sir Rowland's proposals, but she spares his feelings. Like Mr. Woodhouse, Sir Rowland wears his emotions close to the surface. In Richardson's sentimental novel, doing so is an admired sign of "a manly heart" (1: 131). Austen chooses to maintain the sentimental model for Emma's relationship with her father. Both Richardson and Austen modify duty by constructing daughters who treat their fathers tenderly, but nevertheless have their own way.

Sibling Affection

In adopting Sir Rowland as her "papa," Harriet Byron conveniently sticks Mr. Fowler into a safe brother slot. She has a great deal of confidence that the category will preserve her from his viewing her as a potential wife. But her episode with Mr. Fowler and Sir Rowland takes place before her abduction and before she meets Charles Grandison. Safety has its drawbacks. She is grateful that, after the terror-filled ride with Sir Hargrave, Sir Charles lifts her onto the seat of his chariot "with all the tenderness of a brother" (1: 246). Yet as she recovers in his home, attended by Charlotte, Harriet only initially finds solace in his declaration, "I have two sisters: the world produces not more worthy women. Let me henceforth boast that I have three" (1: 211). If that category holds as firmly as she intends it with Mr. Fowler, she will never become Sir Charles's wife. When Lord D. makes a serious proposal for marriage, at the end of the first volume, Harriet is forced to admit, "[I]f I should be *entangled in a hopeless passion*, the object of it would be Sir Charles Grandison" (1: 326). As long as he treats her as a sister, however, Harriet must keep that passion to herself.

Austen frequently explores the strength of pseudoincestuous relationships in her novels. Because, in *Mansfield Park*, Fanny Price is nearly a sister to Edmund Bertram, she understands him with an insight and intimacy never achieved by spouses who meet as adults. Edward Ferrars's proximity as Elinor Dashwood's quasi-brother-in-law, in *Sense and Sensibility*, helps to foster their seemingly hopeless passion. Catherine Morland's relationship with Henry Tilney, in *Northanger Abbey*, flourishes when he treats her with the same freedom she sees in his teasing relationship with his sister. That trio particularly mimics the Harriet Byron, Sir Charles, and Charlotte group, with Austen transferring Charlotte's liveliness to Henry and Sir Charles's seriousness to Eleanor Tilney.

Emma never criticizes the brother-sister quality of her relationship with George Knightley, but, for most of the novel, it masks their desire. Mr. Knightley enters Hartfield with the confidence of a relative, and he argues with Emma without self-consciousness, always more like a brother than a lover. When he pleases her at the ball sponsored by Mr. Weston at the Crown by dancing with Harriet Smith, Emma rewards Mr. Knightley with a dance, both negating and acknowledging their pseudosibling status: "[W]e are not really so much brother and sister as to make it at all improper" (331; 3: ch. 2).

Like Harriet Byron, Emma eventually marries her "brother." Harriet must wait until Sir Charles can disentangle himself from his obligations to Lady Clementina (much as Edward Ferrars has obligations to Lucy Steele); she is saved by the Protestant Sir Charles's unwillingness to convert to Clementina's religion. In a letter to one of her actual brothers, Sir Charles transforms himself into Clementina's "fourth brother"; he acknowledges that his former passionate love for the Italian woman would be displaced by Harriet: "had I never known Clementina, I could have loved her, and *only* her" (5: 337). He marries Harriet in volume 6, and together they welcome Clementina on a visit to England in volume 7, where she begs, "And will *you*, Lady Grandison . . . be my sister? Shall Sir Charles Grandison be my brother?" (215).

Richardson translates "sister" into "wife" by exchanging the roles of Clementina and Harriet. Similarly, Emma changes places with the other women in Mr. Knightley's life. Jane Fairfax and Harriet Smith are competition for George Knightley's attention primarily in Emma's imagination, but perceived Clementinas can produce as much painful jealousy as real ones. Emma rejects Mrs. Weston's suggestion that Jane Fairfax would be a good match for Mr. Knightley, without recognizing her own erotic interest. Emma admits that she is in love only when she believes that her schemes have matched George Knightley and Harriet Smith.

Austen also converts her siblings into spouses, but she sustains the virtues of brother-and-sister love. Mr. Knightley loves Emma precisely because she has allowed him to treat her with a brother's privilege: "I have blamed you, and lectured you, and you have borne it as no other woman in England would have borne it" (430; 3: ch. 13). Even when they agree to marry, Mr. Knightley maintains enough of the brother to agree to live in his father-in-law's home rather than at Donwell Abbey. Harriet Smith believes she loves Mr. Knightley, but her desire is easily reassigned to Robert Martin, her "friend" at the beginning of the novel. Despite Emma's early warning to Harriet that marrying Robert Martin would necessarily exclude Harriet from the Woodhouses' social circle, Emma is happy to regard her former protégée with sisterly affection once she ceases to be a rival for Mr. Knightley.

George Knightley retains none of Sir Charles Grandison's romance attributes: the sword has been beaten into a plowshare; the chariot's horses are needed on the farm. Emma can step out of her coach—an enclosure of sexual tension—without a man's help and without losing consciousness. Yet Austen significantly holds onto Richardson's sensitive male, not only in George Knightley but also in Henry Tilney, Edward Ferrars, Fitzwilliam Darcy, Edmund Bertram, and Frederick Wentworth, in *Persuasion*. In *Emma* Austen invokes *Grandison*'s father-daughter and pseudosibling models of relationships, but she grants her female characters more liberty than Richardson's. In *Grandison* the truly independent women are reduced to caricatures on the margin of society, such as the lesbian, Miss Barnevelt, and the licentious widow, Lady Betty Williams. The echoes of *Sir Charles Grandison* are often inverted in *Emma*, with affectionate improvement. Austen's downplaying of the romantic is at the center of Emma's moral education; she comes to accept the Knight(ley) in her life, without the distorting fantasy.

Exploring Artist and Audience
through Austen's "Opinions of *Emma*"

Annette M. LeClair

Among the earliest comments about *Emma* that have come down to us is Jane Austen's own prediction that readers are likely to have difficulty with it. Even before Austen began writing, she announced her intention to "to take a heroine whom no one but myself will much like" (Austen-Leigh, *Memoir* [Folio ed.] 140). By creating a character of intermingled "blessings" and "evils" (5; 1: ch. 1), and then naming the novel after her, Austen kept the issue of Emma's likability central to readers' response to the work and to the writer herself. Those who find Emma's social outlook offensive and her matchmaking tedious often reject Austen on similar grounds. Her sympathy for her heroine—assumed to be there and seemingly confirmed by her words—suggests to some readers that Austen was also limited in outlook—that her powers, like Emma's, were confined by the social rules, habits, and tastes of her small provincial circle.

Moving new readers of Austen beyond this conclusion can be difficult. But a closer examination of the similarities and differences between Austen and Emma as artists can lead to a deeper grasp of the novel and to a greater appreciation of the pleasures of reading it. For Austen's remarks about the doubtful reception that she expected for *Emma*—even before she began writing it—reveal a consciousness of her audience, and an audacity in facing it, that shaped and elevated Austen's approach to her material and to the act of writing throughout her life. In the portrait-painting scene, Austen endows Emma, too, with artistic audacity. She then dramatizes the reception of Emma's work in ways that tellingly echo the responses that Austen collected from readers of her published works. A careful reading of this episode in *Emma*, in conjunction with the resonant material from Austen's life, can reveal Austen's methods of creating sympathy for Emma, as well as the sophistication of Austen's artistic intentions and control. An explication of the episode also suggests how Austen used her knowledge of her readers' responses to develop an extraordinary partnership with them, to produce works that expect the active, creative engagement of her audience in the process of reading, understanding, and reading again.

The portrait-painting episode is particularly well suited to classroom discussion among first-time readers because it takes place early in the novel and begins and reaches its conclusion in one chapter (vol. 1, ch. 6). A close examination of this small drama is thus possible in a short time, and although students who have finished the novel will bring more to the discussion, even those who have read only up to this chapter should be able to contribute to and learn from the classroom exchange. Indeed, inexperienced readers should realize that Emma's portrait of Harriet, as an artistic enterprise, is an exercise in folly. The episode, therefore, can be used to familiarize students, early on, with the comic structure and playfulness of Austen's plots. It can, as well, help them develop an ear for the diverse voices and preoccupations of the characters around the heroine. Most important, a detailed discussion of the way Emma undertakes the portrait and of the various ways it is received prepares students to participate in and thoughtfully examine the complex dramas in the novel as a whole.

Students who have not already detected problems in Emma's approach to the portrait can be easily alerted to them. A brief review of Emma's conversations with Harriet and Mr. Elton makes clear that the marriage prospects that the portrait is meant to foster exist chiefly in Emma's imagination. Furthermore, Emma's language in announcing her intention to paint the picture reflects the doubtful commercial underpinnings of her scheme. "What an exquisite possession a good picture of her would be!" Emma declares. "I would give any money for it" (43; 1: ch. 6). The terminology is for the benefit of Mr. Elton, who, after all, seeks to make his fortune through a good match. We are also warned that Emma's less than honest motives in undertaking the project will deter her from producing a tolerable likeness of Harriet at all: "she meant to throw in a little improvement to the figure, to give a little more height, and considerably more elegance." The subject of this "pretty drawing" (47; 1: ch. 6) will thus not really be Harriet but Emma's image of an elegant and eligible young woman.

As flawed as Emma's motives may be, instructors might point out that her artistic efforts can be viewed as a sympathetic representation of the creative endeavor in which Austen herself was employed. Like other writers of her time, as well as like Emma (who has often been seen as a kind of "avatar of Austen the artist" [Gilbert and Gubar 158]), Austen considered the "marriage plot" to be engaging material for her work. And she too was cheerful about the commercial value of publishing her books. As Austen remarked in a letter to her niece Fanny, praise for her novels was all very well, but "Pewter" just as welcome (Austen, *Letters* [Le Faye] 287). Hopes for financial returns outweighed even Austen's deeply held desire for anonymity: "I shall rather try to make all the Money than all the Mystery I can of it," she wrote as she finished *Mansfield Park* (Austen, *Letters* [Le Faye] 231).

Also in tune with her heroine, Austen readily defended the fact that while she sought to represent her characters and their stories realistically, "it was her desire to create not to reproduce." She even admitted that the heroes of the marriage plots in her novels are sometimes as idealized as Emma's. Mr. Knightley, in particular, is one of those "very far from being what I know English gentlemen often are" (Austen-Leigh, *Memoir* [Folio ed.] 157). But perhaps their joy in creative endeavor is what Austen and Emma have most in common. Emma's pleasure and absorption in the process of making her portrait—in the business of opening her portfolio, laying out her paints, and setting the scene—are palpable expressions of that joy. Indeed, they take precedence over the marriage that Emma thinks she is promoting. "But as she wanted to be drawing, the declaration must wait a little longer" (46; 1: ch. 6). Emma's dismissal of the imaginary lovers in favor of her own creative work is both selfish and comic. But it also represents a moment of genuine artistic energy and reflects the delight experienced by artists when they take up the brush or the pen. And "the same . . . satisfaction," we are told, "accompanied the whole progress of the picture, which was rapid and happy" (47; 1: ch. 6).

Students who find the marriage plot boring or distasteful may still feel that the similarities between Emma's endeavors and Austen's reflect more negatively on the author than positively on her heroine. Nevertheless, the discussion will have given students a better understanding of the situation in which both artists find themselves and of the confidence with which each undertook her artistic work. Emma's situation becomes even more interesting, however, when her confidence is tested by the reception that her work receives. Initially, once the portrait is released for viewing, its reception seems just as "happy" as the process of painting it. The sentence with which Austen begins her description of the response of Emma's audience starts out promisingly indeed: "Every body who saw it was pleased." But—the very next word in this sentence is a "but"—problems arise immediately. "Every body who saw it was pleased, but Mr. Elton was in continual raptures, and defended it through every criticism." With typical economy—in a single sentence whose end comically undermines its beginning—Austen warns us that what may seem universal praise will be tempered both by meaningless "raptures" and "every criticism"; in fact, both supporters and detractors will largely misunderstand the work she has created (47; 1: ch. 6).

This section of the chapter lends itself to reading aloud in the classroom. In addition to the narrator, five characters—Mrs. Weston, Mr. Elton, Mr. Knightley, Mr. Woodhouse, and Emma—speak in the space of a few hundred words. Having students play the characters can help them identify the differences in tone, preoccupation, and perceptiveness among them. The responses of all the painting's viewers soon fall short of Emma's hopes for her portrait. Mrs. Weston and Mr. Knightley are the first to fail her. They can see that Emma has created and not reproduced, but the effect of their observations is not at all what Emma had in mind. "Miss Woodhouse has given her friend the only beauty she wanted," observes Mrs. Weston to Mr. Elton. "The expression of the eye is most correct, but Miss Smith has not those eye-brows and eye-lashes. It is the fault of her face that she has them not." Mr. Knightley is even briefer: "'You have made her too tall, Emma,'" he says. "Emma knew that she had," interjects the narrator, "but would not own it" (47–48; 1: ch. 6). Although Emma is disconcerted that Mr. Knightley has so easily seen through her, at least she can admit to herself the honesty of his remarks and keep her discomfort private. Mrs. Weston's response presents a much bigger problem. For in blaming not the *artist* but the previously unnoticed "fault" of her *subject* for the portrait's failings, the one member of the audience from whom Emma can be sure of praise actually undermines Emma's cherished artistic intentions. Insult is added to injury when Harriet's shortcomings are pointed out to the very person whose admiration of Miss Smith the portrait is meant to increase.

Of course, one of the purposes of this exchange is to demonstrate that not even Mrs. Weston's mild criticisms can stem the tide of Mr. Elton's "continual raptures." Although we have been informed that Emma is not "sorry to know her reputation for accomplishment [was] often higher than it deserved" (44; 1: ch. 6), she is again honest enough to recognize how ignorant and thus worthless Mr. Elton's raptures are. "You know nothing of drawing," Emma mutters to herself earlier in the chapter. "Don't pretend to be in raptures about mine. Keep your raptures for Harriet's face" (43; 1: ch. 6). In praising the work instead of its subject, Mr. Elton also fails Emma, however, and he does so spectacularly. In a comic reversal of Mrs. Weston's defense of Emma's work that ultimately comes to the same end, Mr. Elton champions the portrait not by defending Harriet but by piling on references to artistic terms whose meanings are clearly beyond him. Suddenly the all too smooth Mr. Elton sounds all too much like another famously rapturous but undiscriminating character in the novel: "'Consider, [Harriet] is sitting down—which naturally presents a different—which in short gives exactly the idea—and the proportions must be preserved, you know. Proportions, fore-shortening'" (48; 1: ch. 6). Students who have read the novel only through this chapter will not be acquainted with Miss Bates's breathless conversational style; Austen does not unleash its full force on her readers until somewhat later. But even for them it is not too early to observe that a variety of characters in *Emma* slip into this style of speech at critical moments in the novel. As Lloyd Brown notes in his study of Austen's narrative technique, it thus becomes a "central point of reference" for examining moral issues and interconnections throughout (132). Here Mr. Elton's remarks serve as a prelude to the larger theme of unperceptive, self-deceiving assumptions that characters continually make as the events in Highbury unfold. Although Emma's own judgment proves unreliable in similar ways, we realize that in her role as an artist, trying to communicate in a work of her own, she faces an unruly audience indeed.

But it is Mr. Woodhouse, that seemingly placid and courteous man, who is the most uncooperative audience member of all. His preoccupation with the imaginary outdoor setting and his immediate concern that the lightness of Harriet's attire in the portrait "makes one think she must catch cold" represents the ultimate in self-absorbed responses. Even Mr. Elton runs out of steam in attempting to bring him around to an appreciation of what Emma has created. To be sure, Mr. Woodhouse finds the drawing as "pretty" as Emma had hoped it would be. "So prettily done! Just as your drawings always are, my dear." But the prettiness Mr. Woodhouse sees is a vague quality common to all the works he praises. It suggests nothing about this particular portrait to distinguish it from any other. In the end, Mr. Woodhouse's obsessions prevent him from seeing Emma's work at all. His conviction that even in a work of art, "it is never safe to sit out of doors" deprives his daughter's painting of any reality of its own (48; 1: ch. 6). Her work becomes, instead, the creation of his patronizing habits and hypochondriacal imagination.

This chapter is so funny, and the joke is so obviously on Emma, that the reader might overlook the care with which Austen explores the vulnerability of Emma's art to the reactions of her audience. But in taking such care, Austen shows that however flawed Emma's intentions may be, her greatest difficulty as an artist is that she cannot control how her work or intentions will be read by others. Soon to be "elegantly framed" and "hung over the mantle-piece of the common sitting-room" (69; 1: ch. 9), the portrait of Harriet becomes a piece of public property, open to misinterpretation and misuse even by those most active in Emma's defense. Her failure to make the portrait serve her matchmaking scheme is undoubtedly a personal disappointment as well as an instance of comic justice. But the way in which her creative work invariably is taken over by members of her audience to suit their own interests is what drives Emma the artist to near-despair. Describing an earlier period of portrait painting, Emma tells Harriet and Mr. Elton that she "did then forswear ever drawing anybody again." Having a portrait of John Knightley (a work she considers among her best, and "only too handsome—too flattering") carried off to London by her sister, Isabella, to be displayed to visitors and "apologized over" as not being flattering enough was simply "more than I could bear" (46; 1: ch. 6). Like her father, her sister views Emma's work only through the lenses of her own preoccupations—in Isabella's case, her devoted but inflated views of her husband's merits. She is thus unable to see, much less appreciate, Emma's work for what it actually is. Emma's frustration with the pressure to produce work that is not so much her own but what her audience is determined to see prompts her for a time to give up drawing "in disgust" (43; 1: ch. 6). Emma discovers that even when she tries to accommodate the demands of her audience, their responses will be shaped more by their own tastes and expectations than by a desire to understand what she creates.

Students can view Emma the artist as a more sympathetic character when they understand how *un*sympathetic her audience is even to what is genuine in her creative work. No one may "much like" Emma's impulse to control everyone around her, but, as this early scene suggests, her efforts to do so are doomed to failure. Austen thus quickly eliminates the suspense of one plot line, which demands that Emma's domineering habits not be allowed to prevail. Instead, by showing, near the beginning of the novel, how impossible it is for Emma to control her audience, Austen introduces a more interesting kind of suspense: Will Emma accept this fact and even, perhaps, learn from it? The portrait-painting episode also subtly underscores Emma's isolation in Highbury as a woman of undeniable intelligence, talent, and spirit. In none of the responses to her work is there a sign that anyone around her is both able and willing to meet Emma on her own ground. No one capable of understanding her work appreciates it, and no one who appreciates her work understands it. Whatever one may think of the ultimate value of Emma's creative work, she is at heart very lonely amid the chatter of the sitting room.

Of perhaps even greater service to first-time readers of the novel, however, is the opportunity that this episode provides for a discussion of the act of "reading" itself, for making the transition from thinking about Emma's audience to thinking about what it means to be a member of Austen's. As we have seen, the similarities between Emma's portrait painting and Austen's novel writing are easy to spot and can help students comprehend the rapport Austen felt toward her heroine. Taking the time to explore the parallels between Emma's "readers" and what Austen knew of hers will reinforce this point; doing so can also help students recognize that Austen is much more skilled than Emma in addressing her audience. Austen, keenly interested in who her readers were and how they responded to her work, used her knowledge of their tendencies not only to represent them with consummate artistry in the portrait-painting episode but also to involve them actively in the way the novel unfolds.

Consulting sources outside *Emma* offers students helpful perspectives on Austen's knowledge of her audience and her strategies for handling it. Useful sources include Austen's "Plan of a Novel" (428–30) and her delectable correspondence with the Reverend James Stanier Clarke over Austen's "own style" and "own Way" in the face of Clarke's highly colored alternate suggestions (Austen, *Letters* [Le Faye] 312; see also 296–97, 305–07, 311–12). But perhaps the most rewarding text for a discussion of Austen's audience in relation to *Emma* is the collection of comments on the novel that Austen compiled in 1816 and 1817 under the title "Opinions of *Emma*" (see appendix to this volume). Because Austen attracted little notice in the literary press of her day, making such a compilation (as she had previously done for *Mansfield Park*) was the only way she had of recording and examining how her own work was being received. Some of the opinions she collected she heard directly from relatives or household members (such as the Austens, Knights, Leigh Perrots, Lefroys, and Martha Lloyd) or from friends with whom she was frequently in touch (such as Anne Sharp, Alethea Bigg, and Fanny Cage). Other comments were from friends of her London-based brother Henry (such as his business partner Henry Sanford and his surgeon Charles Haden), more distant acquaintances of her own (Penelope Lutley Sclater) or complete strangers (Francis, later Lord, Jeffrey), whose opinions must have been forwarded by people she knew. Although Austen's compilation might seem modest and to suggest that her audience was as narrow in scope as Emma's, she draws all levels of society into her readership, giving equal consideration to the views of countesses and impoverished spinsters, professional men and baronets, readers barely out of their teens and members of the literary establishment.

For reasons that will become clear, students will benefit most from a discussion of the "Opinions" if they read and talk about them immediately following a review of the portrait-painting scene. However, they are likely to understand the secondary material only after they have finished reading the novel. The comments that Austen records are brief, sometimes cryptic, and can be fully appreciated only by readers familiar with the plot. Additionally, many of the comments apply to characters who appear after chapter 6. For the "Opinions" to have meaning both on face value and as representations of Austen's audience, students must be able to recognize all the references to the novel, and to a few of Austen's other works, that they contain. Therefore, if the portrait-painting scene is discussed as students are first reading the novel, instructors should probably postpone the examination of Austen's own audience until students have finished the book and a summing up of Austen's work is in order. Little is likely to be lost by such a delay, particularly if the earlier discussion has encouraged students to think about issues of "audience" as they continue to read.

The first thing that one notices about the "Opinions" is the interest that Austen displays in the individual identities of her readers. Each name is carefully set off to the left, preceding what one might have thought more important, the comment about the novel. As Laura Fairchild Brodie notes in her illuminating study of the "Opinions," this structure allows each reader to speak in his or her own voice, much like a character in a play (58)—even, as first-time students of *Emma* may also say, like a character in a novel. For as students read the "Opinions," they should be invited to make connections—and they should easily be able to do so—between Emma's audience and Austen's. (Asking each student to read a selected comment aloud—as, in the scene in which Emma's portrait is unveiled, they read dialogue aloud—can help them "hear" the connections, as well as the differing points of view that the comments represent.) Austen, too, must have recognized, as she compiled the comments, that she was once again in the sitting room at Hartfield, transcribing the voices of the Mr. Knightleys, Mrs. Westons, Mr. Eltons, and Mr. Woodhouses of her own immediate audience. Among those who sent in their opinions, personal preoccupations came first, assumptions were wildly off the mark, and there was no general agreement about anything.

For example, a debate about the "naturalness" of Austen's portrait of her heroine proceeds much like the controversy about the "likeness" of Emma's portrait of Harriet. Austen's brother Francis thinks the novel's "peculiar air of Nature" makes it preferable to the writer's other works, while a Mrs. Guiton finds the novel "too natural to be interesting" ("Opinions" 180). Austen's audience cannot agree about her artistic style, either. James Austen and his wife find the "language different . . . not so easily read" as that of her previous novels, whereas Alethea Bigg finds *Emma*'s "language superior to the others" (179).

It is also clear from the "Opinions" that many of Austen's readers, like the viewers of Emma's portrait, would prefer that she create works to their own specifications for the way life should be. Miss Isabella Herries, for instance, "objected to my exposing the sex in the character of the Heroine" (181). Both Mrs. Wroughton and Mr. Sherer (vicar of Austen's brother's parish at Godmersham) are "Displeased with my pictures of Clergymen" (182, 180). A former governess, Anne Sharp, remarks, more ambiguously, that she is "dissatisfied with Jane Fairfax" (179)—an oblique reference, perhaps, to her expectations for a character whose situation is close to her own. Then there are the readers who, like Mr. Woodhouse, can make no distinction between life and art at all. Mrs. Dickson, who "did not much like [*Emma*]," liked "it the less, from there being a Mr. & Mrs. Dixon in it" (181). Part of the joke here is that the Dixons in *Emma* actually never make an appearance in Highbury. Nevertheless, Mrs. Dickson is so sensitive to her imaginary presence in Austen's novel that she apparently feels wounded by the fun that Emma and Frank have at the Dixons' expense.

That Austen carefully records such self-absorbed responses rather than turning from them "in disgust" provides one kind of evidence that Austen—unlike Emma—is fearless in facing her audience. But the style of the "Opinions" also abounds in the ironic forms of expression and occasional narrative disclaimer that are characteristic of Austen's way of addressing and challenging her readers. Indeed, R. W. Chapman explains his inclusion of the "Opinions" in his edition of *The Novels of Jane Austen* by noting that "the phrasing of some of them, though not their substance, may be hers" (Preface vi). Brodie similarly suggests that Austen's use of punctuation in the "Opinions" provides "ironic commentary" and believes that the italics in particular—such as Mr. Haden's "*quite* delighted with [Emma]"—are actually Austen's, indicating her doubt in the sincerity of the remark (58). Perhaps Austen is telling us that no "continual raptures" will do; a genuine engagement with her work takes more than Mr. Elton's style of empty praises.

We should note that Austen corrects some of her readers' assumptions about her work as she records them. Isabella Herries was "convinced that I had meant Mrs. & Miss Bates for some acquaintance of theirs—People whom I never heard of before" (181). Austen often uses a similar voice in the novels when she suspects that readers may be expecting something other than what she writes: "Seldom, very seldom, does complete truth belong to any human disclosure" (*Emma* 431; 3: ch. 13). More typically in the "Opinions" as well as in the novels, however, Austen relies on irony to make her point. In the "Opinions" she frequently presents the comments in brief, tongue-in-cheek terms that rebound on their sources to hilarious effect. A distant Mr. Cockerelle, for example, "liked [*Emma*] so little, that Fanny wd not send me his opinion" (181). Austen feels no need to elaborate on the point that Fanny conveys Mr. Cockerelle's views quite well by carefully explaining why she won't. Austen—again in contrast to Emma—clearly relishes comments in which the joke is overtly on her. They often reveal more about her audience than about her literary efforts. Mrs. Digweed reports that "if she had not known the Author, [she] could hardly have got through it" (180), and Mr. Fowle "read only the first & last Chapters, because he had heard it was not interesting" (182). But it is perhaps the hapless Mrs. Dickson on whom Austen's irony works most tellingly. As Austen had predicted, she encountered a number of readers who did not "much like" her novel. But Austen reserves her use of this important phrase to characterize the opinion of the one reader who is most clearly not able to "read" at all. An individual who cannot distinguish between *Dixon* and *Dickson* cannot be expected to "much like" the novel or to understand and appreciate its complexities

In Mrs. Dickson students can find warning to all readers of *Emma*. If vague "raptures" are an inadequate response to Austen's work, so is inattentive reading. Unless one is willing to let one's assumptions be challenged, most of the meaning of her work will be missed. Throughout the novel, Austen plays with the expectations that readers bring to the story, in the same way that she plays with the expectations of the inhabitants of Highbury. She continually surprises us with changes in perspective and with revelations that tell us that what we thought we knew is suspect indeed. Gradually both characters and readers learn that it is folly to assume that we are ever in possession of the full truth about what is unfolding before us. By involving her readers in the tangle of "misreading" that pervades life in Highbury, Austen demonstrates both her amused understanding of the habits of her audience and her supreme ability to make those habits work to the benefit of her art. She counts on us to make our customary assumptions so that she can surprise us with their reversal. But only if we are alert to those reversals and enjoy being challenged by them can we begin to understand what Austen's work is really about.

The "Opinions of *Emma*" also suggests the most important kind of liking that rewards readers who enter into the spirit of a novel in which differing points of view are constantly at play. It is perhaps best represented by the fondness that many of Austen's readers express for the despicable Mrs. Elton. Of all the characters cited in the "Opinions," Mrs. Elton ties with Miss Bates and Mr. Knightley for the most favorable mentions (five each). What, students might be asked, do *those* three have in common? As persons, surely little. But as cleverly drawn characters, at least two are wonderfully funny and all three are vividly presented, often surprising, and frequently caught by surprise themselves. By becoming conscious of the artistry at work in such characters and such surprises, readers can develop an appreciation of Austen that transcends their feelings about a particular character's behavior.

Finally, the "Opinions" conveys to new readers the fact that the highest appreciation for Austen's complex artistry may be found in rereading or at least in reexamining what they have read. Some of the opinions that Austen records involve multiple readings—indeed, Alethea Bigg's second reading is given even more space than her first. Subsequent readings can significantly increase students' enjoyment of the novel, and Miss Bigg's comments can point the way. "On reading it a second time," Miss Bigg "liked Miss Bates much better than at first" (180). Miss Bates provides a perfect example of what a second look at the novel offers, for repeated readings of Miss Bates's running commentary on life in Highbury will surely enhance students' pleasure in Austen's skills. Despite teachers' attempts to show how significant Miss Bates's observations in fact are, most rereaders may be left wondering how the characters who are subjected to her monologues in the novel—or any first-time readers of *Emma*—can be expected to separate genuine clues from red herrings from comic piffle. But more important, rereaders acquire a better understanding and appreciation of the adroitness with which Austen interweaves all three in order to create suspense and delight. That kind of artistry is what has made so many of Austen's readers like her work very much, indeed, and what has given generations of them such high opinions of *Emma*—and of the artist Jane Austen.

NOTE

Part of this essay expands work contained in my article "Owning Her Work: Austen, the Artist, and the Audience in *Emma*," published in *Persuasions: Journal of the Jane Austen Society of North America* 21 (1999): 115–27. Used with permission.

Manners in *Emma*

Jonathan H. Grossman

A troublesome question that haunts students of Austen and often makes them impatient is, What are these characters *doing*? Because students are curious about the apparent lack of work ethic in the leisured society Austen depicts in *Emma*, her characters' everyday outings and polite conversations may serve as the subject of an explicit in-class discussion that should help make the novel more accessible.

The way I approach the subject with my students is simply to ask them what manners are. Does everyone have manners? Who has good manners or bad manners? What do such manners mean to you? How do you recognize polite behavior? When have you noticed the importance of manners? Students in general are attuned to and thoughtful about issues of conformity in their lives, and they find such questions provocative. We usually come to an understanding that manners represent both the socialization of the body and a special function of social class, distinct from money, birth, or even position. Thus the stage is set for a discussion of Austen's novel in terms of etiquette.

The point is not just that manners matter in *Emma* but, rather, that they connect individual and society, body and language, everyday customs and world politics. As Pierre Bourdieu suggests, "if all societies . . . set such store on the seemingly most insignificant details of *dress, bearing*, physical and verbal *manners*, the reason is that, treating the body as a memory, they entrust to it in abbreviated and practical, i.e. mnemonic, form the fundamental principles of . . . culture. . . . The concessions of *politeness* always contain *political* concessions."

In Austen, as students readily recognize once they have worked through the quotation, Bourdieu's "concessions of politeness" are not just memory aids for the "content of the culture" (94–95). What for Bourdieu operates broadly through a culture and across classes becomes, in *Emma*, a distinctive class trait. Although etiquette might concern anybody, it is the veritable labor of the leisure class depicted in *Emma*.

Confirmation of this view appears in the book—for instance, from Mr. Knightley's brother, John. As the only character who is rising in a profession (law) in London and also participating in Highbury's polite society, John Knightley draws attention to the fact that maintaining manners in the town is hard work. On one visit he mildly notes the comic extremes of Mr. Elton's manners: "I never in my life saw a man more intent on being agreeable than Mr. Elton. It is downright labour to him where ladies are concerned" (111; 1: ch. 13). And when he observes Mr. Weston paying a visit to Hartfield, John Knightley is "in mute astonishment" that anyone would voluntarily abandon the domestic space that he treasures as respite from his work:

> That a man [Mr. Weston] who might have spent his evening quietly at home after a day of business in London, should set off again, . . . for the sake of being in mixed company till bed-time, of finishing his day in the efforts of civility and the noise of numbers, was a circumstance to strike him [Knightley] deeply. A man who had been in motion since eight o'clock in the morning, and might now have been still. . . . —Such a man, to quit the tranquillity and independence of his own fire-side, and on the evening of a cold sleety April day rush out again into the world! . . . John Knightley looked at him with amazement. . . .   (302–03; 2: ch. 17)

John Knightley is not antisocial, as his warm interactions with his brother, George, and others demonstrate. Rather, he is understandably unwilling to perform the "efforts of civility" required by Highbury's leisured society. In Austen's novels the idea of *leisure* clearly fits Thorstein Veblen's definition in *The Theory of the Leisure Class*: the term "does not connote indolence or quiescence"; instead, it suggests the quite active "non-productive consumption of time" involving in part "a laborious drill in deportment" (46, 50). The "civilizing process," as Norbert Elias calls it, seems to have expanded courteous social conduct into a "downright labour" in *Emma* (111; 1: ch. 13).

The performance of that work is a defining element of class in Austen, separate from wealth and status, and it may be indicated by a behavioral designation—newly minted in Austen's time—such as the "idle" class (as opposed to the "useful" one). Austen critics have traditionally considered class primarily in the terms of position ("upper," "middle," and "lower") that were emerging during this period. At least since Walter Scott's crucial observation that Austen "confines herself chiefly to the middling classes of society" (193), commentators have been creating more accurate positional labels, such as "pseudo-gentry" (Spring 60) and "middle-class aristocracy" (Armstrong 160). Some of the essays in this book focus on the hierarchies that shape the characters' relations and on the material considerations that color their romances. Most obviously, in contrast to that of Elizabeth and Darcy in *Pride and Prejudice*, Emma and Mr. Knightley's marriage unites two characters already occupying the highest social station in Highbury, and it enables Mr. Knightley, "having little spare money" (213; 2: ch. 8), to merge with Emma, "the heiress of thirty thousand pounds" whose Hartfield home is "but a sort of notch in the Donwell Abbey estate, to which all the rest of Highbury belonged" (135–36; 1: ch. 16). When Emma finally realizes "that Mr. Knightley must marry no one but herself" (408; 3: ch. 11), her "epiphany," as Casey Finch and Peter Bowen point out, "marks an uncanny moment of *recognition*: the moment when the individual is brought into alignment with social imperatives" (12). Yet if we believe that the marriage plot is predictable in uniting the two richest, most socially acceptable characters in Highbury, then we might see the novel's story as a case of blueblood fiscal predestination. But to do so is to miss the fact that much of the plot is about the labor of good manners and about Emma's socialization by and through them.

Nowhere, perhaps, is the importance of manners clearer than in the Box Hill episode, and in my class on manners I guide students through a close reading of this scene. At Box Hill, Emma contends with a question that is central to her identity and that has earlier (in vol. 1, ch. 18) been posed in her argument with Mr. Knightley about Frank: What does Frank's defiance of the business of etiquette mean for her? From the beginning, Frank has presented to Emma not so much the possibility of discarding good manners as of *using* them, as Emma herself has done on occasion, and at Box Hill, Frank delivers a metacommentary on the leisure-class work of etiquette, precipitating the novel's central crisis for Emma.

Infuriated with Jane Fairfax, Frank calls for a disruption of etiquette: "Ladies and gentlemen, I am ordered by Miss Woodhouse (who, wherever she is, presides,) to say, that she desires to know what you are all thinking of" (369; 3: ch. 7). Frank's ceremonious but hollow request for members of the group to reveal their thoughts is a demand for speech unregulated by the strictures of politeness, and it points out the mental work that etiquette is called on to do. Less obviously, however, Frank's request itself establishes the disjunction between some of his listeners and their thoughts. He constructs a rupture between manners and the self, making his sharper listeners think as he does— as split beings. Some in his audience (such as Miss Bates), whose identities remain seamlessly constituted by their manners, miss Frank's division. They can simply respond. The others are in turmoil, and Frank's second request is a disingenuous attempt to restore order by explicitly reinstating the business of etiquette:

> "It will not do," whispered Frank to Emma, "they are most of them affronted. I will attack them with more address. Ladies and gentlemen—I am ordered by Miss Woodhouse to say, that she waves her right of knowing exactly what you may all be thinking of, and only requires something

entertaining from each of you, in a general way. . . . she only demands from each of you either one thing very clever, be it prose or verse, original or repeated—or two things moderately clever—or three things very dull indeed, and she engages to laugh heartily at them all." (370; 3: ch. 7)

By closing his request with the promise that Emma will "laugh heartily" at even the dullest remarks, Frank underscores the idea that he is not just asking for entertainment but describing the contract of etiquette, a contract ultimately to be ratified in the nondiscursive bodily reaction of appreciative laughter. After dismissing the work of manners, Frank now calls for the production of politeness. Of course, rather than actually reinstating civility, he once again suggests that ordinary polite conversation is a form of contractual labor.

In this cynically enlightened context, the hapless Miss Bates responds with naively self-conscious certainty: "I shall be sure to say three dull things as soon as ever I open my mouth." To this statement Emma gives a response that she infamously "could not resist":

> "Ah! ma'am, but there may be a difficulty. Pardon me—but you will be limited as to number—only three at once."
>
> Miss Bates, deceived by the mock ceremony of her manner, did not immediately catch her meaning.   (370–71; 3: ch. 7)

Here, even if Emma tells Miss Bates the truth, the "mock ceremony of her manner" signals that she is not just speaking her mind, as the phrase goes. Indeed, the reason that Emma cannot resist her response is not that she is particularly eager to insult Miss Bates; rather, Emma is caught up in Frank's exposé of the production of politeness, and so she cannot "resist" turning etiquette inside out. Under the influence of Frank's perspective, Emma finds herself engaged in parody—standing, in both mind and body, dangerously apart from the labor of etiquette that is her everyday work as a member of Highbury's leisure class. The content of her insult is irrelevant. Even Mr. Knightley berates her only for her abandonment of a politeness that transcends—must especially transcend—Miss Bates's poverty: "[Miss Bates] is poor; she has sunk from the comforts she was born to. . . . You, . . . in thoughtless spirits, . . . laugh at her" (375; 3: ch. 7). What matters for the "thoughtless" Emma at that moment is that power seems to inhere in the knowledgeable position that Frank presents, in which he stands outside the responsibilities of etiquette. Emma discovers, however, that occupying this position means abandoning her identification with her society's efforts of civility. From this perspective, in the course of the novel Emma does not so much choose Mr. Knightley—an esteemed landed gentleman—as reject Frank and the potential loss of her identification with her class that he threatens. For Emma, as for most of Austen's unmarried female characters, choosing between matrimonial possibilities represents a career choice within the leisure class. In this sense, Austen depicts Emma finding not just her proper place but her work. At the same time, on a textual level, Austen directs her novel at the controversial "courtesy books," those conduct manuals for female propriety, whose important rise between 1760 and 1820 Joyce Hemlow called to our attention and whose complex relation to Austen's work Nancy Armstrong so well explains in *Desire and Domestic Fiction*.

As a result of the incident at Box Hill, Emma identifies with the work of manners from which Frank is alienated. Thus, that night, she finds that compared to Box Hill,

> [a] whole evening of back-gammon with her father, was felicity to it. *There*, indeed, lay real pleasure, for there she was giving up the sweetest hours of the twenty-four to his comfort; and feeling that, unmerited as might be the degree of his fond affection and confiding esteem, she could not, in her general conduct, be open to any severe reproach. As a daughter, she hoped she was not without a heart. She hoped no one could have said of her, "How could you be so unfeeling to your father?"
> (377; 3: ch. 8)

As Emma envisions "her general conduct" under surveillance here, she measures herself as a contractual producer—giving up a "whole evening," the "sweetest hours of the twenty-four." But now she is regrounding her identity in the labor of proper conduct. She sees herself succeeding not only at performing the appropriate work of a daughter (something she never dreamed of failing to do) but at having the appropriate feelings toward this work. In other words, her reverie is not concerned so much with the work of politeness (at which she only momentarily failed) as with a state of mind and body ("without a heart" and "unfeeling") that her failure of etiquette has registered. Austen thus shows Emma "heartily" engaging with the work of etiquette, which can then be incorporated and finally forgotten as work. The process might be called a sort of disalienation.

At a broader level, the notion that etiquette is a formality overlaying and sometimes even impeding the characters' struggles for the right relationship needs to be turned upside down: the work of etiquette underpins the marriages in Austen's novels. Frank's marriage to Jane Fairfax, which neatly and obviously unites the one who most needs a lesson in the serious work of manners with the one most accomplished to provide it, portends either his reformation or Jane's misery and, more important, confirms Emma in her choice of Mr. Knightley. (The novel's wedding, between the appropriately—if not quite gentlemanly—mannered Robert Martin and the ingenuously tasteless Harriet, returns them to their places at the nearly invisible margins of Highbury's leisure class, removed from its on-going production of polite society.) The two marriages of the leisure-class characters are not just comedic solutions but the products of a society whose individuals work to embody and reproduce good manners. This is why, at the end of the novel, there is not so much a triumph of weddings (which merit only the briefest descriptions) as a tour de force of the business of etiquette in the shape of "apologies, excuses" (459; 3: ch. 16). The marriage plots, which sensitively register gradations of wealth and rank (as does the rather snobby Emma herself), also represent the activity of a leisure class defined in large part by its capacity to manufacture proper conduct.

Like Austen's other novels, then, *Emma* is a "social history of the landed families, at that time in England" that depicts "the continual making and re-making of these houses and their families," as Raymond Williams observes in *The Country and the City* (113). Williams concludes that the novel depicts a wealthy class whose values are grounded in agrarian capitalism. The "making and remaking of these houses," however, is to be found in the novel's plot of polite society engaged in polite dinners, polite dances, and polite outings. For the leisure class in *Emma*, minding manners is a primary duty, as the charac-ters often straightforwardly call it. Thus, they are engaged in a process both of producing etiquette and of making and remaking themselves as a peculiar class, polite ladies and gentlemen. In a sense, we are no different today: we are equally caught up in the larger process through which class reproduces itself. But the daily lives of Highbury society may feel strange to us, because the function of its leisure class has largely disappeared; its "work" is not meaning-ful in our modern division of labor; and the leisure class today is perhaps more readily identified by conspicuous consumption.

Often my lecture ends at this point. However, if there is time, I push our reading of the novel a bit further, toward something of a surprise ending, by turning to look at Mr. Woodhouse as a secret key to the circulation of manners. For it is no accident that after Box Hill, Emma's reidentification with the ef-forts of civility involves her father. Mr. Woodhouse's fastidious concerns about etiquette and the body may at first seem to be peripheral to the novel's main action, but his hypochondria and civility are actually the front and back of the machinery of social power in Highbury. Together these two oversensitive di-mensions of his character help foster the ongoing production of politeness. And we can see the importance Austen has placed on Mr. Woodhouse if we focus on why, or rather how, Emma—who does not know that Frank Churchill is engaged to Jane Fairfax—arrives at her decision not to marry Frank: for Mr. Woodhouse, in effect, presides over Emma's choice of her husband.

How is it that Emma rejects Frank Churchill? After Frank arrives and im-presses both Woodhouses, he first shakes Emma's opinion by dashing off to London to have his hair cut, an act that she does not know is a cover for his purchase of a piano for Jane Fairfax. Although Emma is then provoked to reit-erate her resolution never to marry, she soon forgives Frank, and over the next few chapters, their relationship generally builds. Emma dines and dances with Frank, and one evening ends with Frank's attending Emma to her carriage. "Miss Woodhouse and Mr. Frank Churchill; I never saw any thing equal to it" gushes Miss Bates to Mr. Knightley soon after (245; 2: ch. 10). Emma will later accurately report to Mrs. Weston: "I will farther tell you, that there was a period in the early part of our acquaintance, when I did like [Frank], when I was very much disposed to be attached to him—nay, was attached—and how it came to cease, is perhaps the wonder" (396; 3: ch. 10).

This "wonder" is illuminated, however, as the story begins a new intrigue. Chapter 11 of volume 2 opens with the words "It may be possible to do without dancing entirely," but Frank is planning another ball. "Frank Churchill had danced once at Highbury, and longed to dance again; and the last half hour of an evening which Mr. Woodhouse was persuaded to spend with his daughter at Randalls, was passed by the two young people in schemes on the subject" (247). After a few paragraphs of brief, festive conversation about the dance floor, Mr. Woodhouse interjects this pronouncement:

> "Oh! no," said he; "it would be the extreme of imprudence. I could not bear it for Emma!—Emma is not strong. She would catch a dreadful cold. So would poor little Harriet. So you would all. Mrs. Weston, you would be quite laid up; do not let them talk of such a wild thing. Pray do not let them talk of it. That young man (speaking lower) is very thoughtless. Do not tell his father, but that young man is not quite the thing. He has been opening the doors very often this evening, and keeping them open very inconsiderately. He does not think of the draught. I do not mean to set you against him, but indeed he is not quite the thing!"
>
> Mrs. Weston was sorry for such a charge. She knew the importance of it, and said every thing in her power to do it away. Every door was now closed.   (249; 2: ch. 11)

At first glance, Mr. Woodhouse's reaction to Frank may seem little more than the ramblings of a petty hypochondriac. Yet when Mr. Woodhouse converts his fear of dancing in drafts into a condemnation of Frank's "thoughtless" and inconsiderate behavior, the older man's authority is quietly asserted. He tells Mrs. Weston that he does not mean "to set [her] against [Frank]," but she is distressed when he pronounces him "not quite the thing." Mrs. Weston, "sorry for such a charge," knows "the importance of it." Mr. Woodhouse's lowered voice is heard by others besides Mrs. Weston, as is shown by the generalized and serious response to it among the partygoers.

Confronted by Frank's disrespect, Mr. Woodhouse acts not as an autocrat but as a seismograph for tremors. He reacts. He was "never able to suppose that other people could feel differently from himself" (8; 1: ch. 1); and, preoccupied with matters that seem irrelevant, Mr. Woodhouse can all the more effectively test and register obedience to the strictures of politeness.

Her father's disqualification of Frank is not lost on Emma, although she remains silent. In fact, her silence may suggest that she is thinking rather than hastening, as usual, to rescue her father from agitation and to smooth over discord. Just after her father's speech, a few contradictory words pass between Emma and Frank about the space of the dance floor, and Emma's thoughts at that time, rendered in free indirect discourse, contain the novel's first specific indication that she is not interested in wedding Frank:

> Had she intended ever to *marry* him, it might have been worth while to pause and consider, and try to understand the value of his preference, and the character of his temper; but for all the purposes of their acquaintance, he was quite amiable enough.   (250; 2: ch. 11)

Thus, just after Mr. Woodhouse's condemnation, the reader learns that Emma does not need to evaluate Frank, or rather "the character of his temper," anymore. The italicization of *marry* indicates that Emma's love is not at issue here. Indeed, the narrator soon announces that "Emma continued to entertain no doubt of her being in love." Nonetheless, Emma then finds that "the conclusion of every imaginary declaration on his side was that she *refused him*" and that "their affection was always to subside into friendship" (264; 2: ch. 13). Thus, rather than realizing that she does not love Frank, Emma discovers that she cannot marry him and therefore must not really love him.

Emma's mental rejection of Frank as an appropriate match is guided by her father's judgment. Emma, of course, is not obeying orders. Her own subjectivity is so bound up in the codes of behavior in Highbury that the decision not to marry Frank is her own, even as it follows Mr. Woodhouse's rendering of the social imperative. Emma herself finally does not want the disruption of etiquette that, in her father's estimation, Frank threatens. Therefore, Emma (echoing her father's pronouncement that Frank is "not quite the thing") soliloquizes about Frank's potential for misbehavior: "I do not look upon him to be quite the sort of man—I do not altogether build upon his steadiness or constancy" (265; 2: ch. 13).

The scene just after Mr. Woodhouse's condemnation confirms the relevance of his reading of Frank's behavior. Frank visits Hartfield and engages in a thinly veiled battle with Mr. Woodhouse, to which Emma is again a quiet spectator. In this scene Mr. Woodhouse expresses persistent concern about dancing with the windows open, to which the "thoughtless" Frank responds with the threatening words: "Ah! Sir—but a thoughtless young person will sometimes step behind a window-curtain, and throw up a sash, without its being suspected. I have often known it done myself" (252; 2: ch. 11). Slyly, Frank suggests his willingness to disrupt the standards of politeness. Their disagreement reveals both Frank's flirtatious selfishness and his lack of candor, but the argument itself represents Frank's primary transgression. He is rude to Mr. Woodhouse. Frank has what Emma calls "that greatest fault of all in her eyes which [John Knightley] sometimes fell into, the want of respectful forbearance towards her father" (93; 1: ch. 11). It is not just that Frank disrespects Mr. Woodhouse's cavils, but, worse, that he disrespects the serious business of etiquette that occupies every respectable person in Highbury. Frank's battle with Mr. Woodhouse, like Emma's later "insolent" (374; 3: ch. 7) insult to Miss Bates, is a rebellious casting aside of the etiquette that structures life in Highbury.

Mr. Woodhouse, then, does not regulate Highbury with the commands and pomp of a hierarchical figure. On the contrary, his "favouring blindness" lends Emma the guise of self-determination and manifests the automation of Highbury authority. "[T]he entire deficiency in him of all such sort of penetration or suspicion" (193; 2: ch. 5) means that Emma's realization that she must marry Mr. Knightley will, finally, appear to her as a self-correction. Yet, while Mr. Woodhouse seems to see nothing, he requires good manners. Again, he does not mandate good manners; rather, he calls upon them, reacts to them, and models them. For example, early in the novel "the scruples of his own civility" (57; 1: ch. 8) cause Mr. Woodhouse to offer elaborate excuses to an entirely accepting Mr. Knightley in order not to appear rude at leaving to take a brief walk. Throughout the novel—as in the dinner scene at Hartfield in which Emma, laughably alert for "a dangerous opening" (105; 1: ch. 7), spends the evening ensuring that conversations run smoothly for her father—Mr. Woodhouse's expectation of good manners guarantees the harmonious continuation of business as usual for Highbury's leisure class. For this reason, he need not overtly interfere with Emma's matrimonial plans: in Highbury, the traditional patriarchal method of controlling the reproduction of society through arranging marriages is replaced by good manners. Mr. Woodhouse, who feels that "[m]atrimony, as the origin of change, was always disagreeable" (7; 1: ch. 1), puts it this way to Emma: "No, my dear, I never encouraged any body to marry, but I would always wish to pay every proper attention to a lady. . . . My dear, you do not understand me. This is a matter of mere common politeness and good-breeding" (280; 2: ch. 14).

Thus we may, suddenly and freshly, also understand the importance of Mr. Woodhouse's hypochondria to the novel: it helps propel Emma's (and the others') participation in the labor of etiquette. As D. A. Miller argues, "the body . . . plays a crucial, even supreme role in the construction of Jane Austen's 'ideology'": for Austen does not aim to treat the body "as a mere echo chamber for meaning, so much as to exploit the body's felt self-evidence in the interests of anchoring within it an ideology" ("Austen" 57). Feeling is believing, and Miller's point that ideology is grounded in the body means also that the body becomes a wellspring for ideology. That is, the body has beliefs, submerged below the level of consciousness—embedded, for example, in muscle memory, speech patterns, or manners—and these beliefs are held more closely, passed along more silently, and expressed more tyrannically than beliefs imposed as doctrines. From the beginning of the novel, good manners ensure that even the independent and leisured Emma will assiduously attend to her father's incessant demands: "Emma could not but sigh over [Miss Taylor's departure from Hartfield] and wish for impossible things, till her father awoke, and made it necessary to be cheerful" (7; 1: ch. 1). At this point, we have come full circle: Emma's semiconscious rejection of Frank exemplifies Bourdieu's meditation on the politics of politeness and the microdiscipline of manners. Bourdieu's suggestion that "the principles embodied in this way are placed beyond . . . consciousness" (94) helps to explain the process by which Mr. Woodhouse's comic complaints of drafts and open doors lead to Emma's realization that she cannot marry Frank.

And therein lies one of my larger aims in teaching about manners in *Emma*: to convey the idea that reading novels as extended artistic dissections of the connections between individual and society enables us to see power as infinitely more complex than, say, one person's control of another. I pair my lecture on manners with a discussion of gossip in *Emma*; students love to anatomize these two topics, which complement each other. Together the two classes, after several discussions on free indirect discourse, explore specific episodes and characters in the novel. At some point—ideally, when the drama feels right—I observe that our discussions of manners, gossip, and free indirect discourse suggest that we are talking about the complicated, subtle ways in which power can flow. And, I add, these issues of power are not ahistorical. Rather, they form a thread leading back to the French Revolution's dismantling of monarchy and the subsequent reimagining of modern social relations—a subject raised at the outset of our course and likely raised in many of the courses of the teachers and students reading this book.

NOTE

This essay is indebted to the students who studied *Emma* with me in a survey course, British Literature, 1789–1925. An extended version of this essay appeared as "The Labor of the Leisured in *Emma*: Class, Manners, and Austen," in *Nineteenth-Century Literature* 54.2 (1999): 143–64, © 1999 The Regents of the University of California. Permission to reprint has been granted by The Regents of the University of California.

Classless, Clueless: *Emma* Onscreen

Carol M. Dole

The mid–1990s saw a remarkable proliferation of cinematic adaptations of Jane Austen's novels, including a new British miniseries of *Pride and Prejudice* (1995), an art-house version of *Persuasion* (1995), and Emma Thompson's widely distributed *Sense and Sensibility* (1995). Most striking, however, was the number of film versions of *Emma*. The first to appear was Amy Heckerling's *Clueless* (1995), an American comedy marketed to teenagers, which updated the novel but acknowledged its source neither in its title nor in its marketing campaign. More reverential period films, bearing Austen's title, appeared in 1996 on both sides of the Atlantic. In Hollywood, Miramax's *Emma*, starring Gwyneth Paltrow, was written and directed by Douglas McGrath. In England, Kate Beckinsale starred in a telefilm written by Andrew Davies and directed by Diarmuid Lawrence.

Such a bounty of *Emma* films offers many opportunities for teachers of Austen's novel. This essay begins with a strategy for using the films to give students more stake in classroom discussion of the novel, and then suggests ways to examine the difficult question of Austen's attitude toward the class system of her society by comparing novel and film(s).

Students Devise a Film Version

Many undergraduates struggle with *Emma*, complaining that the novel is long and repetitious (particularly in its treatment of Miss Bates). Students new to Austen may miss the subtle satire of her tone. An effective way of encouraging attention to tone, and of helping students understand the narrative function of repetition, is to challenge the class to create a film version of *Emma* on paper. Students who find *Emma* long become more alert to the purposes of each character and of each episode when they are faced with making choices for a film. For instance, if they want to slash Miss Bates from the script, they must find other means to reveal Emma's impatience and occasional unkindness— and, in the process, they will probably come to appreciate Austen's use of this "annoying" character.

Since most students are knowledgeable about film as a medium (even if they lack the technical vocabulary), teachers should not have to sacrifice much class time to provide the necessary instruction: explaining how much material can fit into a film of a given length and presenting basic film terms, perhaps in a handout. Depending on the level of the class, I sometimes introduce narrative theory to assist students in selecting the crucial elements of the text to include in the film. (I like to use Bordwell's distinction between story and plot, in Bordwell and Thompson's textbook *Film Art*, but defining "story" and "discourse" would also do.)

Even before the class begins *Emma*, I tell students that they will be developing a plan for their film based on the novel. They can specify that the imagined film have a period setting, or they can choose (or create) a modern location (I advise them not to use a high school setting like the one in *Clueless*, which many students have seen).

Although I will require each student to turn in a paper with his or her own plan, the shared experience of designing a film can serve as the centerpiece for class discussion during the weeks spent on the novel. For instance, an analysis of Emma's or Frank Churchill's character can spark a debate on which actor to cast in the film. A discussion on which episodes not to include in the film can help students focus on the narrative function of scenes in the novel. Likewise, consideration of camera techniques ("If you could use only three close-ups in this conversation, where would you put them?") can point up the crucial subtleties in a dialogue, just as choices about background music can encourage students to consider tone.

When I assign the paper as a major part of a literature and film course, I require a three-part paper, the sections handed in on different days. Of course, few classes afford the time for such an extensive assignment, but I present it in full here so that others can adapt the elements that prove most useful for their needs:

> Part 1: What problems will your adaptation face, and how will you solve them? If the film is an update, will the issues in the novel still be relevant? Since the novel is too long for a two-hour film, which storylines, episodes, or characters could be omitted? What options are you considering for communicating the characters' thoughts to the audience? How would Austen's ironies be translated to the screen? What are the primary themes of the novel, and which will be stressed in your film version? What tone will your film try to achieve? (I read part 1 and make suggestions about possible difficulties before students attempt part 2. Also, at this first stage I sometimes require students to do critical reading on the novel, to help them identify its central concerns.)

> Part 2: *Story outline.* This is your vision of the film as a whole. In an introductory paragraph, explain which themes your film will stress. Then write a synopsis of the story you will use in your film. Include brief sketches of the major characters, specifying your casting choices and explaining how sympathetically you will portray them. Make the chronology clear.

> Part 3: *New scene.* Write a script for one new scene you have designed yourself rather than based on a scene from the novel. Append a paragraph explaining how this scene contributes to expressing the theme(s) of the novel. Explain where this scene occurs in the story outline.

If you lack the time to assign students to write papers detailing their cinematic visions, students could write a short paper on, for instance, whether a certain actress would be a good choice to play Emma. Or groups of students can create a film version and explain their vision to the class. For courses in which time is not a constraint, students may design and videotape a scene from their films (videos are most likely to be successful for updated versions). Even without such time-consuming projects, students will almost certainly engage more fully with the novel if they are invited to see its characters through the camera's eye.

Although the camera's eye will probably have to remain imaginary for students' versions, the adaptations of professional filmmakers offer another option for exploring Austen's novel. The remainder of this essay focuses on how instructors can use *Clueless*, McGrath's *Emma*, and Lawrence's *Emma* to elucidate one of the knottiest problems of interpreting Austen.

The Problem of Class

One of the chief difficulties in guiding twenty-first-century undergraduates through Austen's works is to explain the intricacies of the early nineteenth-century class system—and then to convince young Americans not to dismiss Regency-era social distinctions as mere foolishness. This difficulty is particularly critical in teaching *Emma*, since its marriage plots revolve less around money (a motivation students can understand) and more around status.

Emma does, of course, offer witty attacks on snobbery that can appease readers schooled on democratic ideals. But a perennial challenge in reading the novel, for students and scholars alike, is to determine whether Austen is mocking or endorsing her characters' views. Unlike Elizabeth Bennet of *Pride and Prejudice*, the heroine of *Emma* is herself a snob, capable of feeling insulted that the vicar of Highbury should have "the arrogance to raise his eyes to her" in a marriage proposal (135; 1: ch. 16) or of declaring that the yeomanry are "the order of people with whom I feel I can have nothing to do" (29; 1: ch. 4). In the course of the novel, Emma must learn to abjure such snobbery. However, other elements of the novel suggest that Emma's sense of class superiority is justified. Austen's famous specificity about income and bloodline, in *Emma* as in her other novels, indicates that rank is a paramount part of her characters' lives. Moreover, *Emma*'s most admirable characters give serious attention to class distinctions. Although the exemplary Mr. Knightley is far from a snob, he lectures Emma at Box Hill about her treatment of those who are not "your equal in situation" (375; 3: ch. 7) and urges her to befriend the genteel Jane Fairfax rather than Harriet Smith, "the natural daughter of nobody knows whom" (61; 1: ch. 8). These passages and others suggest that Emma needs to learn how to inhabit her superior class properly. Such features of the novel are cited by those critics who regard Austen as "ultimately an apologist for the landed classes" (Tobin, "Aiding" 425).

Although they cannot solve all the difficulties of determining Austen's attitude toward class, the three films offer rich possibilities for analysis of the novel's treatment of rank.

Emma in Beverly Hills

Ironically, of the three film adaptations, the breezy teen comedy set in a Beverly Hills high school is the most faithful to Austen's project. *Clueless* satirizes America's upper-middle-class consumer culture with a mingling of irony and geniality that comes closer to Austen's approach than either of the period films, which aim to reconstruct and revise the past rather than to scrutinize contemporary mores, as Austen did. Perhaps this is the reason that more scholarly attention has been paid to this teen flick than to the more reverential adaptations (see, e.g., Ferriss; Nachumi; Sonnet; Wald). If time constraints allow you to include only one *Emma* film in the class, *Clueless* is most likely to appeal to students and to help them grasp Austen's insights into human interaction in a class-based society.

For *Clueless* admits to the reverberations of class as neither period film does. Whereas the McGrath and Lawrence films try to discredit or ignore class notions to suit contemporary tastes, *Clueless* finds a modern equivalent of Regency England's social hierarchy in the cliques of a California high school. Cher Horowitz, popular and stylish, is at the pinnacle of student society. Like Emma, Cher is well aware of class boundaries. Once Cher decides to take a transfer student named Tai under her wing, as Emma does for Harriet, her first act is to instruct Tai in the class system represented by the school's cliques: Alaina's group, who think only about the TV station; the "Persian Mafia," who all drive BMWs; the popular boys (the only acceptable dates for a member of Cher's group); and the Loadies, drug users and class cutters whom "no respectable girl actually dates."

This high school social map has limited applicability, of course, to the overall class system in the contemporary United States. In the "multicultural melting pot of happy-go-lucky rich kids" (Looser, "Feminist Implications" 162) that populate Bronson Alcott High, race and money, the most compelling determinants of present-day status in America, are rendered irrelevant. Since ethnicity is ignored and money is apparently ubiquitous, the society that Heckerling has designed is nearly as homogeneous as the gentry of Highbury. (Although the film mocks the ignorant stereotyping of Cher's declaration that her Salvadoran maid speaks "Mexican," it pays little more attention to the maid than Austen does to the Woodhouses' servants.) Popularity, style, interests, and intelligence are the markers of class in *Clueless*. This constellation of traits both reflects actual tendencies in American high schools and provides an appropriate parallel to Austen's insistence on the importance, in the British class system, of genteel manners and of serious-mindedness.

Just as marriage is the surest test of class boundaries in Austen, so dating is a test of the strength of clique divisions in *Clueless*. *Emma* is sometimes regarded as conservative, in part because of its disposition of characters in marriages that do not cross a substantial class divide. Emma's schemes to marry Harriet, the natural daughter of an unknown father, to men of higher status go awry, and Harriet, Frank Churchill, and Emma herself eventually choose spouses of ranks similar to their own.[1] *Clueless* neatly captures the novel's ultimate ratification of social boundaries by ending with similar couplings. Like Harriet, Tai loses Elton to class prejudice: Elton incredulously asks matchmaker Cher, "Why would I go with Tai? . . . Don't you know who my father is?" Although the film dismisses Elton as a despicable snob, with a doubleness akin to Austen's it ultimately pairs characters who belong together based on contemporary mainstream criteria, however unacknowledged. Rich, white, ambitious, intelligent (if ignorant) Cher ends up with her rich, white, ambitious, intelligent ex-stepbrother, Josh. Dionne, who is African American but otherwise all but interchangeable with her best friend, Cher (both were "named after great singers of the past who now do infomercials"), is paired with Murray, who matches her in style, race, verbal agility, and popularity. Tai, like Harriet, aspires higher under the tutelage of a smarter, more self-confident friend; but ultimately follows her early attraction to Travis, one of the Loadies (just as Harriet returns to her original choice, the devoted Robert Martin). Tai and Travis are made for each other: not only do they share a penchant for flannel shirts and illegal substances, but Tai can no more figure out 7 x 7 than Travis can recall the number of steps in his 12-step program. It is worth noting, however, that, unlike *Emma*, *Clueless* underwrites the American myth of upward mobility by giving Tai a fashion makeover, magically freeing Tai and Travis from their drug dependencies, and establishing Travis's expertise at skateboarding, thus erasing their slacker grunge and qualifying the couple to sit at the same table with the high school aristocrats in the film's closing scene.

A screening of *Clueless*—the film should be viewed in its entirety, since it deviates from Austen's plot in several ways—provides an opportunity for students to examine the attitudes toward class in their own society and to probe the realities of rank in Highbury. One way to set up a discussion of class in America is to show the first half of *Clueless*, pausing the video when Cher is in the midst of her misbegotten campaign to attract Christian (the Frank Churchill equivalent). Before learning which matches succed in the film, students can discuss which characters should pair up (ask students who have seen the film previously not to answer). Students' justifications for their choices may provide a basis for exploring their attitudes toward social groupings.

Besides challenging students to reflect on social status, the film offers lessons on shifting ideologies and on narrative economy. The absence of a Jane Fairfax counterpart and the substitution of a gay character for Frank Churchill can spark useful discussions of changing assumptions about gender and inclusiveness. The redistribution of some of Jane Fairfax's functions to minor characters (for instance, Josh's Shakespeare-quoting date serves as a rival for Mr. Knightley/Josh's admiration, as Jane does in the book) helps clarify the distinction between character and narrative function. The comic bite of *Clueless's* lampoon of the moneyed classes, evident when Cher reveals that her mother died of "a routine liposuction," provides an opportunity to look for Austen's more subtle sardonic judgments on the society of her day. Cher's voice-over narration, which invites the audience to smile at her cluelessness, offers an instructive parallel to Austen's use of Emma's thoughts to make the reader both look down on Emma and warm to her.

Instructors teaching *Emma* in a class on film adaptations of literature may be able to screen one of the costume dramas in addition to *Clueless*. Each offers a distinctive treatment of class, and of Austen's irony, that can lead to a deeper understanding of the novel.

The British Emma

The British *Emma*, starring Kate Beckinsale, has little in common with *Clueless*. With its scowling Knightley and sobbing Jane Fairfax, this film sacrifices much of the comedy of Austen's novel to a dramatic examination of the costs of self-interest, whether that of a lover who trifles with others for his own convenience or of a social class whose ease depends on the labor of others.

Like most British heritage films, *Emma* appeals to viewers' sense of authenticity and nostalgia, but it also critiques Regency notions of class from a late-twentieth-century viewpoint. Indeed, screenwriter Andrew Davies aimed to reveal "the fears and evasions of the aristocracy and gentry, living in such close proximity to the great unwashed" (qtd. in Birtwistle and Conklin 13). The film begins and ends with a theft from Mr. Woodhouse's chicken coop, a reminder that hunger and the violence it breeds are abroad in the land. Another early visual image is of a squalid cottage and its downtrodden inhabitants, and the film provides numerous glimpses of servants at work. Transitions between scenes often turn on the movement of servants opening doors or unpacking luggage, and maids silently attend to the ladies' hair while Emma and Harriet chat. One brief action is especially pointed: a bewigged servant is seen stooping to move Mrs. Elton's knee cushion to each strawberry plant even while she rhapsodizes about the "simple and natural" act of gathering fruit for herself.

The film's visual testaments to the price of hierarchical social arrangements, however, are never allowed to counteract the audience's affection for the more likable gentry characters. Unlike the darker 1995 film of *Persuasion*, which provided close-ups of discontented laborers, Lawrence's *Emma* denies subjectivity to its servants by filming them primarily in long shot. The film eliminates the novel's scene of Emma's visit to the poor. And even the squalid cottage's momentary appearance onscreen is undercut by competition from the credit titles and by the underbeat of the sprightly music that accompanies the entire sequence of Miss Taylor's wedding. This downplaying of the less appealing aspects of the early-nineteenth-century class system is necessary, given the imperative to present Emma as "faultless in spite of all her faults" (433; 3: ch. 13) to an audience schooled on more egalitarian notions. Rather than become strident in critiquing the class system as a whole, the film revises the lesson Emma must learn and offers a final fantasy of class harmony.

Both tasks are accomplished in the closing scene, which has no source in the novel: the harvest supper. After a lyrical scene of workers gathering the harvest while children scamper among the sheaves, Mr. Knightley's tenants mingle with the gentry at a bountiful banquet. The impossible Mrs. Elton, whose snobbery is magnified in the film, serves as a scapegoat who bears Emma's erstwhile class attitudes: we are meant to despise her while she smiles graciously to the arriving workers even while muttering about having "to sit down with hobbledehoys." At this harvest celebration, Emma demonstrates that she is now worthy of Mr. Knightley. As at the end of the novel, Emma has learned to renounce snobbery; but this 1990s Emma must also renounce a belief in distinctions of rank. After the supper Emma publicly seeks an introduction to Robert Martin—a moment underlined by a sudden silence on the soundtrack—and invites him to Hartfield, even though Martin's costuming and inarticulateness throughout the film clearly differentiate him from the gentlemen. The final dance testifies that Emma is not alone in embracing egalitarianism. Although the segregated seating during the meal reflects the customs of Austen's era, the dance of the three newly engaged couples (Emma and Mr. Knightley, Jane and Frank, Harriet and Robert) sacrifices Austen's ending, and ordinary class habits, in favor of an image of class harmony.[2]

The American Emma

The approach taken by the American costume production differs considerably from that of Lawrence's film. McGrath's work devotes far less exposition to decoding the Regency class system for modern viewers. Instead, it subjects that class system to the same sardonic treatment it applies to Austen's characters. In the British version, most of the irony of Austen's narrative voice is lost, but McGrath finds broad equivalents for Austen's irony both in visual jokes and in Emma's voice-over narration.

Sight gags about class privilege are pointed. As Mr. Knightley complains that he just wants to stay home "where it's cozy," the camera swings around to reveal the enormous size of his manor. When Harriet joins Emma in visiting the poor, the inexperienced girl performs a comic shtick of bumbling and dropping things. Other jokes are at Emma's expense, as when she secretly searches for an invitation to the Coles' party even after insisting that the couple is beneath her. Likewise, Emma's snobbery, along with her other weaknesses, is the butt of humor through her diary and the voice-overs of her thoughts. Her dialogue too is comically exaggerated, as when, after learning that she and Harriet are rivals for Mr. Knightley, Emma wails to Mrs. Weston that Harriet's unknown parents "could be pirates!"

The mise-en-scène also undercuts hierarchies. Pairs of characters, whether equal or not in rank, are routinely positioned in the frame in a lateral configuration so that neither figure dominates. Harriet and Emma are shown seated on opposite sides of a fireplace, or walking side by side toward the camera; Mr. Knightley and Emma, or Mr. Elton and Emma, are often captured in two-shots. In one scene, Harriet bows her head into Emma's lap; later, Emma makes a similar gesture. Doorways, window seats, and other backdrops reinforce the symmetry of the characters' positioning.

On the one hand, this symmetry reinforces the film's egalitarian views. On the other, it contributes to the film's rejection of historical accuracy in favor of nostalgia and spectacularization. As Nora Nachumi has noted, Gwyneth Paltrow as Emma is often "dressed and posed like a Greek goddess" (135), in flowing gowns that gesture toward their period by incorporating an Empire waist but that expose Paltrow's arms and bosom in a more ancient (and modern) fashion. The film evokes the classical era in numerous other ways as well: most prominently in the symmetrical composition but also in details such as the Ionic style of the settee (Nachumi 136), the costume in which Harriet poses for her portrait, and the strangely summery weather that lingers until Christmas. Overlaid with the glory that was Greece, the historical England that the film conjures up is a fantasy of harmony and plenty calculated to induce nostalgia.

The film also deploys set decoration and cinematography that appeal to the American reverence for the appurtenances of upper-class life. The many exterior shots displaying graceful white tents on spacious green lawns and "bowers of suspiciously rosy apples" (Lane 76) further idealize a locale of imposing manors and picturesque views. Indoors, firelight gleams on tables heaped with silver and delicacies—tables that, as Gertrude Himmelfarb observes, are "far too lavish for the squirearchy of a small town like Highbury" (75). This seductive spectacularizing of upper-class luxuries undercuts the film's raillery of the class system. Moreover, unlike the British *Emma*, the American film essentially hides the working-class labor that enables such luxury. Tea tables with silver services appear on the lawn as if by magic, and even the Box Hill picnic admits only a fringe of servants glimpsed in long shot.

Scene Comparisons

In practice, time constraints will force most teachers to show sections of the two costume dramas rather than both films in their entirety.

To encourage students to notice cinematic as well as verbal methods of creating meaning, instructors might preface a screening with a brief lesson on the visual elements of film. The mute button can come in handy here: deprived of dialogue, students can focus on which characters are given sympathetic close-ups (and how often), which figures dominate in a frame, which brightly colored costumes draw the eye to a particular character, and which actors are glamorized by soft backlighting or given a more realistic look by harsher lighting. When a scene is replayed with sound, students should listen for any background music that sets a comic, sad, or dramatic mood.

One useful pairing is of Lawrence's and McGrath's versions of the Box Hill incident. Visually, these scenes point up the different treatment of servants in the films. McGrath concentrates on the genteel picnickers, allowing only the arms and legs of the servants to intrude into the frame. In contrast, Lawrence emphasizes the workers' immense difficulty in producing the excursion for the leisure class. Servants are shown clinging to the outside of a lumbering cart loaded with hampers stuffed with food and stemmed glasses, and a dramatic shot captures maids and footmen struggling up the hill with chairs and tables for their masters' comfort.

The juxtaposition of the two versions of the Box Hill scene also points up the difference in tone between the two films: McGrath highlights Austen's comedy, and Lawrence emphasizes her drama. Both versions demonstrate the necessity for condensation in film adaptations of novels, for both bring in incidents from other parts of the novel—but the choice of imported events is instructive. The American film, emphasizing picturesque landscape and cheerful action, folds in the joys of berry picking and the giggling of girlfriends about Harriet's newest love. In this version, Frank begins the hapless game that leads to Emma's insult of Miss Bates in a chivalric attempt to shield Jane from Mrs. Elton's nagging. In contrast, the British version imports the "Dixon" anagram game to highlight the tensions between the secret lovers, and even exaggerates the cruel intentions beneath Frank's flirtations with Emma, making Emma look complicit in his tormenting of Jane. Both versions have to be painful, since the Box Hill episode encompasses Emma's greatest cruelty, but the American version softens the pain somewhat, to retain the film's essential comedy and to preserve audience affection for its heroine.

A useful pairing in distinguishing between the tone of the two films, as well as in determining the seriousness with which they address class conflicts, is the confrontation, early on, between Emma and Mr. Knightley over Harriet's refusal of Robert Martin. The British film stages this key argument indoors, where there are no distractions from the dialogue. With costumes in subdued colors and lighting that approximates natural daylight, the film presents its characters as speakers rather than as objects of display. Although at times they stride around the room in anger, long shots work to demonstrate their discomposure rather than to display their figures. Because most shots are close-ups (characteristic of a telefilm, which typically seeks to enlarge faces for the small screen), we tend to concentrate on the characters' clashing words. The scene opens with a close-up of a choleric Knightley exclaiming "She refused him!" and closes with Emma's bitter prediction (spoken after he storms out of the room) that "you will see you are wrong and then you will be sorry!" The minor key music at the end of the scene emphasizes its sourness, and the scene's focus on verbal interplay stresses the fundamental difference between Emma's and Mr. Knightley's assessments of Harriet's social status.

How different the American version is! The substance of the pair's argument is essentially the same, but the mise-en-scène, acting styles, and music create a comic tone that partially obscures the debate on class. The scene opens in a peaceful mood, with Mr. Knightley congratulating Emma on having improved Harriet, and only gradually works into a rancor that is defused by comedy. Taking a cue from the 1940 film of *Pride and Prejudice*, McGrath stages this conversation during an archery practice at Donwell Abbey. Outdoor archery invites spectacle. The wide green lawn and shimmering pond set off Paltrow's handsome pink gown in a glowing display of light and color. Backlighting on Paltrow's close-ups gives a golden halo to her upswept blond hair, further glamorizing her beauty and offering her pouts as charming. In case the spectacle of this scene is not sufficient distraction from the issue under discussion, the director introduces physical comedy. Emma begins as a competent archer, but just as she is insisting that Martin "is not Harriet's equal," her arrows begin to miss the mark; this visual signal that she is in the wrong obviates any consideration by the viewer of the question in dispute. When Emma starts aiming so wildly that Knightley jokes about her not shooting his dogs, the gist of the discussion of class is subsumed by the comic action. Even when the two sit down to finish their conversation at the tea table, a static setup that could invite more contemplation, Mr. Knightley's sulky pose and the jaunty background music extend the comic air of the archery scene.

The Disposal of Harriet

Although in neither film is the disposal of Harriet confined to a single scene, an examination of her fate is an excellent way to grapple with the problem of interpreting Austen's narrative voice and attitudes toward class. One of the primary lessons Emma must learn in the novel is that "[b]irth, abilities, and education" had marked Jane Fairfax, not Harriet Smith, as the proper associate for her (421; 3: ch. 12). Many of Emma's difficulties spring from her failure to bow to Mr. Knightley's insistence that her protégée had no claims "either of birth, nature or education, to any connection higher than Robert Martin" (61; 1: ch. 8)—a lesson borne out by the discovery that Harriet is the illegitimate daughter not of a gentleman, as Emma had insisted, but of a tradesman. Although by the end of the novel Emma is very willing to make the acquaintance of the farmer Harriet is marrying, she nonetheless recognizes that the engagement will take Harriet away from Hartfield:

> . . . which was not to be regretted.—The intimacy between her and Emma must sink; their friendship must change into a calmer sort of

goodwill; and, fortunately, what ought to be, and must be, seemed already beginning, and in the most gradual, natural manner. (482; 3: ch. 19)

As Mark Parker points out, the ambiguous voice of this passage allows for multiple interpretations:

> *Emma* can generate two readings of class: a progressive one, which emphasizes the insidious workings of class in Emma's disposal of Harriet; and a reactionary one, which sees and accepts this working as part of the price of social stability. Each reading turns on assumptions about the narrative voice: whether it is silently indignant . . . or simply complicit.
>
> (358–59)

Is it Emma herself, or the narrator as well, who finds it "natural" that formerly intimate friends should be separated by marriage into different ranks? A close reading of this passage, and others like it, raises crucial questions about the novel's narrative voice.

Comparison of the disposal of Harriet in the film versions suggests that while modern retellings of *Emma* tolerate some maintenance of class boundaries in marriage, for same-sex friendships no class boundaries are acceptable. Each of the three adaptations ends on a note of friendship between Emma and Harriet (or their stand-ins).

In McGrath's version, the estrangement between the two women is fleeting; when Emma's announcement of her engagement is seen in dumb show through a window, Harriet appears to rush out of the room, but in the next scene the two young women warmly reunite over the news of Harriet's own engagement. The sequence ends with an embrace, then cuts to the closing scene of Emma's wedding: Harriet is one of the few friends whom Emma kisses as she leaves the church. Nothing suggests that difference in rank will ultimately separate the two women or that Emma should instead have chosen Jane Fairfax as a friend.

In *Clueless*—which in this case can be shown in part, since its parallels for Harriet and Martin are obvious—Tai and Cher also remain friends. Although Cher's jealousy of Tai's growing popularity temporarily estranges them, in the closing scene Tai and Cher are seated together as friends at the teachers' wedding. Tai and Travis might not be dressed as stylishly as Cher and Dionne and their dates, but character proxemics suggest that they are indeed equals.

The British *Emma* is the only version to admit that Emma might have considered a separation from Harriet. Having given more attention to class issues throughout—for instance, in the ubiquity of servants and in Emma and Mr. Knightley's argument about a suitable mate for Harriet—Lawrence's film must at least raise the question of the endurance of Emma's friendship for Harriet after their marriages. Indeed, although the two friends never fall out as in the novel, the issue of class comes up when Harriet confesses her engagement to

Emma with an apology: "I understand you will have to give me up." But that specter is erased at the harvest supper when Emma pointedly seeks the company of Harriet and Martin, who then join Emma and Mr. Knightley in the dance (as discussed above). And the matter of Emma's more appropriate friendship with Jane Fairfax is never addressed.

Taken together, the three resolutions of the Harriet plot demonstrate the varying approaches of the three films to solving the dilemma of Austen's deference to social boundaries. The updated American film erases the class question by invoking the myth of class mobility to create a near-equality between Cher and a madeover Tai. The Hollywood costume drama dismisses the class issue, along with other dark strains of the novel, through distraction, silence, and prettification. The British film, overtly the most faithful to Austen until its invented ending, dutifully records her class sensibilities only to reject them in the end.

NOTES

Portions of this essay have been adapted from the author's "Austen, Class, and the American Market," which appeared in *Jane Austen in Hollywood*, ed. Linda Troost and Sayre Greenfield (Lexington: UP of Kentucky, 1998). Used with permission.

[1] Although Frank Churchill stands to inherit wealth, whereas Jane Fairfax has to work for her keep, the two were raised to a similar level of gentility by families who were not their parents. Their approximate social equality is a measure of the importance of education—a criterion considered by both Mr. Knightley (61; 1: ch. 8) and Emma (421; 3: ch. 12) in determining status.

[2] Although classes did not usually socialize with one another to this extent, Ruth Perry has pointed out to me that the residue of England's feudal system made it possible for classes to mingle for such seasonal events.

"A Very Kind Undertaking":
Emma and Eighteenth-Century Feminism

Devoney Looser

Published discussions of the teaching of *Emma* describe student responses that are profoundly at odds with one another. Patricia Meyer Spacks writes, "Every time I teach *Emma*, the novel, I run into the same problem: students don't like Emma, the character. Young men and young women alike find it hard to understand why they should interest themselves in the fortunes of such a self-willed, class-conscious, overprivileged individual" (16). Barbara Fisher Williamson reports the opposite response. Her students balk at characters like *Wuthering Heights*'s Catherine Earnshaw and *Middlemarch*'s Dorothea Brooke ("Why doesn't she just leave him and get a job?"), but "Austen's girls they like":

> Lizzie Bennet and Emma Woodhouse are familiar. [Students] are interested to learn how these girls get ahead in love and at the bank. . . . They like Emma for thinking well of herself and easily forgive her for thinking too well. Her snobbism confounds them, and they wish it weren't there. But they are altogether glad to see her win her man, establish her place in society and move into the great house. (159)[1]

For each example like Spacks's or Williamson's, there are essays titled "Is *Emma* Still Teachable?" and "Jane Austen and the MTV Generation" (Zaal; Marshall). Is teaching *Emma* about instilling affection or distaste for its protagonist? Is it about finding a character students can admire, identify with—or condemn?

My approach is to discourage students from labeling Emma as likable or detestable, as well as from judging historical change as an all-or-nothing phenomenon. Teaching *Emma* to advanced undergraduates (primarily women) in courses such as Women Writers of Great Britain or The Novel to Jane Austen, I have found that focusing discussion on the political complexities of feminism complicates inclinations to make knee-jerk assessments of characters and culture. I often use a series of questions: Is Jane Austen a feminist? Should Austen's work be measured in the context of today's feminist politics and practices? Or should she be compared with contemporaries who criticized women's status in late-eighteenth- and early-nineteenth-century Britain—a time when *feminism* did not yet exist in the English language? (I remind students that, according to the *Oxford English Dictionary*, the word first appeared in 1851, although it was not widely used in the sense we now understand until the 1880s.) How do we reach a verdict on Austen and feminism? Should we? Why has Austen's feminism (or lack thereof) been a central issue in the past three decades of literary criticism?

Before *Emma*, I assign texts by Mary Wollstonecraft, Mary Hays, or both, so the groundwork has been laid for further discussion of the rights of woman.[2] The class has studied eighteenth-century women's legal status, employment, and educational opportunities. I introduce the concept of a married woman as *femme couverte*—without a separate legal identity and treated as her husband's property—and about the limited number of respectable opportunities for single, educated women to support themselves. I introduce material to show that privileged girls were encouraged to acquire "female accomplishments," such as music, dancing, and drawing, along with a smattering of academic subjects.[3] Our discussion of what the word *feminism* means today usually produces answers ranging from "man hating" to "women's liberation." An exchange often ensues about who feminists are, what work they do, and on whose behalf. Once we consider the concept of sisterhood, we make a smooth transition to *Emma* and the novel's female characters. The "on whose behalf" issue is one I highlight as we read (and one I find highly unsettling in my own feminist practice).

Emma Woodhouse is the most powerful, privileged woman the novel presents, with the possible exception of Mrs. Churchill, who, although married, "rules" at her estate (121; 1: ch. 14). Emma often means well, but she famously mistreats other female characters, most notably in her manipulation of Harriet Smith's love life and aspirations; her jealousy toward and back stabbing of Jane Fairfax; and her unkind witticism at the expense of Miss Bates, on Box Hill. Ultimately Emma sees her pattern of behavior as wrong. Is her reformation a sign of growth, a feminist awakening, and a discovery of the indignities to which dependent women are subject, coupled with an acknowledgment of her culpability in the exploitation of the three women? Or does the novel reinforce visions of ideal femininity in which women must be modest, kind, and not meddlesome? In my view, the novel presents Emma's growth as an acceptance of her responsibilities as a woman of privilege, rather than as a withdrawal into marital dependency.[4] *Emma* models the ways elite women should wield power over less-privileged females through its protagonist's mistakes, repeated and exaggerated in Mrs. Elton's behavior. Because the novel, as Claudia Johnson concludes, explores "positive versions of female power" (*Jane Austen* 126), it demonstrates, as well, liberal, reformist feminism—in all its possibilities and shortcomings.[5]

I find it necessary to impart to students an understanding of women's relations with other women in early-nineteenth-century Britain.[6] Young men and women were highly segregated socially, a situation that promoted (or, at the least, allowed for) significant emotional and physical bonding among women. Intimacies between unmarried women were much preferred to openly affectionate interactions with men outside the family. Even after marriage, close associations among women were often maintained. It was not uncommon, for example, for a bride to bring her female companion along with her on her honeymoon (Pool 184). Even more germane to female companionship in *Emma* is what we might call patronage, a subcategory of friendship in which "someone . . . has the power to act on one's behalf, for one's protection or advancement"

(Wiltshire, "World of Emma" 85). Another scholar, Betty Rizzo, argues for the cultural centrality of women's patronage of other women.

The bond between patroness and humble companion, Rizzo says, "mirrored the marriage relationship and was often identified with it." The companion was usually single and economically dependent, from a genteel family but without a fortune that would follow her into marriage. The patroness introduced her into good society; in return, the companion entertained or assisted the wealthy mistress by performing menial tasks, serving as confidante, or adding a hand at the card table. A companion was a useful presence on outings that would be considered improper for a woman by herself. Like a husband exercising power over a wife, a patroness could be autocratic or could "work out an equitable relationship such as she herself would have liked to experience in her dealings with men" (1–2).

Would Emma have wanted Mr. Knightley as a husband if he had treated her as she treats Harriet? From the start, Emma uses Harriet to further her own "views, and plans, and projects" (66; 1: ch. 8). She, in fact, had "very early foreseen" that Harriet would be "useful" as "a walking companion"; Harriet would be "a valuable addition to [Emma's] privileges" (26; 1: ch. 4) in perambulations, beyond the grounds of Hartfield, that might have been dangerous or even slightly improper if she had gone alone. Emma's sense of Harriet as "useful" is in keeping with the patron-companion relation, which stressed social form over emotional substance. Harriet was "the *something* which [Emma's] home required"; Emma needed "*a* Harriet Smith (26; 1: ch. 4; emphasis added). Choosing Harriet was, to Emma, "a very kind undertaking; highly becoming her own situation in life, her leisure, and powers" (24; 1: ch. 3). But Emma is deceiving herself when she imagines that her desire to take Harriet under her wing is a "very kind undertaking."

As Rizzo indicates, Emma uses her prerogative as a patroness to assume a powerful role in regard to Miss Taylor and Harriet (8–9). Her determination to mold Harriet derives from the patroness's social role in preparing younger, less wealthy companions for marriage. A governess or a companion could leave her situation most appropriately if, like Miss Taylor, she married—an acceptable form of quitting that was a promotion in status. The idea of twenty-one-year-old (spoiled, undisciplined) Emma becoming a prenuptial guide to (illegitimate, giggling) seventeen-year-old Harriet seems dubious, but even the skeptical Mr. Knightley at first concedes that Emma has "improved" Harriet, when he thinks Robert Martin is about to marry her: Harriet "really does you credit" (58; 1: ch. 8), Mr. Knightley tells Emma, a compliment he rescinds when he learns that Emma has maneuvered Harriet into rejecting Martin's proposal. Emma's interference does neither woman credit.

Austen was no idealist about female communities. She did not espouse a feminist sisterhood in which women from different classes would work together for collective betterment. Although she viewed herself as an important part of a community of women (Kaplan; Perry, "Interrupted Friendships"), she rarely expressed the belief that women should blindly support all women or even women in their own class.[7] In each of her novels, in fact, female characters attempt to foreclose other women's chances for happiness in favor of their own self-serving plans. Elite women come in for particularly rough treatment. As Juliet McMaster laments, "One wishes Austen would sometimes show a powerful woman in a favourable light!" ("Class" 120). The promise of a better Emma at the end of the novel is perhaps the closest we get. Thus Austen's novels illustrate the ways unscrupulous women compete in a society that primarily advances the legal and economic interests of men; in showing the limits of women's alliances with each other in a patriarchal culture, however, the works imply that there are more progressive possibilities.

Many find Austen's (and Emma's) acceptance of rank troubling. Although the novel makes little effort to envision a female community across class barriers, few eighteenth-century feminists did, either. *Emma* does not demonstrate allegiance to the revolutionary bourgeois feminism of Wollstonecraft and Hays, but it does expose what Austen saw as dangers and hypocrisies on the opposite end of the spectrum—the antirevolutionary conservatism of Hannah More (1745–1833). Wollstonecraft and More have been set up in opposition to each other since the 1790s.[8] More, a well-known Evangelical writer who published conduct books, political propaganda, and works of religious devotion, has been called "the most influential woman living in England in the Romantic era" (Mellor 13). In More's view, society is structured in a natural, divinely sanctioned order, although women should be better educated—according to their station—in order to become more pious. Austen, who read More's writings, appears to have disliked her and the Evangelicals. Discussions of More and Austen have usually centered on *Mansfield Park*, but Austen's negative assessments of More may also have prompted the representations of patroness and companion in *Emma*. Although no revolutionary, Austen did not embrace the conservative politics of More, a woman who sought to "defuse radical social protest in England" (Landry 16).

More published one novel, *Coelebs in Search of a Wife* (1808). Because she professed the common belief that novels were immoral, More was criticized by some for bringing out a work of fiction. The reading public, however, seemed not to mind: *Coelebs* was extremely popular.[9] The novel follows its eponymous, worthy, and priggish hero on his search for the right woman. He must rule out a series of flawed women—who serve as warnings—before he finds his virtuous maiden. While it has been assessed in harsher terms, one critic finds *Coelebs* "rigorous though pristine" (Demers 97). Such qualities apparently did not appeal to Austen. In a letter, she tells her sister that "the only merit [the title of the novel] could have, was in the name of Caleb, which has an honest, unpretending sound; but in Coelebs, there is pedantry & affectation.—Is it written only to Classical Scholars?" (Austen, *Letters* [Le Faye] 172).[10] Austen also ridiculed More's novel in a revision she made to a short work in her juvenilia, *Catharine*. Its sensible heroine is accused by her severe, scrutinizing maiden aunt of misbehaving, despite having been given *Coelebs* to read. Austen here pokes fun at the idea that reading More's novel should serve as what we would call behavior modification.

In many ways *Emma* is an anti-*Coelebs*.[11] Austen's work centers on a flawed single female in possession of a fortune, not a flawless single male of great wealth. Most important, Emma does not see herself in want of a husband but on a marriage quest on behalf of others. Flying in the face of More's advice, Austen gives Emma precisely the qualities against which eligible women seeking husbands were to guard: intelligence, confidence, wit, and even arrogance. Austen's twisting of More's plot is worth noting for biographical reasons as well. More, like Austen, never wed.[12] As an unmarried novelist, More preaches to readers about how to mold themselves into perfect wives. The fictional Emma Woodhouse, too, offers endless counsel on marriage, which the novel presents as generic nonsense: "Well, Harriet, whenever you marry I would advise you to do so and so" (340; 3: ch. 4). Although Emma's youth is another impediment to her giving sound advice, her single status also makes her recommendations to Harriet suspect. Rather than heed Emma's advice, Harriet, for her part, mimics Emma's self-declarations, determining that she, too, "shall never marry" (341; 3: ch. 4). That Harriet does as Emma does, rather than as she says, might suggest the uselessness of More's how-to works as well. Why should readers follow the marital wisdom of an unmarried female author? *Emma* indirectly comments on the sophistry of a single woman who moralizes about how to attract a husband.

An examination of More's attempts at patronage is also relevant to *Emma*. An unpleasant, infamous episode in which More intervened to "improve" another woman might be compared with Emma's acts of intercession. Commitment to "patronage of genius, especially female genius" was regarded in More's circle as a "duty and privilege" (M. Jones 73). Her mentoring of a working-class poet, Ann Yearsley, in 1784–85, proved at once successful and disastrous (Ferguson; Landry; Demers; Waldron). Yearsley, a poor married Bristol milkwoman with five children, was an odd choice, because More did not believe that the indigent should be ambitious; their reward for accepting a humble lot on earth would be joy in heaven. Yet More spent thirteen months teaching Yearsley the rules of composition, correcting her poems, and writing more than 1,000 pages of letters appealing for subscriptions to Yearsley's first book (M. Jones 74).

An argument between the two women occurred when the book, enjoying considerable success, netted £360. More and others formed a trust to control the money. They did not want Yearsley to leave her work as a milkwoman, and they feared that the money would be misused if left at her disposal. Yearsley felt that the money belonged to her. Of being denied management of the book's profits, Yearsley wrote, "I felt as a mother deemed unworthy of the tuition and care of her family" (qtd. in M. Jones 75). More resigned from the trust, but the matter was not resolved. Yearsley published criticisms of More and responded to those who accused her of ingratitude. Their friendship was severed. Like Emma,

More "did not see herself as meddlesome," according to a sympathetic biographer (Demers 67). Yearsley was bitter at More's "haughty treatment" (Ferguson 75). In an unpublished poem, Yearsley's speaker advises another woman "not to intervene in the lives of people like herself" (qtd. in Ferguson 77). The More-Yearsley episode serves as a celebrated real-life failure of female patronage.

By the end of the novel, Emma and Harriet appear headed for a More-Yearsley clash. Emma's early belief that she can control Harriet's rise (and gain social credit for it) parallels More's approach to Yearsley. Emma teaches Harriet social aspirations far beyond those expected of her and throws Harriet in the path of the man she desires for herself. Emma fears that a match between Harriet and Mr. Knightley is "far, very far, from impossible"; as Emma puts it, "If Harriet, from being humble, were grown vain, it was her [that is, Emma's] doing" (413, 414; 3: ch. 11). However, Emma "resolved against seeing Harriet" (416; 3: ch. 12). She "felt for Harriet, with pain and contrition; but no flight of generosity run mad, opposing all that could be probable or reasonable, entered her brain" (431; 3: ch. 13). Harriet "would be a loser in every way," but Emma would not wish the "dead weight" of her company (450; 3: ch. 15). Harriet's side of this rift we are not privy to, although we are given to understand that Harriet, too, desired to "avoid a meeting," and Emma "fancied there was a something of resentment" in her letters (451; 3: ch. 16). Emma and Harriet's friendship points toward impending catastrophe.

Emma comes to see what others have long told her—that Jane Fairfax has much more to recommend her as "a delightful companion" (104; 1: ch. 12). Because of her education and social advantages, Jane offers substantial rather than functional companionship and represents Emma's missed opportunity. Emma avoids Jane to sidestep the "misery of having a very particular friend always at hand, to do every thing better than one does oneself!" (202; 2: ch. 6). Jane is Emma's "equal friend, sanctioned by society and the novel," as Janet Todd argues (*Women's Friendship* 275). Emma now recognizes her loss in avoiding Jane:

> Had she followed Mr. Knightley's known wishes, in paying that attention to Miss Fairfax, which was every way her due; had she tried to know her better; had she done her part towards intimacy; had she endeavoured to find a friend there instead of in Harriet Smith; she must, in all probability, have been spared from every pain which pressed on her now.—Birth, abilities, and education, had been equally marking one as an associate for her, to be received with gratitude; and the other—what was she?
>
> (421; 3: ch. 12)

The quotation is not just another example of Emma's snobbery but a demonstration of repentance that the novel asks us to sympathize with. In my experience, students often have trouble determining why they should see Harriet as a much worse choice than Jane for Emma—perhaps because writer-director Amy Heckerling's film *Clueless*, which many students have seen, presents female patronage as more about popularity and makeovers than about social structures or economic disadvantage. Students usually agree that Jane is smarter than Harriet, but the issue of birth is more difficult. Both Harriet and Jane, after all, are attractive women without prospects of independent wealth.

I find it useful to highlight Harriet's illegitimacy in its cultural context. Harriet is introduced as "the natural daughter of somebody" (22; 1: ch. 3). Emma romantically assumes that Harriet is a gentleman's daughter and will be acknowledged as such, at which point she will come into a fortune. Harriet is revealed as the daughter of a tradesman, who could afford to support her only at Mrs. Goddard's mediocre school:

> Such was the blood of gentility which Emma had formerly been so ready to vouch for!—It was as likely to be as untainted, perhaps, as the blood of many a gentleman: but what a connexion had she been preparing for Mr. Knightley—or for the Churchills—or even for Mr. Elton!—The stain of illegitimacy, unbleached by nobility or wealth, would have been a stain indeed.   (482; 3: ch. 19)

The situation of illegitimate children in Austen's era was dismal. According to William Blackstone's *Commentaries on the Laws of England* (1758), such a child could "inherit nothing. . . . neither can he have heirs, but of his own body; for being *nullius filius*, he is therefore kin to nobody, and has no ancestor from whom any inheritable blood can be derived" (qtd. in Pinchbeck and Hewitt 2: 583). Not only legally an outcast, an illegitimate child was also morally tainted. Nineteenth-century orphanages often refused the illegitimate—the largest category of destitute children—because, it was believed, they would pollute other orphans (Pinchbeck and Hewitt 2: 584). In giving Harriet a happy ending with Robert Martin, Austen might even be said to liberalize the discourse on illegitimacy in her time. Mr. Knightley works on Emma, to the end, to change her opinion of Martin:

> His situation is an evil—but you must consider it as what satisfies your friend; and I will answer for your thinking better and better of him as you know him more. His good sense and good principles would delight you.—As far as the man is concerned, you could not wish your friend in better hands. His rank in society I would alter if I could, which is saying a great deal I assure you, Emma.   (472–73; 3: ch. 18)

Emma's oversensitivity to class distinction is something Mr. Knightley is convinced he can alter, even if he cannot change Martin's rank. Conveniently for Emma, her meddling with Harriet has done no long-lasting damage.

Mrs. Elton's potential for doing damage as a patroness is even greater than Emma's.[13] Attempting to out-Emma Emma, Mrs. Elton took a great fancy to Jane Fairfax; and from the first. Not merely when a state of warfare with one young lady might be supposed to recommend the other, but from the very first; and she was not satisfied with expressing a natural and reasonable admiration—but without solicitation, or plea, or privilege, she must be wanting to assist and befriend her.

(282; 2: ch. 15)

Mrs. Elton takes Jane under her wing "without solicitation." There is no familial or community privilege to justify the position she assumes. In her "knight-errantry," Mrs. Elton resolves that Jane, her timid but delightful "inferior," must not remain in "retirement, such obscurity, so thrown away." The vicar's wife alone becomes the "very active patroness of Jane Fairfax," who is represented as a pawn, although, "could she have chosen with whom to associate, she would not have chosen" Mrs. Elton (282, 283, 284, 286; 2: ch. 15).

Mrs. Elton is a sign of what an unreformed Emma might have become. Indeed, Emma shares some of Mrs. Elton's faults: a "vain woman, extremely well satisfied with herself, and thinking much of her own importance; that she meant to shine and be very superior" (272; 2: ch. 14). If Mrs. Elton selects a more appropriate humble companion in Jane than Emma does in Harriet, the vicar's wife more egregiously oversteps her boundaries. Although finding employment as a governess for Jane seems like a selfless act, it may actually be an attempt to prove to her new community (and to her beloved Maple Grove relatives) that she exerts power in Highbury. The cruel extent of her coercion appears through Miss Bates's statement of gratitude, "Yes, our good Mrs. Elton. The most indefatigable, true friend. She would not take a denial. . . . It is not every body that would have stood out in such a kind way as she did, and refuse to take Jane's answer" (380–81; 3: ch. 8). Mrs. Elton represents the female patron as bully.

Patronage exists by definition because of economic inequalities, but *Emma* implies that in a more equitable patron-companion relationship, wealth must be counterbalanced or complemented by accomplishments and merit. Austen does not suggest that privileged women should give up or even share their advantages, but she offers lessons about how women with power might best exercise it. Where a humble companion is concerned, a powerful woman may think she is engaged in "a very kind undertaking," but she would be wise to investigate her motives, as well as her protégée's situation and expectations. The novel does not recommend unquestioning support, pliability, or flattery on the part of a companion (Harriet's mistakes), nor does it endorse rigid paternalism and unrealistic idealism on the part of the patroness (Mrs. Elton's and Emma's follies, respectively). While we may see *Emma*'s portrayal of women's bonds with other women as too individually focused or too limited in scope to offer a model for our time, in its own era the novel showed the need for greater fairness among privileged women.

Teaching *Emma* can introduce discussions about eighteenth-century feminism, in all its complexity. It can demonstrate that there is no such thing as an unbroken line of female or even feminist thinking, then or now. The novel may provoke debate over how far Austen's visions of women and empowerment go. It is a testament to *Emma*'s relevance—although not, perhaps, its so-called solutions—that the issue of "on whose behalf," of women helping women, constitutes a central question in today's feminist practice. As Donna Landry concludes about More's treatment of Yearsley, it is a case of "the liberal feminist dilemma writ large: 'a good heart and an inadequate methodology'" (20).

NOTES

[1]Of course, Emma does not "move into the great house." She remains in her familial great house with her new husband, a deviation from fairy tales itself worthy of classroom commentary.

[2]A great deal of scholarship on Austen, most notably by Sulloway and by Kirkham, links her beliefs to those of Wollstonecraft and Hays. I find the most convincing argument about Austen's relation to 1790s feminism to be C. Johnson's. In *Jane Austen* Johnson argues, "Austen was not able to depoliticize her work—for the political implications of her work [are] implicit in the subject matter itself—but rather to depolemicize it" (xxv). In *Equivocal Beings* Johnson argues that "though Wollstonecraft remained an unmentionable throughout Austen's career, there is ample evidence that she too was a figure Austen reckoned with" (191). See also my anthology *Jane Austen and Discourses of Feminism*.

[3]For instructors who do not have such material, *Women in the Eighteenth Century* (V. Jones) includes brief introductions and primary texts that demonstrate attitudes toward such issues as conduct, sexuality, education, and feminism. McMaster's essay "Class" provides a valuable introduction, as well as a useful discussion of the position of the governess.

[4]Some of the argument that follows is revised from my essay "'The Duty of Woman by Woman': Reforming Feminism in *Emma*," Jane Austen, *Emma*. Case Studies in Contemporary Criticism, ed. Alistair Duckworth, © 2002 by Bedford-St. Martin's, which examines *Emma* as an example of feminist criticism of the novel. I am grateful to Bedford-St. Martin's for permission to use the argument from and some sections of that essay here.

[5]In her *Equivocal Beings*, Johnson argues that *Emma* remakes masculinity and national identity: "Where this novel is concerned with gender transgression, it is from the masculine, not the feminine side" (196). Johnson's work has been enormously influential to my own thinking, although I believe that *Emma* gestures toward how an ideal powerful woman might behave.

[6]For a short introduction to female companionate relationships and Austen, see Castle "Sister-Sister."

[7]She did, however, express sympathy for Caroline, the estranged, ill-treated wife of the Prince Regent: "Poor woman, I shall support her as long as I can, because she *is* a Woman, & because I hate her Husband" (Austen, *Letters* [Le Faye] 208).

[8]Richard Polwhele's poem *The Unsexed Females* (1798), which presents More as diametrically opposed to Wollstonecraft, celebrates the fact that More lives, while Wollstonecraft is dead. See Landry 254–60; Kowaleski-Wallace 41–44; and Demers 81–88. Myers argues that More and Wollstonecraft share many political commitments. Mellor has published a feminist defense of More's "moral or Christian capitalism," calling her a "revolutionary reformer" and likening her to Wollstonecraft (18) but—not surprisingly—making little mention of the Yearsley incident (discussed later in my essay).

[9]It earned £2,000 within its first year, and 30 editions of 1,000 copies each were sold before More's death, in 1834 (M. Jones 193). *Emma*, by way of contrast, was issued in 1816 with a print run of 2,000, of which 1,200 were sold; no further edition appeared until 1833.

[10]Austen proclaims with characteristic irony that when she reads *Coelebs*, she is certain to be delighted as much as other people, but until then she will dislike it.

[11]A "sequel," describing the life of a virtuous heroine and a decaying prostitute, titled *Coelibia Choosing a Husband: A Modern Novel* (1809), was written by Robert Torrens. See Demers 97–98. Johnson calls Mr. Knightley the "very reverse of Coelebs" (*Jane Austen* 141–42).

[12]More was betrothed at twenty-two, but her fiancé refused to marry her after six years of engagement. When the engagement was canceled, the terms of its forfeiture provided her an annuity of £200 and a lump sum of £1,000 (Demers 6). More vowed never to marry and later turned down a proposal, making good on her pledge.

[13]On Emma and Mrs. Elton as "Lady Patroness," see Johnson, *Jane Austen* 129–30.

The Sexual Politics of *Emma*

Ruth Perry

Students often want to know if readers can discern whether a book has been written by a man or a woman and, more generally, how gender affects authorship. After explaining the pitfalls of "essentialism" and summarizing what Virginia Woolf says in *A Room of One's Own* about the material conditions for work, I tell students that certain themes are more likely to show up in women's writing. Literary representations of women's friendship, for example, are rare in works by men. In texts by women, the complicated feelings of female characters as they recognize one another's powers and identify with each other can reveal the authors' attitudes about themselves as writers and as women.[1] Women's friendships, essential to psychic survival and often the most significant mirror for the self—yet constantly undermined, conditioned, distorted, and discouraged in patriarchal culture—can thus be read in fiction as representing a woman's reaction to her society's gender prejudice. Women's friendship tests the power of women in a society: in cultures in which women are weak, friendship among them is inhibited; in societies in which women are strong, it flourishes. In addition to reflecting the possibilities, in any culture, for connections among women—whether erotic, maternal, sororal, comradely—the quality of their relationships can indicate society's attitudes toward femininity, heterosexuality, conventional marriage, and what Adrienne Rich calls the "lesbian continuum."[2]

Emma is a splendid work for seeing how a woman writer understands the determining nature of gender and how she inscribes, in her text, its effects on her heroine's relations with other women characters. Austen herself lived in what amounted to a women's enclave in a patriarchal system and understood the consequences of doubled loyalties. In *Emma* she chronicles the relations among Emma, Miss Taylor/Mrs. Weston, Harriet Smith, Mrs. Goddard, Robert Martin's sisters, Jane Fairfax, Miss Bates, and her mother and shows how the complications of friendship and dependence among these women are distorted by their absorption in various, often imaginary, marriage plots. Indeed, Austen uses the marriage plot to comment on the situation of women in her society and not merely to reinscribe the plot; the essentials of her commentary are contained in the story of the relations among women.

From the outset, the sexual politics of this novel strike the feminist reader as irritatingly patronizing: Emma must be brought down a peg, must be cured of her vanity and arrogance, and by a man—Mr. Knightley—who has watched over her, corrected her faults, and given her advice and guidance since she was a little girl. Emma must be taught not to manipulate people, not to interfere in their lives, not to think she knows what is good for them better than they do. Critics have varied in their assessments of Mr. Knightley's priggishness and Emma's culpability, but everyone recognizes that, from his more realistic vantage grounded in economic realities, he keeps reining in Emma's imagination and criticizing her romantic scripts for Harriet. Emma imagines that Harriet, with her blond beauty and sweet temper, might aspire—like the heroine of a sentimental novel—to a match far above her station as a parlor boarder in Mrs. Goddard's school. As Austen has taken care to point out in the case of Mr. Weston, a man of financial independence may choose an amiable woman without money or connections. But Mr. Knightley, the ranking man in town, thinks Emma's romantic schemes for Harriet unrealistic and insists on the importance of birth and breeding. When Emma tells him pertly, "I am very much mistaken if your sex in general would not think such beauty, and such temper, the highest claims a woman could possess" (63–64; 1: ch. 8), Austen gives the authoritative Mr. Knightley a reply favoring the still higher claims of women's reason, education, and lineage.[3]

Although there is truth in the cliché of male correction and improvement, with its easy ironies, a more sensitive index of the effects of patriarchal values on women's lives is to be found in an examination of the problematic relations among the women in this novel, as they are affected by the need to negotiate the heterosexual marriage market and to find a secure place in society.

To begin with, Austen sets up Emma as a woman who does not have to get married. Among Austen's heroines she is unique: handsome, clever, *and* rich. The cards are stacked in this game; Emma's situation cannot be improved materially by marriage. As she laughingly tells her naive young friend Harriet:

> I have none of the usual inducements of women to marry. . . . Fortune I do not want; employment I do not want; consequence I do not want; I believe few married women are half as much mistress of their husband's house, as I am of Hartfield; and never, never could I expect to be so truly beloved and important; so always first and always right in any man's eyes as I am in my father's.   (84; 1: ch. 10)

Yet finally, at the end of a series of misguided and failed female friendships, Emma realizes that she too must marry, with no less inevitability than Austen's other heroines.

What, then, was Austen's attitude toward marriage and toward friendship with other women? Does the biographical information furnish any clues about her thinking? Let us recall that Austen spent her adult life essentially with other women. True, she often enjoyed the society of her brothers and nephews as well, and she was especially fond of the younger, adventurous ones. But she shared a bedroom with her sister, Cassandra, all her born days, and Cassandra was her first, last, and most constant love.[4] In their life together, like the best of companionate unions, they shared the minutiae of domesticity, gossip and news of neighbors and friends, concerns about the rest of their family, and their literary judgments about whatever they were reading. I have no doubt but that Cassandra, whom Jane termed "the finest comic writer of the present age" (Austen, *Letters* [Le Faye] 5), functioned as a literary sounding board for the author, if not as a more active editor. Cassandra's clear-eyed, unsentimental comments on the literary efforts of their scribbling nieces and nephews can occasionally be found in Austen's letters. The intimacy of Austen's writing—the sure, confident, direct simplicity of her prose—may be the result of this first and most ideal reader: the appreciative, keen-eyed, upright, reliable, humorous, loving Cassandra. When Jane died, Cassandra wrote to their niece Fanny: "I *have* lost a treasure, such a Sister, such a friend as never can have been surpassed,—She was the sun of my life, the gilder of every pleasure, the soother of every sorrow, I had not a thought concealed from her & it is as if I had lost a part of myself" (Austen, *Letters* [Le Faye] 344).

During the years in which she revised and published her earlier works and drafted *Mansfield Park*, *Emma*, and *Persuasion*, Austen lived with her mother and Cassandra in an all-woman household. In 1805 they added to their ménage Martha Lloyd, whose mother had just died and who had grown up with them in the neighborhood of Steventon. Jane wrote to Cassandra, "I am quite of your opinion as to the folly of concealing any longer our intended Partnership with Martha" (Austen, *Letters* [Le Faye] 105). Such partnerships were not unusual in eighteenth-century England. It was a common enough arrangement for single women to pool their resources and to make a family of friends. A favorite niece, either Anna Austen or Fanny Knight, was occasionally added to this intimate circle. As Jane once wrote to Cassandra, Fanny was "almost another Sister,—& could not have supposed that a neice would ever have been so much to me. She is quite after one's heart" (Austen, *Letters* [Le Faye] 144). In the novel, Emma says gaily to Harriet of her intended spinsterhood: "I shall often have a niece with me" (86; 1: ch. 10).

In Austen's own life, then, marriage was not a sovereign good, nor the lack of it a determining disappointment. In 1808, at thirty-three, writing to Cassandra about a ball she had just attended, she took stock. "It was the same room in which we danced 15 years ago!—I thought it all over—& in spite of the shame of being so much older, felt with thankfulness that I was quite as happy now as then" (Austen, *Letters* [Le Faye] 157).

While some critics have commented on the intensity of sisterly feeling in Austen's works, others have directed our attention to different kinds of relations between and among women.[5] When we examine *Emma* in this light, we find many testimonies to the pleasures of women's friendship. The most obvious of these is the relation between Emma and Mrs. Weston. Mrs. Weston tells Mr. Knightley, "perhaps no man can be a good judge of the comfort a woman feels in the society of one of her own sex, after being used to it all her life" (36; 1: ch. 5). In her unstinting fondness for Emma, in her idealized motherliness, Mrs. Weston is described as "well-informed, useful, gentle, knowing all the ways of the family, interested in all its concerns, and peculiarly interested in . . . [Emma's] every pleasure, every scheme of her's;—one to whom she could speak every thought as it arose, and who had such an affection for her as could never find fault" (6; 1: ch. 1). Emma could tell "nothing of Hartfield, in which Mrs. Weston had not a lively concern; and half an hour's uninterrupted communication of all those little matters on which the daily happiness of private life depends, was one of the first gratifications of each" (117; 1: ch. 14).

Indeed, the precipitating cause of the action in the novel, such as it is, is the separation of these friends because of Mrs. Weston's marriage, a marriage that leaves Emma in need of companionship. The story of Emma and her governess is as old as the story of the separation of Demeter and Persephone, the first of many pairs of women divided by marriage. By the end, we have lamented the separation of four sets of friends: Jane Fairfax from Miss Campbell, the inevitable cooling of the friendship between Emma and Harriet, and the double estrangement of Emma from Mrs. Weston when the latter has a baby girl to engross her.

But the great unfinished business of the novel is the never-quite-managed friendship between Emma and Jane Fairfax, the two superior young women for whose association we wait and whose conversation promises the most delightful equality of taste and interests, but who are parted on the eve of their goodwill by their marriages. All through the novel we long for an improvement in their relations, for the sake of each differently deprived young woman. Austen scarcely misses an opportunity to emphasize how desirable this friendship is, not only for the two principals but in the eyes of their friends and relatives. If the first half of the novel is devoted to the misuse of friendship—exemplified by Emma's manipulation of Harriet's romantic feelings and marital expectations—the second half piles pressure on pressure for a warm bonding between Emma and Jane. Isabella assumes it to be a most eligible connection, and Mr. Knightley urges Emma several times to befriend Jane Fairfax. In the end, Emma does move closer to Jane, making three symbolic overtures only to have them rejected: she invites Jane to Hartfield, she puts her carriage at her disposal, and she sends her some arrowroot. She signals her willingness to share with Jane Fairfax her home, her neighborhood, and—because arrowroot is a colonial product of the British West Indies—the commodified benefits of the empire. But these symbolic gestures come too late, and the narrative repeatedly, pointedly, evades the looked-for friendship.

Emma's exclusive attention to marriage plots of her own devising is consistent with her inability to enter into a relation of equality with other women. Her obsession with arranging marriages blinds her to other relational possibilities—including friendships in which one is neither patron nor dependent. Grateful as she is to her governess and friend Mrs. Weston for her guidance and education, their connection was never based on equality. And the great attraction of Harriet Smith, beyond her blond beauty and pliant temper, is that "everything" could be done for her. Emma's subsequent failure to connect with Jane Fairfax (her equal in age, abilities, and sense), along with her enthusiasm for those unequally structured relationships, might be interpreted in the light of her preoccupation with the marriage plot.

Friendship between women is problematic in a genre designed to fulfill the marriage plot—that has to justify a woman's subordination to a husband, either by demonstrating his worthiness as an authority or by proving her need for his power, his money, or those equivocal substitutes, his moral and spiritual guidance. Destined to play the heroine in her own marriage plot, Emma must be made to acknowledge her dependence on Mr. Knightley. The relations she has with other women in the meantime prepare her for the unequal one she will inevitably enter. Determined by that necessity, the deformations of women's friendship can be read as a running commentary on the marriage plot.

First, Emma's marriage scenarios for Harriet distort their relationship. Harriet, sweet seventeen, is herself a conventional heroine of sentimental fiction: guileless, true, and passionate, with beautiful blue eyes. Emma's mistake is to confuse her with a character in a book—to write romantic scripts for her and to paint an idealized portrait of her. Austen's appreciative reading of Eaton Stannard Barrett's burlesque *The Heroine* (1813) when she was working on *Emma* may have heightened her satiric sense of the effects of novel-reading on life.[6]

Second, Emma, who takes credit for having engineered the marriage between Mr. Weston and her governess and who imagines several different endings for Harriet Smith's story, also conceives marriage plots for Jane Fairfax that replace any real association with her. She convinces herself of an entanglement between Jane and Mr. Dixon while Jane is, in fact, living out a romantic scenario as improbable and romantic as any in a novel, undetected by Emma. And the dissembling and reserve required of Jane to play her part in that drama effectively bar the possibility of any intimacy from her side.

Austen's message at this level would seem to be that women who imagine themselves and one another only in marriage plots—as romance novels teach one to do—will miss the opportunities for friendship with other women. At every turn, marriage is inimical to women's friendship. The friendship between Emma and Jane, which we expect and even come to long for, is not only blocked by their marriage plots, but is confounded by competition and envy. Emma resents Jane's superior discipline and accomplishment because it spoils her self-idealization, and Jane is hurt by Frank Churchill's open flirtation with Emma. Competition between Emma and Jane is possible to the same extent as their friendship and for the same reason: because Jane Fairfax is Emma's only peer. But ultimately the novel evades their recognition of equality, whether in friendship or in competition.

The visibility of women's competition in *Emma* serves as a reminder of the patriarchal structures in which women live. Mrs. Elton's marriage places her in competition with other women in her society and gives her precedence even over Emma. Throughout most of the novel, Emma imagines that she competes with other women only for intellectual or artistic distinction. In elegance of mind and manners she recognizes that she is better than Harriet but less disciplined than Jane. (Indeed, it is Jane as much as Mr. Knightley who sets in motion Emma's recognition of her shortcomings.) At the same time, Jane and

Harriet, each in her own way, are aware from the start that, despite the self-referential nature of Emma's perception of their competition, they are, in fact, competing for men—for husbands—for Mr. Elton, for Frank Churchill, and for Mr. Knightley. Emma's eventual recognition of this common object simultaneously precipitates her entry into womanhood and cuts her off from other women. Furthermore, her moments of jealousy of Jane and Harriet lead her to her "true" good: Mr. Knightley. Her competitive feelings toward them—and her admiration—are turned to account for the marriage plot.

Both Emma the author and Austen the author are restricted by the novel's standard romance script. The way Austen handles this limitation and the way she resolves the tension between the marriage plot and the friendship plot constitute a metanarrative worth paying attention to. Jane's desperate dependence on marriage foreshadows the finale of Emma's story, since, inevitably, Emma must stop being an author and submit to becoming a heroine in someone else's script, in order for the book to end. Self-conscious about how overdetermined that ending is, Austen ironically undercuts her own authorial hand as Cupid in describing the immediacy of Emma's recognition: "It darted through her, with the speed of an arrow, that Mr. Knightley must marry no one but herself!" (408; 3: ch. 11).

Emma's first intimations of the harsh imperative of the marriage plot come when she sees Jane's prospects narrowing. Then she relents in her dislike and empathically puts herself in Jane's place; fellow feeling supersedes all earlier reactions. But just as the possibility of friendship between them emerges, it is foreclosed by marriage. As in the case of Harriet, the marriage plot inhibits the friendship plot.

There is a literary-historical reason for sensing a close identification between Emma and Jane and for reading their missing connection as symptomatic. In the first version of the novel, in the fragment *The Watsons*, they were combined in a single character—Emma Watson, a heroine with Emma Woodhouse's healthy, blooming looks and openhearted manner, but with the constricted financial and material circumstances of Jane Fairfax.[7] Emma Watson, living with difficult, garrulous relatives in a house that is too small, on the brink of going into service as a governess, has no dowry and no prospects; her family cannot afford to keep her indefinitely. A woman would be lucky to make £30 a year beyond room and board as a governess. Under the circumstances, marriage was, of course, the best advancement to be hoped for. Although *The Watsons* was never finished, one can guess that Emma Watson was to be saved from service by a marriage with the genteel and intelligent clergyman, Mr. Howard. "Single Women have a dreadful propensity for being poor" remarked Austen in a letter to her niece Fanny Knight,—which is one very strong argument in favour of Matrimony" (Austen, *Letters* [Le Faye] 332).

Splitting the character into Jane Fairfax and Emma Woodhouse, she who has little and she who has everything, permitted Austen to use these women to comment on one another and on the destiny they share. Emma Woodhouse, in no need of marriage, has health, wealth, and a comfortable house, whereas Jane Fairfax, living in cramped quarters with her grandmother and unmarried aunt, realizes she must apply to an office "for the sale—not quite of human flesh—but of human intellect" (300; 2: ch. 17). Although Emma and Jane represent the economic poles among women of the gentry, in fact their situations are merely opposite sides of the same coin. Jane's story is a darker version of the truth that both must face: women by themselves are insufficient to face the world. The unwritten story of Jane's relationship with Frank Churchill, which casts its shadow on the novel, is a grim reminder of women's dependence on men, no matter how intelligent, gifted, or disciplined the women may be; of their vulnerability; and of their subjugation to men's values and pleasure. This is the real condition of women, not the fairy tale version of the spoiled, rich, pampered girl who is the apple of her father's eye and has no need of men.

The socioeconomic force of the comparison between Jane's lot and Emma's lot is to show that class is not everything—that gender is the primary determinant of status. By the time *Emma* is finished, every woman in the novel is cured of her vanity, and every man is confirmed in his right to choose and be accepted. At twenty-one, which Jane Fairfax designates as the age of sacrifice, Emma too must learn to forgo authorial control and play, to temper her self-love, and to submit to the will of her betters—in her case, Mr. Knightley; that is, she must accept her position as a woman. Structured like a fugue, in which the themes of marriage, independence, friendship, service, and submission rise and mingle and subside, the novel also twins Jane Fairfax with Mrs. Weston, about whose life before she was Emma's governess we know nothing and who is also saved from service by marriage.

Unmarried women parade through these pages as counterpoint and corroboration of the marriage theme. All three of the younger women—Emma, Jane, and Harriet—declare at one time or another that they will never marry. Miss Bates, Jane's aunt, is the perennial reminder of the social helplessness of an old maid. Like a dependent child, she is a burden at best, despite her sterling character and cheerful disposition. Carriages must be sent for her, she must be fed—with hampers of apples and loins of pork—and her endless repetitive chatter must be patiently listened to.

As everyone knows, the turning point in Emma's moral development—her apotheosis of self-disgust—comes from Mr. Knightley's rebuke when she insults Miss Bates for being tiresome, when she says what everyone knows is true. Mr. Knightley is here the agent of Emma's personal maturation, of her recognition that she has acted badly. The form of his chastisement is instructive; it reminds Emma of the realities of rank and station. "Were she a woman of fortune, I would leave every harmless absurdity to take its chance. . . . Were she your equal in situation—but, Emma, consider how far this is from being the case. She is poor; she has sunk from the comforts she was born to; and, if she live to old age, must probably sink more" (375; 3: ch. 7). As in Austen's other novels, the humiliation of the heroine precedes her capitulation. Emma must learn to accept the world as it is before she is fit to be a wife. She must sort out the conventions of fiction from those of society and from the self-indulgence of youth.

There is another insult, unwritten and unheralded in the submerged novel, that dawns on us only on a second reading or with second thoughts. It is the insult offered Jane Fairfax on this same occasion at Box Hill by her secret fiancé, Frank Churchill, and that unwitting flirt, Emma Woodhouse. Their chatter about marriage, in Jane's helpless presence, is cruel beyond the explicit denigration of Miss Bates and no less a reminder of the dependence and vulnerability of single women. Indeed, to Jane herself their chatter is the sternest of reminders of the rock bottom reality of her situation and drives her to accept servitude in Mrs. Smallridge's establishment as governess to three little girls.

This, then, is the lesson learned on that most disagreeable of days: women must marry, they must not be old maids if they want to protect themselves from insult and scorn. This social pressure effectively divides women from one another even if they are not in direct competition for economic subsistence— for it directs women to find their comfort in submission to a benevolent husband rather than in equal intercourse with others of their own sex.

In this essay I have been arguing that although the marriage plot provides the frame for *Emma*, certain elements of the action call attention to the ways in which compulsory heterosexuality disrupts and distorts the relations between women. The novel structurally protests the overdetermination of the marriage plot by repeatedly raising and then undercutting our romantic expectations and by locating the real romantic story offstage where we cannot indulge ourselves in it. What romance there is, played out where we can see it, turns out to be illusory—whether it is the romance that Emma offers Harriet with Mr. Elton or the romantic flirtation carried on between Emma and Frank Churchill. When Austen sketched women in their associations with one another, she made visible a dynamic of women's frustrated need for each other. If one takes seriously both that need and its disappointment, another pattern of meaning emerges from the juxtaposition of friendship plots with marriage plots. Where critics have failed to see this pattern of meaning, it is because they have failed to take Austen seriously as a *woman* writer. They are satisfied that Emma needs to be made vulnerable, whether to social hierarchy, contemporary gender roles, or male authority. But they do not imagine that a woman writer might feel differently about that vulnerability.

The metanarrative of *Emma* reveals how much the imperative to marry costs women: it inhibits their range of relations with other women, makes them dependent on male approval, and limits their imaginative and social autonomy. As a writer, Austen was aware of the limitations of the marriage plot in a formal, literary sense too. Her resistance can be felt not only in her evasion of romantic scenes and her disingenuous misleading of the reader as to where to look, but in the discomfort she makes us feel about Mr. Knightley's unremitting paternalism, the serious lack of beaux in Highbury, or Jane Fairfax's match with a man clearly her moral inferior. Trapped as an author, as her characters are trapped as women, Austen underscores the inevitability of their narratives in the claustrophobia of Highbury, in the discussions in the novel of the limited possibilities for women outside of marriage, and in Emma's marriage—a marriage in which she never even leaves home. None of Austen's women characters, not Emma, nor Jane Fairfax, nor Mrs. Weston, can outwit her destiny. Their stories only repeat themselves as these women become wives and mothers, raising their daughters, preparing the next generation for their parts in the marriage plot.

I have argued that Austen's ironic undercutting of romance in this novel, together with the unresolved but repeated plea for friendship between women, constitutes a subversive message. In the separation of Emma from Mrs. Weston, from Harriet, and especially from Jane Fairfax, Austen provides a critique of her society and of the conventions of the romance plot in the sentimental novel. She may not have replaced the conventional story for women, but she knew, more profoundly than perhaps we have understood, what was wrong with that old narrative.

NOTES

This essay is a shorter, revised, and updated version of my essay "Interrupted Friendships in Jane Austen's *Emma*," *Tulsa Studies in Women's Literature* 5 (1986): 185–202. Used with permission.

[1]The first—and still the best—systematic treatment of this subject in eighteenth-century English literature by women is Todd's *Women's Friendship in Literature*. This essay is much indebted to her discussion of *Emma*.

[2]The phrase "lesbian continuum" was coined by Rich to encompass the range of woman-identified experience, not simply genital experience. It signifies the intense links "between and among women, including the sharing of a rich inner life, the bonding against male tyranny, the giving and receiving of practical and political support" (648–49).

[3]In his splendid reading of *Emma*, Booth argues that despite the ostensible sexual politics of the novel, in which the reader is reinforced in the belief that "women are indeed the weaker sex, that unlike men they cannot be whole, cannot find maturity, without the protective instruction and care from the right kind of man," the seeds of critique can be found in our resistance to Knightley, however mild, and in the other ironies of the ending (34).

[4]In a review of Le Faye's edition of Austen's letters (Castle, "Sister-Sister") and in Castle's subsequent rejoinder to protesting letters (Letter), Castle went so far as to suggest that Jane's intense bond with Cassandra had "its unconscious homoerotic dimension" (Letter). Castle offers as evidence Austen's frequent observations about women's physical qualities and the cut and fit of their clothes. "Unlike men, women have bodies," Castle wrote ("Sister-Sister" 5). This review called forth a storm of controversy from Austen readers and scholars in subsequent issues of the *London Review of Books*. The most sensible reply, to my mind, was the comment made by Claudia Johnson in the 5 Oct. issue, in which she remarked that Austen criticism has always been divided

between those who find in Austen's fiction a "reassuringly orthodox world" and those who suspect Austen of "sexual abnormality" because she "does not particularly privilege the representation of sexual passion with men in her fiction." As evidence of the latter tradition, Johnson refers to Mudrick's observation that Emma, "in love" with Harriet, experiences "a love unphysical and inadmissible, even perhaps indefinable in such a society" (11) and Wilson's essay "A Long Talk about Jane Austen," in which he notes that "Emma, who was relatively indifferent to men, was inclined to infatuations with women" (39).

[5]In addition to Todd's work, important early feminist work on Austen was done by Deborah Kaplan, Susan Lanser, Jane Lilienfeld, Judith Wilt, and Nina Auerbach—all of whom contributed significantly to the reinterpretation of the link between Austen's life and writings. The most controversial essay about the sisters Marianne and Elinor in *Sense and Sensibility* is Eve Kosofsky Sedgwick's "Jane Austen and the Masturbating Girl," which reads Marianne's restless, disturbed behavior against a Victorian treatise on masturbation. Sedgwick argues for a "homoerotic matrix not yet crystallized in terms of 'sexual identity'" (826). Marianne's erotic identity, she writes, is not exactly a "same-sex-loving one or a cross-sex-loving one (though she loves both women and men), but rather the one that today no longer exists *as* an identity: that of the masturbating girl" (827)—which Sedgwick particularizes as a combination of excessive sexuality and "autoerotic inaccessibility" (829).

In the nearly two decades since the original version of this essay argued that women's friendships in Austen's novels provide a running commentary on the emotional deformations of a heterosexist society, a number of feminist critics have asserted Emma's homoerotic tendencies. Tiffany Potter makes a case for analyzing the novel with Adrienne Rich's "lesbian continuum" in mind and compares Emma's diction with that of Anne Lister, a contemporary of Austen's and a practicing lesbian. Lisa Moore notes the physical appreciation among women in *Emma*: Emma is susceptible to Harriet's beauty and Mrs. Weston admires Emma's face and figure, her blooming complexion and her pretty form. Insisting on Emma's homoerotic desire, Moore writes: "With Harriet, Emma takes on too much the role of the lover; to learn to be a heroine, she must learn to be beloved" (125). Susan M. Korba, elaborating on a point made earlier by Susan Morgan, argues that sex is imbricated with issues of power. Reading *Emma* against Jessica Benjamin's "Master and Slave: The Fantasy of Erotic Domination," Korba diagnoses motherless Emma as desiring those she can dominate or wishing to dominate those she desires. This dynamic of erotic domination is apparent in Emma's sexual inaccessibility to men, she argues, in her relation with Harriet, and in the fact that Emma's interest in Jane Fairfax increases when Jane's autonomy is threatened.

[6]For Austen's reading of Barrett's *The Heroine*, see Austen's letter to Cassandra 2 Mar. 1814 (Austen, *Letters* [Le Faye] 255). For a fuller treatment of Barrett's influence on Austen's novel, see Kirkham, ch. 18.

[7]Q. D. Leavis first proposed the view that the basis of Emma was *The Watsons*, drafted when Austen was living in Bath.

Teaching about Free Indirect Discourse

Dorice Williams Elliott

"First and foremost let Jane Austen be named, the greatest artist that has ever written," wrote George Henry Lewes in his well-known review (359). However, when I read this statement to my students and ask them why Austen is such a great artist, most are baffled. Unequipped to deal with issues of literary style and technique, they often resort to comments about Austen's funny characters—if they respond at all. Certainly, Austen's ability to make us laugh at but still sympathize with her characters is central to her art. As Lewes explained it, "To read one of her books is like an actual experience of life: you know the people as if you have lived with them, and you feel something of personal affection towards them" (359). But how does she do it? Much of this effect is attributable to Austen's skillful use of what theorists of narrative call "free indirect discourse."[1] Because of her complex intermingling of the humorous, satiric voice of the narrator and the inner voice of a character's thoughts, we as readers get a double view—both inside and outside—that makes the character not only someone we recognize but someone we seem to know better than we know our friends or even ourselves.

Free indirect discourse, as I explain to my students, is a literary technique in which the author subtly shifts the point of view back and forth from omniscient narrator to character until it is difficult or even impossible to separate the two voices.[2] It is often used, especially in Austen, together with direct interior monologue and with what Dorrit Cohn calls "psychonarration," or the narrator's description of what a character is thinking. [3] In psychonarration, for instance, the narrator might explain to us that "Anne was feeling sad as she remembered her mother's death." In direct interior monologue, the author gives us the thoughts in the character's own words, like quoted speech: "Ah, mother. How I miss you." A clue that the author is using free indirect discourse instead of psychonarration or interior monologue is that, although the character seems to be speaking (or thinking) in his or her own words, the writer uses the past tense and third person pronouns instead of present tense and the first person, the form used in expressing one's feelings or thoughts. As Austen uses it, free indirect discourse is often marked by distinct punctuation, particularly increased use of dashes and exclamation points. The technique enables the author to represent not only a character's conscious thinking but also his or her semiconscious or even unconscious feelings as well. Although not the first to employ free indirect discourse, Jane Austen handled it so adroitly and frequently that she is often credited with introducing it as a literary technique. And although Austen used free indirect discourse to some extent in her earlier novels, in *Emma* she developed it into a supple tool for representing her characters' thoughts and feelings. It is largely through her use of this technique, I contend, that Austen could take a heroine she predicted that "no-one but myself will much like" and make her into a sympathetic character with whom the reader feels a sense of intimacy despite her evident flaws and mistakes (Austen-Leigh, 1870 ed. 157).

To demonstrate how Austen combines the voices of narrator and character in free indirect discourse, we can begin by identifying the recognizable characteristics of the narrator and of the primary focalizer, the character Emma. The narrator, of course, is the primary voice telling us the story in the novel, whereas the focalizer is the character through whose eyes we see or whose point of view we share at any given moment. The narrator of *Emma* makes her entrance in the famous first sentence: "Emma Woodhouse, handsome, clever, and rich, with a comfortable home and happy disposition, seemed to unite some of the best blessings of existence; and had lived nearly twenty-one years in the world with very little to distress or vex her."[4] The narrator, obviously omniscient, seems here to speak for the community, in observing that Emma "seemed to unite some of the best blessings of existence," and to have an inside knowledge of Emma's life, telling us that she has had "very little to distress or vex her." The narrator also seems to view her heroine with just a hint of satire; the subtle emphasis on "nearly twenty-one years in the world" suggests a youthful sense of self-importance. The narrator goes on to give us an affectionate but slightly critical view of Emma in phrases like "highly esteeming Miss Taylor's judgment, but directed chiefly by her own" and the "real evils indeed of Emma's situation were the power of having rather too much her own way, and a disposition to think a little too well of herself" (5; 1: ch. 1).

The narrator knows a great deal not only about Emma but about the other inhabitants of Highbury, and she details her knowledge in an instructive but chatty tone, with a sly undercurrent of humor and social criticism. Mrs. Bates is "a very old lady, almost past every thing but tea and quadrille." Her daughter, Miss Bates, "enjoyed a most uncommon degree of popularity for a woman neither young, handsome, rich, nor married" (21; 1: ch. 3). The narrator also points her satire at the community generally. When the vicar's new wife is introduced, the community's response is summarized thus: "Mrs. Elton was first seen at church: but though devotion might be interrupted, curiosity could not be satisfied by a bride in a pew, and it must be left for the visits in form which were then to be paid, to settle whether she were very pretty indeed, or only rather pretty, or not pretty at all" (270; 2: ch. 14). On other occasions Austen's narrator can be coy, as when she withholds description of the climactic moment in which Emma replies to Mr. Knightley's proposal. The narrator's wisdom and experience of human nature is also evident in statements like the one she uses to sum up the proposal scene: "Seldom, very seldom, does complete truth belong to any human disclosure; seldom can it happen that something is not a little disguised, or a little mistaken; but where, as in this case, though the conduct is mistaken, the feelings are not, it may not be very material" (430, 431; 3: ch. 13). With such examples, students can easily pick up the distinctive features Austen gives to her narrator's voice.

Emma's own voice is characterized by a combination of good breeding, or propriety, and a youthful sense of humor and playfulness. Her playful tone comes across especially in her conversations with Mr. Knightley, as in her mock-serious depiction of Miss Taylor's wedding: "you want to hear about the wedding, and I shall be happy to tell you, for we all behaved charmingly. Every body was punctual, every body in their best looks. Not a tear, and hardly a long face to be seen" (11; 1: ch. 1). Austen frequently breaks up Emma's speeches with dashes, giving a sense of spontaneity and freshness: "And have you never known the pleasure and triumph of a lucky guess?—I pity you.—I thought you cleverer—for depend upon it, a lucky guess is never merely luck" (13; 1: ch. 1). But Emma is also decided in her opinions and willing to speak authoritatively, particularly on the subject of social distinctions. Attempting to shape Harriet's opinions about the farmer Robert Martin, Emma makes her own view very plain: "What has he to do with books? And I have no doubt that he *will* thrive and be a very rich man in time—and his being illiterate and coarse need not disturb *us*" (34; 1: ch. 4). A significant feature of Emma's dialogue is that it varies according to her auditor; with her father, she is kind and straightforward, while with characters like Miss Bates or Mrs.Elton, she is polite but ironic. As one might expect from a young woman barely past adolescence, Emma is also prone to emphatic, even exaggerated statements: a match between Harriet and Mr. Martin would be a "degradation"; Harriet herself is not merely pretty but "a beautiful girl, and must be thought so by ninety-nine people out of an hundred" (62–63; 1: ch. 7). Yet despite her enthusiasm, quick wit, polish, and self-confidence, Emma has her self-doubts. Although Emma vehemently disagrees with Mr. Knightley over the relative merits of Harriet and Mr. Martin, the narrator tells us that "she had a sort of habitual respect for [Mr. Knightley's] judgment in general, which made her dislike having it so loudly against her" (65; 1: ch. 7). Such misgivings are not generally spoken aloud but form the subtext of some of Emma's most notable speeches.

Once we have discussed the specific nature of both the narrator's and Emma's voices, we are ready to look at how Austen blends them in free indirect discourse. Examples of free indirect discourse can be found on almost every page, but the technique is especially effective in representing Emma's state of mind following each of her major humiliations. I often use the passage just after Mr. Elton's proposal to Emma, because it skillfully combines psychonarration and interior monologue with free indirect discourse:

> (1) The hair was curled, and the maid sent away, and Emma sat down to think and be miserable.—(2) It was a wretched business, indeed!—(3) Such an overthrow of every thing she had been wishing for!—(4) Such a development of every thing most unwelcome!—(5) Such a blow for Harriet!—(6) That was the worst of all. (7) Every part of it brought pain and humiliation, of some sort or other; but, compared with the evil to Harriet, all was light; and she would gladly have submitted to feel yet more mistaken—more in error—more disgraced by mis-judgment, than she actually was, could the effects of her blunders have been confined to herself.
>
> (8) "If I had not persuaded Harriet into liking the man, I could have born any thing. (9) He might have doubled his presumption to me—(10) But poor Harriet!"
>
> (11) How she could have been so deceived!—(12) He protested that he had never thought seriously of Harriet—never! (13) She looked back as well as she could; but it was all confusion. (14) She had taken up the idea, she supposed, and made every thing bend to it. (15) His manners, however, must have been unmarked, wavering, dubious, or she could not have been so misled.   (134; 1: ch. 16)

The first sentence is obviously the narrator's description, although it veers into psychonarration when she says that Emma "sat down to think and be miserable." I point out that Emma, of course, would not actually say to herself, "I am going to sit down now to be miserable," but the narrator's description clearly describes Emma's state of mind. Sentence (2) is less clear; it could be the narrator speaking, but the word "wretched" and the exclamation point are, as we have seen, characteristic of Emma's voice. The dashes that set off the sentences also suggest a train of thought running through Emma's mind. Similarly, sentence (3) seems to come right out of Emma's thoughts, except that a character would not say "she" and "had been wishing" in referring to herself. Because those words are clearly the narrator's, the sentence is our first obvious example, in the passage, of free indirect discourse, the blending of the narrator's and the character's language in the same sentence. Sentences (4) and (5) could be either the narrator's or the character's direct words, but in (6), again, the past tense suggests the narrator's voice. In (7) the third person pronouns and the past tense verbs indicate the voice of the narrator, but the three repetitive phrases, separated by dashes, seem to come directly from Emma: "more mistaken—more in error—more disgraced by mis-judgment." The pattern of restating, in different words, the most humiliating aspects of her behavior is, by the way, characteristic of Emma's thought patterns in other sections of the novel as well; it occurs again here in sentence (15).

The paragraph that includes sentences (8), (9), and (10) is clearly interior monologue, marked by the use of quotation marks and first person pronouns, with contrary-to-fact and conditional clauses referring to Emma's recent experience ("If I had not persuaded . . . I could have born"). Sentence (11) is, again, free indirect discourse, with the question Emma asks herself switched to a third person exclamation by the narrator, while (12) could be either free indirect discourse or interior monologue—at this point, the narrator's voice and Emma's have become unified, so that it is impossible to tell. The next two sentences are psychonarration, but even here a phrase like "all confusion" could perhaps be Emma's words. Again, I point out that Emma is not likely to say to herself, "I am looking back as well as I can"—the narrator can describe the thought process more naturally and succinctly. But the conclusion Emma comes to as a result—it is "all confusion"—could be either her own words or the narrator's description of the tangled state of her thoughts and feelings.

By using free indirect discourse, combined with psychonarration and interior monologue, Austen gives the reader a more complete and natural-sounding portrayal of Emma's feelings than any of the three could if used by itself. Interior monologue, as we have seen, represents only those thoughts and feelings that the character actually articulates, while psychonarration alone puts more distance between the narrator and the character and lessens the sense of immediacy and intimacy. Using all three lets us know not only what Emma feels or decides but how she arrived at her reaction—how her thoughts flowed from and connected themselves to each other. Readers feel as if they are inside Emma's head, thinking and feeling along with her, not just looking in from the outside.

By analyzing a passage in this way, students should learn to pay careful attention not only to the words of the literary text but also to the punctuation, the tone, even the graphic presentation of the text on the page; such practice makes students more sensitive to the way meaning is created. Many of them find the process intriguing and are excited to locate other passages in the novel that use free indirect discourse, as well as the other methods for representing thought. Along with passages suggested by students, I often have the class look at the one that follows Emma's discovery that she has unwittingly encouraged Harriet to fall in love with Mr. Knightley. To render this climactic moment, when Emma first realizes that she is in love with Mr. Knightley herself, Austen again uses a skillful blend of interior monologue, psychonarration, and free indirect discourse to take the reader inside Emma's mind to experience, with the heroine, her new self-knowledge. Once they recognize and analyze such passages, students have answers to questions about Austen's style and artistry. They realize that she not only wrote an entertaining story about a young woman and her mistakes and misjudgments but also pioneered an important literary technique that has had a major influence on writing. Even students who didn't like *Emma* as a character, or who first saw the book only as a woman's romance, can understand Lewes's assessment of Austen as a great artist.

Focusing on the way Austen represents Emma's thoughts and feelings leads to a discussion of the students' thought processes. I sometimes ask the class to take a moment to pay attention to what is going on in their own minds—to ask themselves how much of what they are experiencing mentally is in the form of articulated thoughts and how much is sensation of which they are aware semi-consciously but have not put into words. Students quickly realize that thinking and feeling are complicated processes, not simply divisible into conscious and subconscious elements. I then ask them to think about how they might represent their thoughts in writing, perhaps by trying out free indirect discourse themselves. After this discussion, I ask students to contribute to our class e-mail list. Composing for e-mail allows them to write quickly and, in a sense, to imitate thinking aloud. Becoming more sensitive to their thought processes adds to their appreciation of what Austen accomplished when she used free indirect discourse in *Emma*.

Close reading of passages of free indirect discourse can also be a useful springboard for talking about other authors, both contemporaries and descendants of Austen. For instance, I often teach *Emma* in survey courses, and students are usually at a loss to understand how Austen could have anything in common with her contemporaries the Romantic poets. When we discuss this question, I have them look back to the Preface to *The Lyrical Ballads*, in which Wordsworth explains that poetry should "follow the fluxes and refluxes of the mind when agitated by the great and simple affections of our nature," and recall his interest in exploring and representing thought processes in poems like "Tintern Abbey" and *The Prelude, or Growth of a Poet's Mind* (158). Coleridge, too, was obviously fascinated by the workings of the mind, not only in his *Biographia Literaria* but in his poetry—his preface to "Kubla Khan" or his rendering of the power of imagination in "Frost at Midnight" and "This Lime-Tree Bower My Prison." While Austen focuses on the mind of a twenty-year-old girl rather than an illustrious poet, she certainly shares her contemporaries' interest in tracing the processes of thought and imagination.

Austen's use of free indirect discourse in *Emma* can, moreover, be compared with later nineteenth-century novels, many of which use the technique as Austen developed it. However, I often contrast Austen with Dickens, who seldom uses free indirect discourse. After our close reading of *Emma*, students can spot this key difference in their styles and comment on the resulting difference of effect and tone in the two writers, who both were writing comedic satires. Unlike Austen, the Dickens narrator, who rarely cedes authority to a character, relies much more heavily on psychonarration or direct interior monologue than on free indirect discourse in representing the thoughts of his characters.

In my experience, though, the most effective comparison with Austen's use of free indirect discourse is Virginia Woolf's handling of the technique in either

Mrs. Dalloway or *To the Lighthouse*.[5] I may begin the study of a Woolf novel by bringing in photocopies of the passage from *Emma* that we used earlier to discover and define free indirect discourse. Students have often heard the term "stream of consciousness" applied to Woolf's writing, but reminding them of Austen's use of free indirect discourse calls their attention to the way Woolf employs the same technique that Austen used so deftly over a hundred years earlier. Recognizing what they already know about free indirect discourse from *Emma* makes Woolf's modernist experiments less formidable and is a good lead-in to a discussion of influence, especially since Woolf's literary criticism makes it evident that she much admired Austen's novels.[6]

Learning about Austen's use of free indirect discourse in *Emma* thus makes students not only better readers of Austen but better readers of other authors as well. Focusing on this aspect of literary technique makes them more aware of matters of style in general and helps them articulate their responses to the characters and situations they encounter in literature.

NOTES

[1]Mezei's article contains a helpful summary of the different terms that have been used for this narrative technique (67–69). I follow Mezei's practice in adopting the term "free indirect discourse" for my discussion here.

[2]There is a long history of scholarship on free indirect discourse and related techniques for representing consciousness. For a brief overview, see Fludernik's "Discourse Representation" and other, related articles in the *Encyclopedia of the Novel*. Some of the major theorists who have written about free indirect discourse and narrative theory more broadly include Fludernik, Bakhtin, Bal, Banfield, Barthes, Chatman, Cohn, Genette, Lanser, Pascal, Prince, and Tannen.

[3]Cohn's *Transparent Minds* is an excellent, accessible book-length discussion of interior monologue, psychonarration, and free indirect discourse, which Cohn calls "narrated monologue."

[4]Although it is important for students to understand that the author and the narrator are not identical, I find it more natural to use "she" in speaking of Austen's narrator. The knowledge and concerns of the narrator seem to indicate that it is a woman's voice speaking.

[5]See Mezei's article for a discussion of free indirect discourse in both *Emma* and *Mrs. Dalloway*.

[6]See Woolf's assessment of Austen in *The Common Reader* (134–45) and *A Room of One's Own* (66–68, 74–75).

Learning to Listen:
Teaching about the Talk of Miss Bates

Pamela S. Bromberg

Miss Bates describes herself as "a talker, you know; I am rather a talker" (346; 3: ch. 5). While Emma readily concedes that Miss Bates is good-natured, kind, and generous in her thoughts and actions, she finds her company tedious, primarily because she "was such an eternal talker" (166; 2: ch. 2). Students often share Emma's judgment; they, too, find Miss Bates "so silly—so satisfied—so smiling—so prosing" (85; 1: ch. 10) that they quickly learn to skim her long, rambling monologues, eager to shift to the wittier, more entertaining voices of the other characters and the narrator. If they do so, they fall into a carefully prepared authorial trap; like Emma, they fail to take Miss Bates seriously.

In volume 1, chapter 10, Austen positions Miss Bates as a foil to Emma, who firmly rejects Harriet's suggestion that she could become "an old maid at last, like Miss Bates" (84). As Emma herself recognizes, Miss Bates, "a woman neither young, handsome, rich, nor married" (21; 1: ch. 3), and not clever or beautiful, is in all respects her antithesis. Because Miss Bates is clearly not a heroine but rather a talkative old maid whose marginal social and economic status makes her ineligible for the canonical nineteenth-century marriage and adultery plots, readers (especially first-time ones) may be tempted to ignore her. The novel teaches us, however, as it teaches Emma, that we do so at our peril. Miss Bates plays a pivotal role as the focal point for Emma's climactic lesson in moral growth and awareness and as a source of important narrative information. If we look at Miss Bates not only from Emma's youthful viewpoint but also from Austen's perspective in dramatizing this nuanced character, we discover that Miss Bates is at the center of an expanding, increasingly democratic society. As Julia Prewitt Brown argues in her essay in this volume, Miss Bates's "characterization makes her a symbol of Highbury itself," representative of its emerging "fluidity and mobility." To become accurate interpreters of texts and of human character and responsible members of the reading community, we ourselves, like Emma, should pay careful, respectful attention to the Miss Bateses of the world.

Readers do not actually meet Miss Bates until the beginning of volume 2, but they hear about her well in advance. Early in chapter 3 of volume 1, the author, strategically positioning the two women as part of the second social tier in Highbury, introduces Miss Bates and her mother, the widow and daughter of a former vicar who must now live "in a very small way," endeavoring "to make a small income go as far as possible." Austen sketches Miss Bates here as Emma's opposite in economic position, age, appearance, and social status. For students who disapprove of Emma's arrogance and privilege, Miss Bates, along with her niece, Jane Fairfax, provides an important counterweight. While she lacks Emma's gifts of fortune, face, and intellect, Miss Bates, we are told, is extremely popular because, despite her relative poverty and lack of social power, she is unfailingly cheerful. She is "interested in every body's happiness, quick-sighted to every body's merits," and demonstrates a "contented and grateful spirit" to her many neighbors and friends. The narrator also informs us that she "was a great talker upon little matters . . . full of trivial communications and harmless gossip" (21; 1: ch. 3).

The reader learns about Miss Bates again in chapter 10, but this time from Emma's more critical and condescending point of view. Amused at being compared with Miss Bates as a potential "old maid," Emma informs Harriet of the significant distinctions between them. Although she acknowledges Miss Bates's good nature, generosity, and popularity, Emma emphasizes her "silliness," her limitations of intellect and judgment and her tendency to see the world through rose-colored lenses. Emma then offers a clear-eyed analysis of her own power as "a single woman, of good fortune," as well as a surprisingly mature recognition of the ways in which "a very narrow income" can make people small-minded and cross. Emma admits that poverty has not soured Miss Bates; "she is very much to the taste of everybody, though single and though poor." But Emma is more demanding in her standards; as she tells the eager Harriet, Miss Bates "is only too good natured and too silly to suit me" (85; 1: ch. 10). The reader, identifying with Emma's commanding and persuasive tone and viewpoint, has been prepared to dismiss Miss Bates.

The reader's encounter with Miss Bates in the first chapter of volume 2 is also mediated through Emma's point of view as she and Harriet walk to the small apartment Miss Bates shares with her mother. The passage begins with Emma's pained recognition that she has been remiss in her obligations toward these "tiresome women" and continues with free indirect discourse which reveals Emma's impatience with Miss Bates's talkativeness throughout their visit (for more on free indirect discourse, see Dorice Williams Elliott's essay in this volume). When we finally hear from Miss Bates ourselves, we discover that her speech consists of a minutely detailed account of everyday activities and recent conversations, punctuated by moralizing exclamations about her kind neighbors and her own good fortune. Miss Bates is a chronicler, as opposed to a narrator. She gathers information without looking for significance or seeking explanations. Rather than develop her stories thematically, she moves from one point to the next by means of simple chronology, random association, and frequent digression. A few guiding principles characterize her speech: she emphasizes the kindness of others, praises her talented niece, refers often to her deaf mother, and defers to her audience. Although excruciatingly accurate about facts, she fails to interpret them or place them in perspective. Her monologues become tedious because they lack artful construction; the tonally flat language lacks the irony and wit of Austen's narrative persona. Deficient in social power, authority, and observational skill, she offers no analysis of her information and suggests no insights into the motives of the characters whose words and actions she rehearses.

In this particular conversation, Miss Bates thanks Emma for calling on her, commends Mrs. Cole's kindness, and shares news of Mr. Elton's stay in Bath before arriving at her central topic, a letter from Jane Fairfax, who is soon to arrive for a three-month visit. Over the course of her breathlessly rambling account of the Campbells' trip to Ireland to visit their newly married daughter, Miss Bates repeatedly mentions the new husband, Mr. Dixon, "a most amiable, charming young man" (160; 2: ch. 1). Emma, supplying the narrative shape that Miss Bates has omitted and taking the facts in a direction that Miss Bates would never have contemplated, mistakenly imagines that Mr. Dixon has an adulterous interest in Jane. Miss Bates unknowingly feeds this narrative impulse when she lauds Mr. Dixon in her typical manner and eagerly tells Emma how he saved Jane from being dashed into the sea at Weymouth. The clever Emma shrewdly picks up on the fact that Jane prefers visiting her aunt and grandmother to joining the Campbells and Dixons in Ireland. But Emma, although a much better narrator than Miss Bates, has chosen the wrong plot to explain this interesting information.

The first-time reader, viewing the scene from Emma's vantage point, is tempted to share her impatience with Miss Bates and to accept the young woman's narrative hypothesis. A couple of pages later, Austen reveals that Jane's letter about not accompanying the Dixons to Ireland "contained nothing but truth, though there might be some truths not told" (166; 2: ch. 2). Such moments of ironic narrative layering make *Emma* particularly rewarding to reread. The challenge for teachers is to help students notice Emma's construction of meaning from facts without giving away the real story. One way is to compare Emma's narrative invention with Miss Bates's outpourings, whose formlessness is often indicated by lengthy paragraphs; lack of scene setting, commentary, summary, or argument; and the copious use of dashes and digressions. Students enjoy the discovery that Austen has installed Miss Bates as a comic counternarrator, the foil to her own highly inflected, precisely plotted, and deeply meaningful storytelling.

Miss Bates's monologues perform several functions. They contain important, although unmediated, often hidden information; they provide comic counterpoint to Emma's and Austen's sophisticated, inventive storytelling; they perform social and economic work for Miss Bates's little household and for Highbury as a whole. Chapters 9 and 10 in volume 2, which illustrate these functions, repay the reading aloud of selected passages. Chapter 9 opens with Emma at the height of self-satisfaction; reflecting on the success of her appearance at the Coles' dinner party the previous evening, she congratulates herself on "her condescension" and takes pleasure in having pleased the Coles, "worthy people, who deserved to be made happy!" (231) Emma then accompanies Harriet, who has business at Ford's, to Highbury. An encounter with Frank and Mrs. Weston, who are on their way to hear the new piano, is followed, a few minutes later, by an invitation from Mrs. Weston and Miss Bates, who have run across the street from the Bateses' apartment to ask Emma and Harriet to join the others for

Jane's performance. Miss Bates's self-effacing plea for their company provides a welcome contrast to Emma's smugness in the chapter's opening paragraphs; after detailing the decision made minutes earlier to invite them over, she interrupts herself to give a long-winded account of Frank's repair of Mrs. Bates's spectacles and the great civility of the Wallises, who have generously baked and delivered their apples. This topic, in turn, leads to a disquisition on Jane's delicate appetite and the healthfulness of baked apples. Her "medley" (237) resumes as they walk in the street; she returns to the subject of Frank's kind repair job and his enthusiasm for baked apples, the question of how best to bake apples, and Mr. Knightley's generous annual gift of a sack of his best fruit. Miss Bates then gives a word-for-word account of Mr. Knightley's discovery that the Bateses had run out of his apples and his prompt decision to send more. After the apples arrived, Miss Bates relates, she learned that Mr. Knightley had none left. At this point in her monologue, she interrupts herself to warn her visitors of the dark and narrow staircase up to their apartment (239).

Also at this point, the reader, taking Emma's cue, probably feels impatient at Miss Bates's meanderings. Austen herself condones that response by extending it to other characters. In chapter 10, when Miss Bates spies Mr. Knightley on horseback and stops him to thank him for the apples, the reader (along with the guests in the Bateses' sitting room) becomes an amused audience overhearing Mr. Knightley politely but "resolutely" cutting Miss Bates off and riding away before she can thank him (244). Later, in chapter 15, Mrs. Weston, reflecting on Jane's growing intimacy with Mrs. Elton, remarks: "Her aunt is a good creature, but, as a constant companion, must be very tiresome" (286).

Why, the reader (and Emma) may ask, does Miss Bates (and Austen) subject us to this barrage of trivia? It is a question worth posing in the classroom. If we slow down and read Miss Bates's speech carefully, what do we learn about Highbury, about the Bates family past and present, and about the other characters and their activities? First, her chronicle of Frank's attentions provides one of many clues to his secret engagement that Austen sprinkles throughout the text. A skillful first-time reader (unlike Miss Bates) may notice this pattern. The reader knows that Miss Bates is slow to observe people's romantic interests—in polite reference to Mr. Elton's earlier interest in Emma, she says, "I do not think I am particularly quick at those sort of discoveries. I do not pretend to it. What is before me, I see" (176; 2: ch. 3)—but Miss Bates's orations reflect her focus on more pressing issues: the critical business of encouraging her friends and neighbors to maintain their generosity to her and her mother.

Thus, in subtle ways Miss Bates's monologue reveals the poignant details of the decline in her economic position: her apartment is located across the street from Ford's, presumably above another commercial establishment; the staircase is dark and narrow; the sitting room is small. But, as she repeatedly illustrates, the people of Highbury extend kindness and generosity to this household of single women. Although the three women no longer have much "custom," or business, to give Mrs. Wallis, she continues to give them "the greatest attention" (236–37; 2: ch. 9). As she details the kindnesses extended by the Wallises, Frank Churchill, Mr. Knightley, William Larkins, and many others, Miss Bates repeatedly expresses heartfelt gratitude, thus trumpeting particular acts of kindness to the larger community. Her enthusiastic praise not only rewards her benefactors; it establishes a standard of philanthropic good behavior for her other friends. In so doing, this dependent woman, who can offer no other return for the gifts, exerts a not-so-subtle moral pressure on Highbury and gives herself social and economic leverage. Miss Bates's loquacity, which is determined at least in part by her economic marginality, makes her presence felt, even if only through self-effacing reportage and obsequious gestures of obligation and approval. The sheer volume of her speech effectively transmits every instance of kindness, and prompts her listeners to be as worthy of her praise as those she reports on.

Yet another purpose of Miss Bates's talkativeness is to allow Austen to shed ironic light on Emma's more thoughtful, disciplined conversation. Emma, at the other end of the socioeconomic and intellectual spectrum from Miss Bates, has the ability to speculate, imagine, and create plots not only for herself but also for others, such as Harriet, who have less power. But Emma arrogantly oversteps the boundaries of her privilege when she attempts to arrange Mr. Elton's marital destiny, and the reader enjoys the climactic discovery that Frank has deployed Emma herself as a bit player in his plot of secret engagement to Jane Fairfax.

Finally, reading Miss Bates's monologues aloud can help students shift their attention from the marriage plots to the wonderfully detailed portrait of Highbury that Austen gives us in *Emma*. These chapters convey the sense of ordinary life in the village. As Emma stands in the door of Ford's looking out at the "traffic," Austen sketches a typical scene, complete with pedestrians, carriages, "dawdling children . . . eyeing the gingerbread," and "two curs quarrelling over a dirty bone" (233; 2: ch. 9). We might judge how long it takes to cross the street from Ford's to the Bateses' apartment by estimating the length of "the medley" after Miss Bates, Mrs. Weston, Emma, and Harriet leave the store. Students, after finishing *Emma*, enjoy returning to these chapters to see how carefully Austen has staged the subplot of Frank and Jane's secret alliance. Rereading reveals that Miss Bates's sociable invitation to Harriet and Emma, followed by her voluble "medley" as they cross the street, has given Frank and Jane a few precious minutes together while Mrs. Bates snoozes. Her daughter's warnings to Harriet and Emma on the stairway ironically serve the unintended effect of alerting the lovers to return to their putative activities so that the "appearance of the little sitting-room . . . was tranquillity itself." Frank laughs at Emma as he says to her (for the benefit of Jane) that seeing her "is a pleasure . . . coming at least ten minutes earlier than I had calculated" (240; 2: ch. 10).

After these scenes in volume 2, we hear less from Miss Bates. Having established her character and dramatized her style of speech, Austen still employs Miss Bates as an important source of information but replaces her character's rambling conversation with her own condensed and focused prose. In chapter 2 of the third volume, Austen tightens Miss Bates's speech, substituting the brisk tempo of free indirect discourse for the syntactically complete, more labored speech of the earlier scenes. By truncating Miss Bates's sentences to fragments, often eliminating verbs or nouns, Austen renders "the incessant flow of Miss Bates, who came in talking" but uses her more as a focalizer—Austen narrates from Miss Bates's point of view without subjecting the reader to the onslaught of her monologues, as in volume 2, chapters 2 and 9. In volume 3, chapter 2, rather than employ third person description to set the scene of the ball at the Crown Inn, Austen uses Miss Bates as her viewpoint, dramatizing the heightened emotion and activity of this social gathering of all Highbury with her breathless exclamations about the brilliant lighting and transformed rooms: "Oh! Mr. Weston, you must really have had Aladdin's lamp. Good Mrs. Stokes would not know her own room again" (322; 3: ch. 2). As the guests arrive, we hear Miss Bates greet each party in turn. Her broken sentences and incomplete phrases convey the general air of excitement, and as she interrupts herself to repeat her hellos, we note the names not only of the main characters but also of townsfolk whom we have not yet encountered. The attentive reader realizes that Miss Bates is no longer a marginal character in Highbury society, as it has broadened in the novel's second volume. We perceive that while Emma snobbishly resists the expansion of her social world by the vulgar Mrs. Elton and the newly well-to-do Coles, Miss Bates is gratefully in touch with a much wider social group in an early nineteenth-century town that has reached a new stage of inclusion. In fact, as Miss Bates greets the partygoers, she is at the center of an emerging social realignment in Highbury. She retains her connections with the elite landowners, including the Woodhouses and Mr. Knightley, while reaching out to members of the middle class as it grows in numbers and in power.

Throughout *Emma* Miss Bates's talk functions as a medium for connecting her friends and neighbors and thereby strengthening the bonds that make up the community. Although she has little income, wit, or beauty, Miss Bates is popular because of "her own universal good-will and contented temper" and a self-effacing concern for others: she "loved every body, was interested in every body's happiness, quick-sighted to every body's merits" (21; 1: ch. 3). Miss Bates retains her central position in Highbury through her good character and the power of her speech to represent and foster the values of community, connectedness, and generosity.

When Emma mocks Miss Bates in the climactic seventh chapter of volume 3, wittily suggesting that it will be hard for this loquacious friend to limit her remarks to "three things very dull indeed" (370), we cringe not only because Emma has been unkind to a well-meaning, good-hearted, and defenseless woman but because her offhanded attack imperils the basic values of caretaking and concern for others that underlie community. First-time readers may also cringe because Emma expresses their own irritation with Miss Bates's long-windedness. More careful reflection, however, suggests that Austen has egged on the reader to make this mistake. As I noted earlier, she has sanctioned our intolerance of Miss Bates by having Mrs. Weston and Mr. Knightley give voice to it. In volume 3, chapter 5, as the characters' misunderstandings, schemes, and misbehavior build up to their climax at Box Hill, even the narrator seems to lose patience with Miss Bates, noting that "after a pretty long speech from Miss Bates, which few persons listened to," she accepted Emma's invitation to join her father for tea. Then, when Miss Bates is revealed as the source of Frank's mysterious knowledge of "Mr. Perry's plan of setting up his carriage" (344), she acknowledges, "I am a talker, you know; I am rather a talker; and now and then I have let a thing escape me which I should not" (346).

When Austen's trap is set in volume 3, chapter 7, the reader is prepared to fall into it. As Mr. Knightley reproaches Emma for her unfeeling insolence toward Miss Bates, a woman whose poverty ought to solicit compassion, the reader shares her mortification and regret. By the end of the novel, the reader, along with Emma, has learned to take Miss Bates more seriously, to enter into her life and words with imagination and respect, and to recognize that she is at the heart of the community. Paying attention to Miss Bates suggests how we may become both forgiving judges of human nature and active readers. We have to work hard and patiently to interpret her chronicles, but as detectives of human nature, we can rely on her for the facts, in contrast to the fancy, or even the deception, that better narrators, such as Emma and Frank, may supply.

Language and Gender in *Emma*

Patricia Howell Michaelson

One of the many pleasures of teaching Austen's novels is the way they reward students' attentiveness to nuances of language. When reading Austen, I tell my students, the rule is the slower the better, and best of all is reading aloud. Few writers' prose invites the kind of close study we practice with verse, but Austen's every sentence can be examined for ironies and ambiguities. This is especially true, of course, of her dialogue, and students can (with a little prodding) discern the idiosyncratic voices, or idiolect, of Austen's characters and the judgments Austen asks us to make of them as they speak.[1]

But students may be less adept at understanding Austen's use of sociolect—that is, the speech that identifies a character as a member of a social group. Indeed, today's students may be so committed to individualism that they need help in seeing that speech, inflected by markers of one's region, class, age cohort, religion, and so on, reflects the overlapping social categories to which individuals belong. Sociolects can be reduced to caricatures ("teen-speak" is one), but they are an essential component of language use; competent speakers utilize a mixture of sociolect and idiolect to present their identities. In *Emma*, as in all her novels, Austen uses sociolect strategically: she invests her minor or absurd characters with stereotypical dialogue while demonstrating by contrast the nuance and flexibility of the language used by intelligent, thoughtful people. This point is especially true in reference to gendered speech. Although writers on language in Austen's time imagined that women, in particular, all spoke in the same debased sociolect, Austen creates characters who can recognize linguistic norms and use them to construct complex identities.

Spending some class time on sociolect in *Emma* can be especially rewarding. First, dialogue plays a major role in forwarding the action in the novel. Second, the important social history that becomes visible in close reading makes the work eminently teachable. Literature may be the best, if not the only, opportunity for students to experience the pastness of the past as they articulate what is at stake in a narrative. In studying *Emma*, students can gain insights into the relation of language and identity in Austen's time and into the subtlety with which Austen used and stretched linguistic stereotypes. Finally, I hope that studying sociolect in *Emma* can make students more conscious of the ways in which their own speech helps construct their social identity—especially their identity as gendered beings. For while Austen's texts (famously) depict a limited range of language that differs by region or class, the novels make masterful use of the norms of language and gender that had developed in her time. These norms survive relatively unchanged today.[2]

When asked which of *Emma*'s characters are most differentiated by their use of language, students will probably name Miss Bates first of all. Indeed, Austen invites this reading, introducing Miss Bates in part by telling us that "she was a great talker upon little matters . . . full of trivial communications and harmless gossip" (21; 1: ch. 3). Every specimen of Miss Bates's dithering speech confirms that judgment. But students will need to be told that Miss Bates's loquacity and the littleness of her topics are not just idiosyncrasies: they exemplify the stereotype of "woman's language" in the period. The singular "woman" is significant, since the sociolect was described as something that "all" women spoke. While individual women, like Emma herself, might be good conversationalists, the stereotype of "woman's language" posited a norm of undisciplined chatter. Austen puts the term (not without irony) into Mr. Knightley's mouth, when he contrasts Harriet Smith's volubility with his own no-nonsense version of Mr. Martin's proposal: "Your friend Harriet will make a much longer history when you see her.—She will give you all the minute particulars, which only woman's language can make interesting.—In our communications we deal only in the great" (472; 3: ch. 18).

The stereotype of the talkative woman is an ancient one, but in the eighteenth century there was an intensified effort to describe and control women's loquacity through language texts, scientific works, essays, and conduct books. Early in the century, in an unusually unkind *Spectator* essay, Joseph Addison satirized the quantity and emptiness of women's conversation: "there are many among them who can Talk whole Hours upon nothing. . . . With how many different Circumstances, and with what variety of Phrases, will they tell over the same Story?" And what is the cause of such empty verbiage? "A Friend of mine, who is an excellent Anatomist, has promised me by the first Opportunity to dissect a Woman's Tongue, and to examine whether there may not be in it certain Juices which render it so wonderfully voluble and flippant" (Addison and Steele 2: 458–59, 460). Woman's language was "natural" in the lowest sense, disruptive, ungrammatical, and unedifying; women could not control their tongues. The conduct books respond by urging women to be silent. Maria Edgeworth utilized the stereotype differently. *Belinda*'s Mrs. Freke speaks in compressed sentences: "How do, dear creature! . . . How do? Glad to see you, 'faith! Been long here? Tremendously hot to day!" (225). Because woman's language was stigmatized as long-winded but mindless, Mrs. Freke's curt directness becomes part of her transgressive mannishness.

In addition to empty volubility, woman's language was characterized by its reliance on exaggerated modifiers like "vastly," "amazingly," and "monstrous." In Samuel Johnson's *Dictionary*, a few words are described as women's "cant." But in the essays about the *Dictionary* that evoked Johnson's anger, Chesterfield devotes more than half his commentary to woman's language, exemplifying the cultural importance of defining women as a single class of speakers. In his focus on the words made up by women in "the torrents of their eloquence," he cites terms minted by women (*flirtation, fuzz*) and others given new meanings (*vastly* is so degraded that we hear "vastly little") (*World* 2: 299–300).

This aspect of woman's language was especially useful for literary representations, because it is so easily imitated. Austen, as we might expect, skillfully employed woman's language, often to signal inanity or insincerity. We must be on our guard against a character like *Northanger Abbey*'s Isabella Thorpe, who speaks in exclamations and exaggerations: "Oh! Heavens! You don't say so! Let me look at her this moment. What a delightful girl! I never saw anything half so beautiful! But where is her all-conquering brother?" (57; 1: ch. 8). In *Emma* Austen's attack on this vocabulary is most obvious in the overly familiar Mrs. Elton, who says things like "Jane Fairfax is absolutely charming, Miss Woodhouse.—I quite rave about Jane Fairfax" and "My dear Miss Woodhouse, a vast deal may be done by those who dare to act" (282, 283; 2: ch. 15). Thus Miss Bates and Mrs. Elton, far from being exceptional speakers, represent the caricatured norm against which Emma should be measured.

If students have little trouble with Miss Bates and other female characters, they may need more help in seeing that the speech of the male characters is also inflected by gendered norms. (It is, of course, typical of both Austen's period and our own that women's language is described as a deviation from a male norm that is perceived as neutral, or "unmarked.") When asked about men's language, students may first point to Emma's father, Mr. Woodhouse, whose linguistic practice is certainly significant and significantly *not* masculine. Indeed, as a rather sweet hypochondriac, whose domestic orders are nearly always subverted, Mr. Woodhouse epitomizes a kind of "feminine" powerlessness. And his speech exemplifies the "littleness" of the woman's language, with his repetitive exclamations and his focus on bodily functions. Even his vocabulary is "feminine." Here is a conversation with Mr. Knightley:

> "It is very kind of you, Mr. Knightley, to come out at this late hour to call upon us. I am afraid you must have had a *shocking* walk."
> "Not at all, sir. . . ."
> "But you must have found it very damp and dirty. I wish you may not catch cold."
> "Dirty, sir! Look at my shoes. Not a speck on them."
> "Well! that is quite surprizing, for we have had a *vast deal* of rain here"
>   (10; 1: ch. 1; italics added)

Mr. Woodhouse is a good place to begin a discussion of men's speech in *Emma*; students easily see that he uses elements of woman's language and that (more generally) linguistic practices help construct gendered identity. With this base, students can define the linguistic differences between the two major male characters, Frank Churchill and Mr. Knightley. In the classroom, I would move from having students do close readings (to examine individual speeches), to providing background on social norms, to encouraging a discussion of Austen's specific use of those norms. For ease of presentation, I follow a different order here.

The tension between Frank Churchill and Mr. Knightley is multifaceted, but one important aspect is the way Austen represents them as adhering to different linguistic norms. *Emma* plays out a conflict between two modes of language, an older one of gender-neutral politeness and a newer mode of "manly" plain sincerity. On the largest scale, the conflict can be seen as part of a move toward a separate-spheres ideology, as linguistic norms become more defined in terms of a gendered binary. But, significantly for an interpretation of *Emma*, the shifting norms also entailed a redefinition of masculinity. Behavior that had been praised as polite became effeminate or effete; the plainspokenness that had been seen as bourgeois or typical of Puritans and Dissenters became the model for manliness among the gentry. Thus Mr. Knightley can reject Frank Churchill as less than masculine largely because of Frank's linguistic practice. Claudia Johnson has argued that "remaking English manhood" is vital to *Emma*—that older forms of masculinity depicted in the sensitive Mr. Woodhouse and the gallant Mr. Elton and Mr. Churchill are rejected in favor of the landed but businesslike and uncourtly Mr. Knightley (*Equivocal Beings* 191–203). Historical shifts in linguistic norms support this reading.

The older, gender-neutral mode leans on a long tradition in polite conversation, going back to Cicero at least, that was codified in sixteenth- and seventeenth-century conversation manuals, in eighteenth-century pieces like Fielding's "Essay on Conversation," and even in modern theories like those of H. P. Grice. The emphasis on pleasing, cooperation, and turn taking results in rules such as that no one should dominate or use specialized, exclusionary vocabulary. Emma herself is extraordinarily skilled in managing conversation so that everyone feels welcome and included; she also knows when to steer the conversation away from potential conflicts and when reticence is the most tactful option. We are told that Emma changes the topic, "feeling [the old one] to be an unsafe subject" (101; 1: ch. 12); that Mr. Knightley's vexation "made Emma immediately talk of something else" (150; 1: ch. 18); that in an uncomfortable moment she was "always putting forward to prevent Harriet's being obliged to say a word" (156; 2: ch. 1); that Emma did not protest combining two parties because "it could not be done without a reproof to [Mr. Weston], which would be giving pain to his wife" (353; 3: ch. 6); and so on.

Emma's politeness is never criticized, because it is motivated by benevolence and appropriate to her position and her sex. For Austen's male characters, politeness is treated with ambivalence. Certainly Mr. Woodhouse's formal politeness to his guests isn't taken quite seriously; politeness signals insincerity in *Pride and Prejudice*'s Mr. Wickham and stupidity in Mr. Collins. By the late eighteenth century, "pleasing" politeness accrued connotations of artificiality and superficiality. As Michèle Cohen has argued, such courtesy was condemned as French, aristocratic, and effeminate, in contrast to a preferred mode of plain sincerity, which was considered manly and English. This dynamic was played out in the negative reactions to Chesterfield's *Letters*, while the model of straightforward, honest speech and behavior was promulgated by rational Dissenters like Richard Price and by radicals like Mary Wollstonecraft and William Godwin.

In *Emma*, the conflict between politeness and sincerity is an important component of the tension between Frank Churchill and Mr. Knightley. Austen utilizes the vocabulary of nationhood in contrasting these characters' linguistic practices. When John and George Knightley greet each other with a simple, "How are you," they speak "in the true English style" (99; 1: ch. 12). Even more telling, when Mr. Knightley criticizes Frank Churchill's "professions and falsehoods," he attacks Frank's Gallic civility: "No, Emma, your amiable young man can be amiable only in French, not in English. He may be very 'aimable,' have very good manners, and be very agreeable; but he can have no English delicacy towards the feelings of other people: nothing really amiable about him" (149; 1: ch. 18). Unlike Mr. Knightley, Emma appreciates Frank's "well-bred ease of manner," his "readiness to talk," and the fact that "he knew how to make himself agreeable," the "proof of his knowing how to please" (190, 191; 2: ch. 5). But if Emma does not engage Mr. Knightley's national vocabulary, she does recognize the traditional connection of politeness and class: part of Frank's appeal for her is that he is decidedly aristocratic.

By contrast, Mr. Knightley's plain speech is rather bourgeois, most often associated with men a notch below him like Robert Martin (whose speech we never hear directly). For Mr. Knightley, this speech has to do only with manliness, and he explicitly rejects Frank Churchill's language as less than masculine. Yet Austen highlights Emma's sensitivity to the ways in which conversational interactions reflect class—and Mr. Knightley's obliviousness to them—when the two discuss Frank's difficulty in leaving his demanding aunt to pay an overdue visit to his father. While she argues it is unfair to judge Frank's conduct without knowing the social context, Mr. Knightley says plainly:

> "There is one thing, Emma, which a man can always do, if he chuses, and that is, his duty; not by manœuvring and finessing, but by vigour and resolution. . . . A man who felt rightly would say at once, simply and resolutely, to Mrs. Churchill—'Every sacrifice of mere pleasure you will always find me ready to make to your convenience; but I must go and see my father immediately. . . . I shall, therefore, set off to-morrow. . . .'"
> . . . "Such language for a young man entirely dependent, to use!—Nobody but you, Mr. Knightley, would imagine it possible. . . . Standing up in the middle of the room, I suppose, and speaking as loud as he could!"
> (146–47; 1: ch. 18)

Emma sees clearly that Mr. Knightley's devotion to sincerity is a luxury not available to the less fortunate. While Mr. Knightley asserts that his behavior is simply manly, his financial independence is what enables him to practice forthrightness. Indeed, early in the book, Emma tells Harriet that Mr. Knightley's "downright, decided, commanding sort of manner" is acceptable only because of "his figure and look, and situation in life" (34; 1: ch. 4).

As I teach this aspect of Austen's novel, students first identify the linguistic norms as they are represented in the novel and then appreciate the way Austen strikes a balance between the modes. For example, Emma may tease Mr. Knightley for his bourgeois sturdiness, but Frank's Gallic civility is not necessarily preferable. Frank's insincere courtliness toward Emma, while he is secretly engaged to another woman, deserves the censure it receives at the end of the novel. And Mr. Elton's gallantries, although at least intended as courtship, are vague enough that Emma and Harriet are confused as to their object. Civility has its dangers, yet it may protect feelings; sincerity risks hurting them. At the end of the novel, after Emma and Mr. Knightley are engaged, Emma performs one of her kindest actions in keeping a secret: she never tells Mr. Knightley that Harriet was in love with him. Here, Emma's discretion is nobler than Mr. Knightley's sincerity, although it causes her some discomfort:

> "Mystery; Finesse—how they pervert the understanding! My Emma, does not every thing serve to prove more and more the beauty of truth and sincerity in all our dealings with each other?"
>
> Emma agreed to it, and with a blush of sensibility on Harriet's account, which she could not give any sincere explanation of.   (446; 3: ch. 15)

In *Emma* neither plain sincerity nor polite civility is an absolute good: either may be used for good or for ill. Austen invokes her period's characterizations of the two modes of language, especially as they differ in their construction of masculinity, but both forms may be the target of either her admiration or her wit. Although Austen engages the contemporary gendered sociolects, then, students should be aware that Austen questions these stereotypes. Various eighteenth-century commentators explored the conflicts between pleasing politeness and plain sincerity, but Austen is perhaps unique in challenging the stereotype of woman's language with which I began, by making her women characters display complexity.

Her challenge to the stereotype of woman's language is evident in the Box Hill episode, which students do not always recognize immediately as a crucial scene. As every reader of this volume knows, in the midst of an idle flirtation pursued by Frank Churchill, Emma commits a breach of etiquette in insulting Miss Bates for her volubility. (Emma had mocked Miss Bates before, but never to her face.) When Mr. Knightley criticizes her, Emma responds that Miss Bates is indeed ridiculous. But Mr. Knightley cannot accept that defense:

> Were she a woman of fortune, I would leave every harmless absurdity to take its chance, I would not quarrel with you for any liberties of manner. Were she your equal in situation—but, Emma, consider how far this is from being the case. She is poor; she has sunk from the comforts she was born to; and, if she live to old age, must probably sink more. Her situation should secure your compassion.   (375; 3: ch. 7)

The foolish speech of women may be a legitimate target for criticism, Austen tells us, but the woman who speaks foolishly must, like any other woman, be seen as a whole person, a situated being. Miss Bates's language is silly, but her pitiable condition should protect her from ridicule. The stereotype of woman's language that Austen finesses treated women, consistently, as a single, undifferentiated class of speakers; Austen reminds us of the distinctiveness among them. It is this interplay of sociolect and idiolect, of social identity and individuality, that I hope my students will observe in Austen's dialogue and, by extension, in their own.

NOTES

Parts of this essay appeared in my *Speaking Volumes: Women, Reading, and Speech in the Age of Austen*, © 2002 by the Board of Trustees of the Leland Stanford Jr. University. Used with the permission of Stanford University Press.

[1]Among the many excellent studies of dialogue in *Emma*, see especially Babb; Dussinger; Hough; McMaster, "The Secret Languages of *Emma*"; J. White. Scholars paying special attention to gendered speech include Armstrong; Meyersohn.

[2]For an overview of modern scholarship on language and gender, see Cameron or Coates. On language and gender in Austen's period, see Cohen; Michaelson.

Teaching Emma's Narratives
and the Narrative of *Emma*

Jo Alyson Parker

Since the mid-1990s, I have been teaching *Emma* during the first few weeks of Seminar in Narrative Form, an undergraduate course taken primarily by upper-division English majors. Austen's novel of "3 or 4 Families in a Country Village" (Austen, *Letters* [Chapman] 401) may seem a rather staid narrative compared with some of the texts that follow it in the seminar—selections from Laurence Sterne's convention-subverting *Tristram Shandy* and Marcel Proust's time-enchanting *Swann's Way*, William Faulkner's multiperspectival *Absalom, Absalom!*, Italo Calvino's self-reflexive *If on a Winter's Night a Traveler*, and, more recently, Shelley Jackson's nonlinear *Patchwork Girl*, a hypertext on CD. (Teachers may prefer to use different works of fiction after *Emma*.) But the ostensibly traditional narrative structure of *Emma*—the linear chronological movement, the overt guidance of the savvy omniscient narrator—is precisely what makes Austen's novel a good starting point for discussing the basics of narrative form. I am not suggesting that *Emma* serves merely as a counter to the more innovative or experimental narrative structures that follow. *Emma* is in itself a complex text; its seemingly straightforward story of female reformation is disrupted by countervailing elements that highlight gender and authority. Furthermore, because *Emma* is a narrative about making narratives, it serves as a vehicle for examining narrative form and function, and it anticipates the issues foregrounded in the texts that follow in the course.

The course description for Narrative Form is as follows: "Through a close examination of several fictional and theoretical texts, we explore how narrative attempts to give meaning and coherence to experience, and we consider how we process narrative." During the semester, my students and I progress from straightforward, linear narratives to chronologically disordered narratives, from narratives presented in an apparently assured, authoritative voice, to works that explicitly call into question the authority of the narrator or narrators. At the same time, we examine pertinent theoretical texts, progressing from early theories of narrative to structuralist, poststructuralist, and contemporary feminist theories; we examine the effect of hypertext on our reading and the application of chaos science to studies of narrative. As my syllabus states, "Ideally, the course will offer a synthesis between theory and practice, the theoretical texts enhancing our readings of the fictional texts by enabling us to understand how and why we read." I have found that students respond to the abstractions of theory more positively when they can make links with the concrete evidence in the literary text.

In the course, I encourage students to explore not simply what a narrative is but what it does, the three major purposes it serves: the epistemological function—to provide a means of ordering what might seem to be random, unrelated events into a coherent whole and thus to make sense of them; the rhetorical function—to select and order events so as to persuade us to adopt a particular point of view; the ideological function—to enforce or reinforce a particular set of beliefs.

As a story about storytelling (the stories Emma makes up about others, the stories they make up about her), *Emma* enables us to make some preliminary assessments about the functions of narrative. Emma's unsuccessful plots drive the plot of *Emma*. To appreciate the complexity of Austen's narrative, the students and I examine the text from several directions: we identify its cause-and-effect structure and closure; we observe Emma's proclivity for creating narratives; and, when students have finished the novel, we read a traditional and an early feminist argument about her plotting (an essay by Booth and one by Gilbert and Gubar) as a means of launching the students' own interpretations (this activity is discussed later in this essay).

As we pursue these approaches, we discuss several concepts that relate to the study of narrative. For example, we differentiate between telling and showing—that is, does the writer include explicit commentary by an omniscient narrator or let the characters' words and actions speak for themselves? The scene in which Emma encourages Harriet to reject Robert Martin's proposal (vol. 1, ch. 7) is especially useful for establishing this distinction. Although primarily a dialogue between the two women, the passage includes several intrusions by the narrator; the effect of the whole is to reveal the extent of Emma's manipulation of her pliable young friend. We also discuss the use of free indirect discourse (particularly significant in Austen studies), in which the language and thoughts of a character are filtered through and thus tempered by the words of the narrator. The scene in which Emma chastises herself for the Elton debacle (vol. 1, ch. 16) provides an opportunity for examining this technique. We consider, too, the distinction between what Gérard Genette has termed "mood" and "voice"—a distinction between who sees the narrative events and whose voice recounts those events. Although the voice of Austen's narrator recounts the events, much of the action is seen through Emma's eyes, or focalized through Emma, as students discover. Shifts in focalization, such as when Mr. Knightley observes the game of scrambled letters between Frank and Jane, can be significant. Throughout our discussions, I urge students to bear in mind that *how* the narrative is put together enables the reader to formulate conclusions about *why*.

The Plot of Emma

Before we tackle *Emma*, students read the Grimms' fairy tale "King Thrushbeard" and a selection from Aristotle's *Poetics* (chs. 1–26) to prepare them for talking about plot. The plot of "King Thrushbeard" bears a serendipitous relation to that of *Emma*. Like Emma, who has "a disposition to think a little too well of herself" (5; 1: ch. 1), the princess in the tale experiences a series of humiliations instigated by her well-meaning suitor before she attains the humility necessary for a proper wife. Traditionally, the plot of *Emma* has been regarded as following a similar sequence. While reading the tale, we read Aristotle's discussion of plot; we focus on his notion that the unified plot has a beginning, "after which something is or comes to be"; a middle, "which follows something as some other thing follows it"; and an end, "which itself naturally follows some other thing, either by necessity, or as a rule, but has nothing following it." I ask the students to write a response to this assignment: "What, according to Aristotle, makes a good plot? Using Aristotle's terminology, chart the plot structure of 'King Thrush-beard.'" By examining a simple fairy tale in the light of Aristotle's strictures on plot, students can consider in what way traditional narrative structure depends on, in Aristotle's term, "causal necessity"—that is, how the ending of a tale appears to develop inevitably from the seeds planted at the beginning (ch. 12). They also come to realize that they have already—through their twenty-plus-years' immersion in stories—developed a narrative competence that encourages them to read plots by discovering causal connections between episodes.

After our initial discussions of plot, we turn to *Emma*. As an in-class writing exercise, students predict the outcome according to the various plot seeds laid down in the first chapter: the spoiled but good-natured heroine who tends "to think a little too well of herself"; the "knightly" hero who rescues her from "a long evening" (6; 1: ch. 1) of entertaining her valetudinarian father and who, we soon learn, is "one of the few people who could see faults in Emma Woodhouse, and the only one who ever told her of them" (11; 1: ch. 1). Most students, even those who have not read an Austen text before *Emma*, make accurate predictions. They know enough about Austen to expect a courtship motif and a comic conclusion. More important for the purposes of the class, they identify the plot seeds that will flower by the end of the text: that what Emma lacks—whether tender-heartedness, good judgment, ladylike behavior, or a suitable object of affection—must be supplied in the final pages. Although the students recognize that the plot of *Emma* is as predictable as that of the Grimms' fairy tale, they can, by comparing the two texts, discern how narrative voice and shifts in point of view (how the story is presented) affect our understanding of what occurs. Austen may put forward a fairly straightforward plot structure, but the narrative techniques on which she draws provide a more complex reading experience and a far less clear-cut moral than the fairy tale does.

We revisit notions of plot causality and closure once we reach the conclusion of *Emma* by looking closely at what is not conventionally resolved. Despite her seeming accession to a Knightley-like view of her misjudgments and her subsequent repentance (expressed to Mr. Knightley during the proposal scene), Emma withholds from Mr. Knightley two of her most egregious indiscretions: encouraging Harriet to set her cap for someone far above her in the social sphere and spreading malicious rumors about Jane Fairfax. I ask my students to scrutinize the line following Emma's acceptance of Mr. Knightley's proposal—

"Seldom, very seldom, does complete truth belong to any human disclosure" (431; 3: ch. 18)—and Mr. Knightley's paradoxical assessment that Emma is "faultless in spite of all her faults" (433; 3: ch. 18). While discussing these passages, I introduce D. A. Miller's poststructuralist reading of *Emma*. In his study of nineteenth-century novels, including *Emma*, Miller argues that narratives "are never freely or finally governed by [closure]" (*Narrative* xiv). What might seem to be a tying-up of loose ends depends on the suppression of what does not quite fit: for example, "complete truth." As Miller states about *Emma*, "at the moment of closure, the novel arranges to put in parentheses the inherent instability or suspense of character and situation that has initiated the narrative movement" (*Narrative* 97–98).

Students can consider whether they agree with Miller's point. Does Austen's final pronouncement on "the perfect happiness of the union" (484; 3: ch. 19) follow from what has come before and preclude further developments, or will Emma continue to fall into error? Does Austen, in effect, impose a conventional happy ending on material that does not seem to warrant it, thus suppressing the social ambiguities that threaten to disrupt Emma's world? My students generally do not agree on a response, either in classroom debate or in the papers they write. Many, I must admit, argue that Emma will continue meddling.

Emma's Plotting

Students' assessment of the finality of the conclusion depends a great deal on how they have judged Emma herself. As we work through the novel, we pay particular attention to the narratives that Emma creates. It is, after all, Emma's propensity for narrating others' lives that serves as the main problem with which the text deals. Emma's matchmaking plans are indeed *plots* in two senses of the term—"stories" and "schemes." Emma creates her fantasies from the romantic elements that swirl about her: an illegitimate young woman who might turn out to be "a gentleman's daughter" (62; 1: ch. 8), a gallant clergyman who writes tender missives on a beloved's "ready wit" and "soft eye" (71; 1: ch. 9), an elegant but languishing young woman who has received a mysterious gift of a pianoforte, and a dutiful daughter who must regretfully refuse her sorrowing lover with "delicate negatives" (264; 2: ch. 13). Students examine the following passage and consider what it tells us about the workings of Emma's mind:

> Such an adventure as this,—a fine young man and a lovely young woman thrown together in such a way, could hardly fail of suggesting certain ideas to the coldest heart and the steadiest brain. So Emma thought, at least. Could a linguist, could a grammarian, could even a mathematician have seen what she did, have witnessed their appearance together, and heard their history of it, without feeling that circumstances had been at work to make them peculiarly interesting to each

other?—How much more must an imaginist, like herself, be on fire with speculation and foresight.   (334–35; 3: ch. 3)

When the students take into account the materials that Emma is working with, they understand why she jumps to the conclusions she does; Emma's narratives follow a cause-and-effect pattern that parallels students' ability to predict the ending of *Emma*. As they discern, however, the fact that Emma's plots are logical does not guarantee that they will come to fruition. Emma is, after all, surrounded by other plotters.

Students read the scenes in which Emma imagines that Mr. Elton's words and actions stem from his love for Harriet (vol. 1, chs. 6–7, 11). Even before they arrive at his ill-fated proposal (ch. 15), most students realize that, while Emma is convincing herself that her plot is succeeding, Mr. Elton is advancing another plot entirely, one in keeping with Mr. Knightley's astute pronouncement that Elton "knows the value of a good income as well as anybody" and will not "throw himself away" (66; 1: ch. 8) on a pretty but poor "natural daughter of somebody" (22; 1: ch. 3). When students reread these scenes and passages once Mr. Elton's plot has been revealed, they are amused to see how skillfully Austen demonstrates two opposing interpretations of the same words and events.

As an in-class or take-home writing assignment, students consider some of the other plots advanced by various characters in the novel. We generally come up with the following list: Mrs. Elton's plot to get Jane Fairfax a situation and thus cement her own position as the grande dame of Highbury; the Westons' plot to marry Frank Churchill to Emma; Mrs. Weston's plot to marry Mr. Knightley to Jane; and Frank's plot to pay court to Emma and disparage Jane so as to mislead Highbury society about his true intentions. The list drives home the fact that Emma is not the only "imaginist" in Highbury; the other characters, however, may not "take so active a part" (137; 1: ch. 16) in attempting to make people conform to their assigned roles.

The list also suggests the way in which we shape the inchoate materials of our lives into narratives that may flatter our desires, although we may invoke notions of the "natural" and the "right," to obscure the role that desire plays in our schemes. Students should see that Austen demonstrates, through her emphasis on Emma's narratives, how we tell stories both to make sense of the events in our lives and to employ those events in service of our desires—motives that clash when we are faced with social realities. I ask students to consider how Emma's facetious comment to Harriet sums up the basis of her plotting: "When Miss Smiths and Mr. Eltons get acquainted—they do indeed—and really it is strange; it is out of the common course that what is so evidently, so palpably desirable—what courts the pre-arrangement of other people, should so immediately shape itself into the proper form" (74–75; 1: ch. 9). From the materials at hand, Emma plans outcomes that are "palpably desirable, natural, and probable" (35; 1: ch. 4). As students realize, Emma's invocation of what seem to be Aristotelian notions of naturalness and probability are skewed by her desires and those of the other plotters—for example, Mr. Elton. Emma's narratives fail, however, because she has an incomplete knowledge of the facts and wants to shape what she sees according to her own *should be* rather than society's *is*, the unhappy result of fashioning a narrative from "real" rather than made-up materials.

At this point in our discussions, we reflect on the implications of formulating plots around actual events rather than those we make up—and we consider the distinction between Emma as "author" and the author Jane Austen. In her plots, Austen, after all, bestows the richest and handsomest man on a financially distressed heroine (in *Pride and Prejudice*) or have the hero (in *Persuasion*) return after an eight-year absence to discover that the heroine is as lovely as ever. At the same time, we remember that Austen spent her adult life in fairly reduced circumstances and if, as critics surmise, she entertained a youthful passion, no Wentworth returned to encourage a second bloom in her. Unlike Austen, Emma does not arrange the materials of her life into imaginative fictions but imposes imaginative fictions on those materials. Students can explore Austen's point in choosing an imaginist as a heroine. Although critics such as Sandra Gilbert and Susan Gubar argue that Austen punishes Emma for her plotting as a way to convey her divided views on the assertive nature of female authorship, Austen's point may be more playful than polemical. Austen's likely suggestion that only in fiction can the happily-ever-after be achieved is a wry acknowledgment of the wish-fulfillment aspect of her own fiction making. Perhaps she is also implying that successful plotting involves a selectivity and an ordering unavailable in the real world, a point that students grasp when I ask them to devise a plot for even one day of their lives.

Answering the "So What?" Question

In his essay "Narrativity in the Representation of Reality," which students read after finishing *Emma*, Hayden White discusses the process by which historical events are selected and organized into narratives that fulfill ideological agendas. The essay enables students to see that, in formulating a plot, we would, like Emma, emphasize certain events in order to "prejudice the outcome of the story we would tell in favor of the moral in general." That is, our choices as to what is important depend on the particular agenda that we wish to put forward.

The White essay concludes with a question, "Could we ever narrativize without moralizing?" (25), that can spur students to consider whether Austen's narrative moralizes. Although there are several ways in which Emma's plotting can be read, I have had success in presenting two extreme positions advanced by critics of the novel: (1) Emma is vain and manipulative; her plots derive from her faulty judgment and lead to potential heartbreak for herself and others. (2) Emma is imaginative and assertive, and her plots derive from a desire to escape boredom; they require suppression because of their disruptive effect on patriarchal society. The first scheme posits the ending of *Emma* as happy, with Austen championing the values of her society, whereas the second interprets it as unhappy, with Austen challenging those values. Certainly there are many positions between these two poles; *Emma* is arguably Austen's most complicated and ambiguous text, and we do the work a disservice to suggest that its message may be reduced to a simple *either-or*. In focusing on the extremes, however, I hope to make students realize that, although narratives may have morals, readers cannot facilely sum them up and, indeed, several students may draw on the same evidence to arrive at entirely different conclusions.

I raise this issue early in our reading by having my students examine the quarrel between Emma and Mr. Knightley in volume 1, chapter 8. I then have them do an in-class writing assignment on the following question:

> In the quarrel between Emma and Mr. Knightley, which side do you take? Is Mr. Knightley acknowledging social reality (that an illegitimate young woman with few charms other than beauty cannot expect to rise in society), or is he perpetuating class hierarchies? Is Emma completely blind or does she promote a subversion of these hierarchies?

Aware of Emma's clueless reading of Mr. Elton's behavior and troubled by her snobbery regarding Robert Martin, most students side with Mr. Knightley during the ensuing classroom debate, but some, particularly those who have read feminist literary criticism, side at least in part with Emma. They notice her shrewd comment about Harriet that "till [men] do fall in love with well-informed minds instead of handsome faces, a girl, with such loveliness as Harriet, has a certainty of being admired and sought after" (63; 1: ch. 8). They observe, too, that Mr. Knightley assumes the rightness of his opinions in a way that Emma, perhaps because she is a woman, never can: "[Emma] did not always feel so absolutely satisfied with herself, so entirely convinced that her opinions were right and her adversary's wrong, as Mr. Knightley. He walked off in more complete self-approbation than he left for her" (67; 1: ch. 8). Often the debate leads to a consideration of whether, in treating *Emma* as an example of patriarchal oppression, we are imposing modern-day sensibilities on the text or simply bringing to light a subtext that has always been there.

Once the students have finished the novel, as I noted, we read two influential pieces of Austen criticism (one traditional, one early feminist) as springboards for students' own interpretations: Wayne Booth's 1961 essay "Control of Distance in Jane Austen's *Emma*," from *The Rhetoric of Fiction*, and Gilbert and Gubar's 1979 essay "Jane Austen's Cover Story," from *The Madwoman in the Attic*. These works epitomize the two opposing views of Emma—the manipulator who needs to be reformed versus the imaginist who needs to be repressed—and each essay highlights the weaknesses in the other. Booth's essay, which provides students with a way to discern Austen's manipulation of point of view at crucial junctures, encourages them to consider how Austen's narrative strategies may guide readers in assessing Emma—and, in effect, in becoming better readers than the heroine. Although Booth's notion of "implied author" finesses the New Critical injunction against the intentional fallacy, his concept is nonetheless useful in helping students avoid conflating the historical personage who wrote the book (Jane Austen), the message that comes across in it (the implied author), and the narrator, who may or may not convey that message. From Gilbert and Gubar's essay, students acquire several concepts that have become integral to feminist work—for example, notions of gender constraints, which force the woman writer to deal with societal injunctions against female authorship; and female double-voicedness, an approach in which the woman writer creates a text that explicitly pays allegiance to prescribed gender roles and a subtext that implicitly calls them into question. The essay encourages students to see that what initially appears to be a straightforward message may be complicated when we consider the subject position of the writer and learn to read for a subtext. For students new to feminist and narrative theory, the works provide a starting point for their understanding of *Emma* and of the more recent narrative theories that we examine later in the course.

After the students have debated the merits and demerits of the opposing positions, they do the following written assignment:

> In volume 3, chapter 11, Emma realizes that her hints and encouragement have led Harriet to fall in love with Mr. Knightley. She exclaims to herself, "How to understand it all! How to understand the deceptions that she had been thus practising on herself, and living under!"(411). We might regard this chapter as lending support to Booth's argument that the "blows to [Emma's] self-esteem produce at last a genuine reform" (248)—one, Booth suggests, that the "implied author" directs us to find desirable. Or this chapter might be, in the words of Gilbert and Gubar, "[d]ramatizing the necessity of female submission for female survival," providing Austen "with a 'blotter' or socially acceptable cover for expressing her own self-division" (154–55). By analyzing this chapter (and drawing on other pertinent passages in the text), provide your own argument about the implications of Emma's realization of her own insensitivity and desire to reform. Take into account the issues of narrative structure, point of view, and textual authority we have addressed in the course.

The essays that result from the assignment cover the spectrum; the more robust students tend to argue against the Booth and Gilbert and Gubar essays and to launch their own, often astute interpretations. Students have argued, for example, that Knightley displays the same sort of imaginative thinking for which Emma is faulted; that Emma's flaws and subsequent humiliation are gender-neutral; and that Austen derides the feminine ideal in the person of Jane Fairfax.

Because I want students to wrestle with the issues we have discussed and to avoid thinking, as many undergraduates do, that there must be one correct reading of every text, I hesitate to impose my own interpretation of *Emma*. As I listen to their debates and read their papers, however, I find myself, like many of the students, tending toward a middle-ground position: that is, I regard Emma as faulty, but I consider that many of her shortcomings result from her constrained existence; I see her "submission" to Knightley balanced by his submission to her wishes to remain the dutiful daughter of Hartfield. I have lately, in fact, proposed the question whether Emma, rather than possessing too much imagination, has too little. After all, the narratives she creates are highly conventional; she might very well have read novels along these lines. She cannot write a narrative for herself because she cannot come up with the unconventional plot that would allow her both to be a dutiful daughter and to gain a loving husband—a plot that felicitously manages to balance what is and what should be. It takes that daring imaginist Mr. Knightley to do so. Austen thereby demonstrates that, to reconcile the various demands put on the women of her time, someone must come up with imaginative solutions that go beyond the conventional. Interestingly, the solution comes from the one character who most exemplifies the status quo; Austen acknowledges that only a Mr. Knightley can author such a "[s]hocking plan," as Mrs. Elton terms it (469; 3: ch. 17).

Provisional Conclusions

Although we move on to other texts, our consideration of *Emma* does not achieve closure, for we return to it as a touchstone narrative. When we read *Tristram Shandy* and *Swann's Way*, for example, we contrast their chronologically nonlinear structure with the linear one in *Emma*; we explore how the ordering of events affects our understanding of them. When we read *Absalom, Absalom!*, we compare the narrative voice and the voices in the metanarratives with the voice of Austen's narrator, reflecting on the seeming abdication of narrational authority in works such as Faulkner's. When we read structuralist, poststructuralist, and contemporary feminist theories of narrative, we draw on *Emma* to illuminate some of the points raised. We even contrast our reading experience of *Emma* with our reading experience of literary hypertext, as we return, once again, to issues of causality, closure, and narrational authority.

For their final paper, students have the option of rewriting one fictional narrative that we have read in the form and style of another. Significantly, many students come back to *Emma*, even those who expressed frustration with the text while we were reading it. I have received some inventive, even brilliant, reworkings of *Emma*: a poignant multiperspectival narrative à la *Absalom, Absalom!*, with Emma's daughter and Jane's attempting to discover the source of the now-dead Emma's unhappiness; a Calvino-esque musing on the experience of reading *Emma*, with Emma becoming the antiheroine of interrupted computer role-playing games; a Proustian reworking, with Emma's destiny, like that of the hero of *Swann's Way*, lying between her own Guermantes and Swann's Ways. One ambitious student has developed a hypertext, which she put on her Web site, in which Emma interacts with other fictional characters, such as Tristram and Marcel. Such reworkings go beyond simple exercises, encouraging students to consider the ways in which narrative form and structure influence meaning. By the end of the term, even the most resistant students have, I think, come to understand the complicated narrative structure that underlies the simple courtship plot in *Emma* and to realize that Austen's text has a great deal to tell us about the how and why of storytelling.

NOTE

I would like to thank the students of the Seminar in Narrative Form, who continue to make me rethink Austen's *Emma*, and particularly the students of the 2001 version, who helped me work through the ideas in this paper.

A Likely Story:
The Coles' Dinner Party

Joseph Wiesenfarth

When I teach *Emma*, I find that students identify issues of gender, race, and class more easily than they do the art of the novel or its aesthetic values. It seems immediately clear to them that men are independent and women not; that a single Englishman is more than a match for a band of Gypsies; that scions of rich gentry families have more fun than indigent orphans and poor bastards. But it's not immediately clear to them that a pianoforte can be more than a piano or that a chapter that features it might develop akin to a musical structure. So I tend to draw students' attention to what they don't immediately see clearly rather than to what they do.

My first step in that direction is to indicate to them that Jane Austen writes a novel of manners and that those manners shape the way characters deal with basic needs. Northrop Frye calls those basic needs "the primary concerns of human beings." They are food, sex, property, and freedom of movement. "The need to eat, love, own property, and move about freely must come first, and such needs require peace, good will, and a caring and responsible attitude to nature" (6).[1] In other words, primary concerns require codes of conduct. And we know from Norbert Elias that manners are intimately related to basic needs. As society developed, so did table manners, courtship rituals, property rights, and conventions of travel, as he demonstrates in *The History of Manners*. Consequently, although Jane Austen's style might at first be somewhat foreign to students, what she writes about—the stuff of everyday life—is not. They still eat, make love, have dorm rooms or private digs, and walk or ride or drive in and out of town. These things that are vital to every one of us are the stuff of *Emma* mediated through a code of manners. And occasions like the Christmas dinner at Randalls, the Crown Inn ball, the Donwell strawberry party, and the Box Hill picnic bring them together intensely. Another such occasion is the Coles' dinner party (212–30; 2: ch. 8), which I like to look at in some detail when I teach the novel.

But before I do so, I try to give this chapter a context by looking briefly at the way that primary concerns enter the novel as it begins. Mr. Knightley walks over from Donwell Abbey to Hartfield, where Emma and Mr. Woodhouse are discussing Miss Taylor's marrying Mr. Weston earlier in the day. She is attempting to console her father, who sees no need for weddings, on Miss Taylor's becoming Mrs. Weston. He is fretting because Miss Taylor has gone to live at Randalls; he will fret further, in chapter 2, because he is sure that her wedding cake was too rich. We are immediately, if minimally, dipped into the world of food, sex, property, and freedom of movement. When Mr. Knightley disagrees with Emma about her role in making the Taylor-Weston marriage, we find Jane Austen introducing her principal subject (matchmaking) and its opposite (the danger of matchmaking) and initiating their contrapuntal development:

> The major expositions of the subject and countersubject occur with Emma projecting marriages between Harriet and, successively, Mr Elton, Frank Churchill, and Mr Knightley, and with Harriet on her own accepting and marrying Robert Martin; with Mrs Weston projecting a marriage between Jane Fairfax and Mr Knightley, and with Jane on her own accepting and marrying Frank Churchill; and with Mr and Mrs Weston projecting a marriage between Emma and Frank, and with Emma on her own accepting and marrying Mr Knightley.   (Wiesenfarth 208)

These events are resolved in the last ten chapters of *Emma*, which function like an epithalamium, as Harriet and Robert Martin are engaged and then marry in September; as Emma and Mr. Knightley are engaged and then marry in October; and as Jane Fairfax and Frank Churchill announce their engagement and set their wedding for November. The sexual significance of these romantic preludes to actual marriage is emphasized and celebrated when Mrs. Weston has a baby just nine months after her wedding (461; 3: ch. 17).[2] Thus Austen works out the many sexual games of the novel—played out in visits, dinners, dances, riddles, charades, and mysteries—against a mature sexuality that takes its own undisturbed course and issues in the birth of Anna Weston. When the birth takes place in the midst of the engagements and wedding announcements, students can see how Austen configures an important meaning for sex and love in the shape of her novel.

This then is the context in which the Coles' dinner party might be satisfactorily discussed because it is an event that contributes to the outcome of the novel. The chapter has two principal parts that are framed by an introduction and a conclusion. The first part gives us Emma's conversation with Frank Churchill about Jane Fairfax's pianoforte, their settling on it as a love token, and their agreement that Mr. Dixon is the lover who sent it. The second part gives us Mrs. Weston's conversation with Emma about Jane's new square Broadwood, Mrs. Weston's insistence that it is a love token from Mr. Knightley, and Emma's forceful disagreement with her about that. These two parts carefully mirror each other, with Mrs. Weston giving back to Emma an image of herself as a discoverer of secrets and a conjurer of lovers.

The introduction to the chapter shows us Frank just returned from London, where he has gone on the pretext of getting a haircut but actually for the purpose of buying a piano for Jane. That he has bought the piano, of course, is known only to him and to Jane. Consequently, his allowing Emma to speculate on its sender compromises both her and Jane. That is why, when the secret is revealed late in the novel, Emma calls him treacherous and feels mortified.[3] But at this point in the novel, none of this is evident. Only Frank Churchill's haircut excites attention at the moment. It is seen to be a young man's folly, and Emma concludes that "silly things do cease to be silly if they are done by sensible people in an impudent way" (212; 2: ch. 8). His impudent silliness seems to carry the day. The scene then switches to the Coles' house, where Emma sees Mr. Knightley arriving and praises him for acting like a gentleman by coming in a carriage. He insists that a carriage doesn't make a gentleman and good humoredly calls her a "nonsensical girl" (214). And as if to prove that she is nonsensical, Emma immediately engages Frank in conversation about Jane's piano and lover. And Churchill is impudent enough to encourage her erroneous speculation because it gives cover to his and Jane's secret engagement.

When Mrs. Weston enters into a similar conversation with Emma, she says to her, "My dear Emma, I am longing to talk to you. I have been making discoveries and forming plans, just like yourself, and I must tell them while the idea is fresh" (224). She has discovered that Mr. Knightley arrived in a carriage so he can later send it for Jane Fairfax. This convinces Mrs. Weston that he also sent the piano to Jane. Given the shakiness of the logic, Emma denies the conclusion. Although discovery and conjecture are what Emma is all about, as her recent conversation with Churchill demonstrated, she denies there is any resemblance between Mrs. Weston's speculations and her own. Nonetheless, even though Emma thinks herself sensible, Mrs. Weston allows us to think that she is not. Emma has been mistaken about Mr. Knightley's arriving in a carriage. Since Emma got that wrong, Jane Austen hints, subtly, that Emma has got Mr. Dixon wrong too. But Emma is not ready to admit that just yet.

The chapter's conclusion brings the Coles' new grand pianoforte to the fore. In this coda Emma plays and sings less well than Jane does. Mrs. Weston follows them to play country dances for the assembly. Afterward Frank returns to Emma to compare her dancing with Jane's. But Churchill's gallantry—his praising Emma at Jane's expense—sharply contrasts with Mr. Knightley's

taking care of Jane by sending her home in his carriage. Moreover, as if to emphasize the point, Austen allows Emma to get one important thing right at this
party. That is her characterization of Mr. Knightley: "He is not a gallant man,
but he is a very humane one" (223). The same cannot be said of Churchill, who
has allowed Emma to expose her nonsensical self shamelessly and who has
used Jane Fairfax badly by allowing Emma to think evil of her. By pointing out
this contrast between the two men, we can bring students to understand in a
specific, concrete instance Mr. Knightley's distinction between "amiability" as
the French and the English define it:

> No, Emma, your amiable young man can be amiable only in French, not
> in English. He may be very "aimable," have very good manners, and be
> very agreeable; but he can have no English delicacy towards the feelings
> of other people: nothing really amiable about him   (149; 1: ch. 18)

The "young man" he is speaking about is, of course, Frank Churchill. This distinction further allows us to remind our students that the name Frank "is cog-
nate with *France* or *French*" (Gay, "Emma" 34).[4] Indeed, Frank is French
enough not only to be a "gallant," a ladies' man,[5] but also to want to leave England as fast as he can: "I am sick of England—and would leave it to-morrow, if
I could"(365; 3: ch. 6). He says this at Donwell Abbey, George Knightley's estate; and, as Joseph Kestner remarks, "Knightley IS England" (150).[6] Once a
statement like that is put into play, another whole dimension of the novel—its
historical and allegorical implications—can be evoked.

Having got these basics on the table in taking a first look at the Coles' dinner
party with students, I find it useful next to relate this chapter more broadly to
other chapters in the novel before completing its analysis more minutely.
Events at the Coles' house recall Emma's taking Harriet Smith's likeness
(42–49; 1: ch. 6) and anticipate Emma's visiting the Bateses with Mrs. Weston
to see Jane Fairfax's new pianoforte and hear her play it (240–46; 2: ch. 10).
When Emma takes Harriet's likeness to make her appear elegant the better to
attract Mr. Elton's attention, some who look at the picture say it isn't "like"—
say it doesn't resemble Harriet exactly. Mrs. Weston sees that the "eye-brows
and eye-lashes" are not Harriet's, and Mr. Knightley tells Emma that she's
made Harriet "too tall" (47–48; 1: ch. 6). As it turns out, Austen uses the very
features that Emma exaggerates in drawing Harriet to characterize Jane Fairfax: "Her height was pretty, just such as almost everybody would think tall, and
nobody could think very tall"; furthermore, "her eyes, a deep grey, with dark
eye-lashes and eye-brows, had never been denied their praise" (167; 2: ch. 2).
So Emma, who has always neglected Jane, gives Harriet her features because
Jane is an elegant lady whom Emma cannot manage and Harriet is a giggling
girl whom she can manage. In addition, Harriet is no threat to Emma's superiority in any way: for instance, she cannot play the piano at all. These hints
about the relation of Harriet's portrait to Jane's personal features show us that

Emma is jealous of Jane Fairfax because, as Mr. Knightley says, she sees in Jane "the really accomplished young woman, which she wanted to be thought herself" (166; 2: ch. 2). Emma knows that he is right. The pianos at the Coles' house and the Bateses' house are indications of it.

When, then, Mrs. Weston decides that Mr. Knightley sent the Broadwood to Jane Fairfax as a love token, Emma dislikes the conjecture for two reasons. First, it confirms Mr. Knightley's sense of Jane's accomplishments as superior to her own: a pianist as accomplished as Jane deserves a piano as excellent as a Broadwood. Second, Mrs. Weston's conjectures as imitations of her own about the piano and a lover give Emma a very unflattering picture of herself. Mrs. Weston has, in effect, taken Emma's likeness by becoming her double even though Emma turns critic and says that Mrs. Weston isn't "like" at all. But I think you will find that your students will say the same as mine: in this instance, Mrs. Weston is very "like" Emma indeed.

And there is another likeness of Emma too. One that on the face of it is highly improbable because it is Mrs. Bates whom we meet in a senseless condition—she can't hear, she can't see—the morning after the Coles' dinner party. When Emma goes with Mrs. Weston to see Jane's pianoforte and hear her play it, she finds Mrs. Bates asleep. Frank Churchill has taken her glasses in hand, supposedly to repair a rivet; really to blind her to his love-making with Jane. As Emma later remarks, "It was his object to blind all about him." Because Mrs. Bates is also hard of hearing, she can neither see nor hear Jane and Frank together. Seeing nothing and hearing nothing, she goes to sleep. And Emma, as she enters the room, is no more aware of what is going on between Frank and Jane than Mrs. Bates is: "no one," Emma also later remarks, "could be more effectually blinded than myself" (427; 3: ch. 13). Thus when Jane plays the piano for her guests, Emma readily attributes the passion of her playing to her passion for Mr. Dixon, who, Emma just knows, has to have sent that piano. And Frank promotes Emma's wrong conjecture further by complimenting Mr. Dixon on sending along his and Jane's favorite music too. With Mr. Dixon so firmly fixed in her mind, Emma can sense nothing going on between Frank and Jane. Mrs. Bates may be asleep, but it's Emma who is snoring.

Showing students and eliciting from them relations like these between chapters should heighten their awareness of many other connections from chapter to chapter in *Emma*. It should also prepare them to return to the Coles' dinner party for another look at the way Austen has assembled its elements.

After rampant speculation on who sent the pianoforte to Jane Fairfax, we are asked to turn our attention to the Coles' new grand piano, which none of the family can play, but which Mr. Cole, loving music, bought anyway. This long chapter, filled with varied moments of complex social intercourse, has a very tight structure of motifs that form a musical pattern that we could describe as antecedent and consequent phrasing, a term that musicians sometimes use for a structure that repeats itself with some variations. This is quite appropriate, of course, in a novel in which "likenesses," some of which we've already seen, are prominent. A chapter that is presided over by two pianofortes, one square and one grand, one absent and one present, has something akin to a musical structure that might be described as A-B-C-D // A-B-C-D.

The chapter begins with a discussion of Frank Churchill's haircut (A), which leads to Emma's thoughts on sensible people and impudent actions. Emma then sees Mr. Knightley arrive in a carriage (B) at the Coles' house, which leads to her observations on him as a gentleman and his on her as a nonsensical girl. The long discussion between Frank and Emma of the person likely to have sent the piano (C) follows, with Frank's compliance demonstrating his gallantry and suggesting his preference for Emma. A slight hiatus follows with little or no recorded conversation as the second wave of women arrives before the larger company of men and women begins to mingle (D).

Frank is the first man to arrive from the after-dinner conversation among the men, and he seeks out Emma to comment unfavorably on Jane's hairdo (A): "Those curls! This must be a fancy of her own. I see nobody else looking like her!" (222; 2: ch. 8). He leaves Emma to go and discuss "those curls" with Jane. Mrs. Weston rushes to Emma's side to tell her that Mr. Knightley arrived in a carriage so that he could be of service to Jane Fairfax and Miss Bates (B), which Emma attributes to his humanity and Jane's ill health but which Mrs. Weston attributes to his love for Jane, as his supposed gift of the pianoforte underlines (C). As this conversation ends the men join the women (D) to listen to Emma and Jane play the new grand piano and sing with Frank Churchill. A coda finds five couples dancing before the chapter ends with Frank talking to Emma, just as he did as it began. His last word to Emma is one of praise for her dancing at the expense of Jane's, which he finds "languid" (230; 2: ch. 8). Thus Emma, who has played the piano less well than her rival, finds herself superior to Jane—a position that she has assumed throughout the novel—at the chapter's end.

If I can finish a discussion of the Coles' dinner party this way, I can return immediately with the students to the art of primary concerns in the novel. These four motifs and the variations on them, though presented in the trappings of a social event, are evocations of the primary concerns of food (dinner), sex (piano), property (the Coles' opulent house), and freedom of movement (arrivals and departures). But the emphasis is on sex, love, and what often attends them, jealousy. That is why the pianoforte is central to the chapter. The piano is coded feminine and associated with women's emotional life. As Laura Vorachek has shown, the piano "offered opportunities for representations of women's active sexual desire" (37). Maria Edgeworth advised readers of *Practical Education* (1798) "that musical skill improves 'a young lady's chance of a prize in the matrimonial lottery.'" And H. R. Haweis wrote in *Music and Morals* (1876) that "a good play on the piano has not infrequently taken the place of a good cry upstairs" (qtd. in Vorachek 32, 28). This is certainly the case with Marianne Dashwood in *Sense and Sensibility* and with Anne Elliot in *Persuasion*, both of whom cry over lost lovers while playing the piano. Austen, devoted to the piano herself, never seats a man at the keyboard. Men may sing while women play the piano, but they don't play the piano themselves. At least Englishmen don't; foreigners are another matter altogether, as Franz Liszt vividly demonstrated. Not even the Frenchified Frank Churchill, who sings with both Emma and Jane, plays the piano. The pianoforte in *Emma*, in the tradition of manners at Austen's time, explicitly belongs to female passion.

Pianos, absent as well as present, reveal Jane Fairfax's deeply stressed emotional life, which is also manifested in her ill health and in Emma's jealousy of her. Jane appears to be Emma's rival for Mr. Knightley and actually is her rival for Frank Churchill. The mystery that surrounds the gift of the pianoforte to Jane allows Emma to use the very thing which shows Jane's musical superiority to her (and perhaps her passionate superiority as well) as something that demonstrates Jane's moral inferiority to Emma. To be the beloved of the husband of her best friend would be shameful and casts a shadow altogether over the elegance of Jane Fairfax, which Emma both envies and deplores. The dominating presence of the one musical instrument that was ineluctably associated with a woman's life of feeling, then, is an inspired choice on Austen's part to make private passions as close to public revelations as decorum allows.

If I've managed to teach the chapter on the Coles' dinner party at all well, students should see by the time they've finished with it that the novel relentlessly reveals jealousy as an important aspect of sex and love. If that's the case then one can further point out to them that just as Emma is jealous of Jane, Mr. Knightley is jealous of Frank Churchill and that their jealousy bodes well for their inevitably finding each other's love. That's why he flies out at Churchill as not being amiable even before Frank arrives in Highbury. That's why he has Miss Bates put a stop to Frank's singing with Jane to show himself off. That's why late in the novel he leaves Highbury to visit his brother, John, in London. In a word, a careful reading of sexual attraction and dislike in the chapter set at the Coles' house promotes a good reading of the novel altogether. It even leads us to Mrs. Elton.

When Emma's jealousy of Jane Fairfax manifests itself at the Coles' dinner party, it brings Emma to deplore the possibility of Mr. Knightley's marrying Jane Fairfax: "A Mrs. Knightley for them all to give way to!—No—Mr. Knightley must never marry" (228; 2: ch. 8). This exclamation, ironically enough, is very like that prompted by Mrs. Elton's jealousy when she learns that Emma is engaged to Mr. Knightley: "Oh! no; there would be a Mrs. Knightley to throw cold water on every thing"(469; 3: ch. 17). Students with an instinct for form will find here one more instance of a likeness being taken between the elegant Emma and the awful Mrs. Elton. They will also see yet another instance of the likenesses, prominent at the Coles' party, that dominate the novel. These serve Austen well because they place everyone in the novel (and everyone outside it too) in a matrix of desire and repulsion basic to sexual instinct. And the final manifestation of Austen's genius and of her art gives us both desire and repulsion one more time in the final paragraph of the novel:

The wedding was very much like other weddings, where the parties have no taste for finery or parade; and Mrs. Elton, from the particulars detailed by her husband, thought it all extremely shabby, and very inferior to her own.—"Very little white satin, very few lace veils; a most pitiful business!—Selina would stare when she heard of it."—But, in spite of these deficiencies, the wishes, the hopes, the confidence, the predictions of the small band of true friends who witnessed the ceremony, were fully answered in the perfect happiness of the union.   (484; 3: ch. 19)

Those students who are brought to understand that sex in Austen's fiction always has a social dimension and who remember, as Mr. Woodhouse said, "A bride . . . is always first in company" (280; 2: ch. 14), will know, as the novel ends with Mr. Elton's bride giving way to Mr. Knightley's bride, exactly why Augusta Elton—who "swelled at the idea of Miss Woodhouse's presiding" (369; 3: ch. 7)—is now so jealously sad, and Emma is now so wondrously happy.

NOTES

[1]Frye writes, "Human beings are concerned beings, and it seems to me that there are two kinds of concern: primary and secondary. Primary concerns are such things as food, sex, property, and freedom of movement: concerns that we share with animals on a physical level. Secondary concerns include our political, religious, and other ideological loyalties" (6). In this categorization, political and ideological concerns like gender, race, and class are less important than food, sex, property, and freedom of movement.

[2]Preus writes that *Emma* "begins, then, not only with a marriage, but with a sexual act whose result is Anna Weston." And he argues, further, that "Mrs. Weston's pregnancy becomes a metaphor for a socially positive sexuality. The frequency with which Mrs. Weston is shown to be taking exercise, to be out in public, cheerful, healthy and enjoying herself, is an indication that sexuality and pregnancy are to be taken as positive individual and social conditions" (208).

[3]Emma asks Mrs. Weston of the secret engagement of Jane to Frank, "What has it been but a system of hypocrisy and deceit,—espionage, and treachery? To come among us with professions of openness and simplicity; and such a league in secret to judge us all!" (399; 3: ch. 10). And when Emma reflects on how she has allowed herself to be led astray and how she has willfully led herself astray, she is mortified: "that she had been imposed on by others in a most mortifying degree; that she had been imposing on herself in a degree yet more mortifying" (412; 3: ch. 11).

[4]Kestner further emphasizes the Englishness of George Knightley and the Frenchness of Frank Churchill.

[5]A "gallant" is one "who pays court to ladies, a ladies' man. Now somewhat *rare*. Also, a lover; in a bad sense, a paramour" (*OED* B.*sb*.3). This use of the word was not remarked as rare until 1886, according to the *OED*. The use of "gallant" as "a ladies' man" was still common in Austen's time.

[6]Gay discusses *Emma* as an allegory and presents Donwell Abbey as "the epitome" of England ("Emma" 33–36).

"I Wish We Had a Donkey": Small-Group Work and Writing Assignments for *Emma*

Marcia McClintock Folsom

In my introduction to this volume, I mentioned the hospitality of Austen's *Emma* to many kinds of interpretation. It seems appropriate, near the end of the volume, to offer some ways in which our students might experience the novel's responsiveness to new readings—*their* new readings. Various essays in this volume suggest possibilities for writing assignments: Carol M. Dole describes a wonderful opportunity for students to develop a movie version of *Emma*. Julia Prewitt Brown recommends that students "try, for one day, to see their own lives through Austen's eyes" and suggests that writing a character study will give students access to the novel's moral structure. Dorice Williams Elliott gives students the chance to represent their thoughts in writing (perhaps in a class e-mail) as a way to become aware of the indivisibility of conscious and unconscious thought.

I begin this essay with some observations about Austen's depiction of travel in Highbury. Noticing Austen's attention to the way the characters get around in their village is just one means of entering the "close and intricate world the novel constructs," but my comments are intended as an invitation to discussion in other teachers' classes and in their students' essays. I hope that highlighting such motifs will encourage students and teachers to notice other patterns in the novel, to find "something new and interesting to observe in Highbury" (Wiltshire, *Body* 110), and to come up with their own ways of entering the world of *Emma*.

Austen also describes, in considerable detail, the planning of the guest lists for the community's social events. Austen's commentary on invitations, like her portrayal of transportation in Highbury, may be nearly invisible on a first reading but exemplifies the fascinating material that students will discover when they select a detail to trace throughout the novel. As I consider the two patterns, transport and guest lists, I include ways of developing class discussions and writing assignments to help students read the novel with a greater feeling of mastery. The goal is to have students experience the novel by pursuing projects they have devised, so that they can offer their own imaginative, ingenious interpretations of *Emma*.

Getting Around in Highbury

In the last volume of *Emma*, Mr. Knightley spontaneously invites various characters to pick strawberries at the Donwell estate. His gracious offer gives Mrs.

Elton an alternative outing, at which horses will not be needed, since a lame carriage horse has upset the plans to visit Box Hill. Nevertheless, when Mrs. Elton seizes on the invitation, she says, "I wish we had a donkey. The thing would be for us to come on donkeys, Jane, Miss Bates, and me—and my caro sposo walking by. I really must talk to him about purchasing a donkey. In a country life I conceive it to be a sort of necessary." With immortal silliness, Mrs. Elton dreams of a Marie Antoinette pastoral, imagining herself in costume on a gray donkey with a gentleman walking beside her on Donwell-lane. The comedy is heightened by the image of Miss Bates on a donkey, too. The artificiality of Mrs. Elton's vision is revealed by her thought of pestering her husband to *buy* the donkey to complete this imaginary scene of country life.

Mr. Knightley's amusing response indicates that there is nothing inherently wrong with Mrs. Elton's scheme. He assures her that the road will not be dusty, but he says, "Come on a donkey, however, if you prefer it. You can borrow Mrs. Cole's. I would wish every thing to be as much to your taste as possible" (356; 3: ch. 6). In this funny exchange, the idea of going on an outing wearing a "large bonnet," carrying "this basket with a pink ribbon," and arriving on a donkey is a comic variation on a motif that Austen pursues throughout the novel (355; 3: ch. 6). Woven into the fabric of the work are vivid accounts of travel to the parties, dinners, visits, expeditions, and other festivities that bring the villagers together in this most sociable book. In fact, a distinctive quality of *Emma* is its quiet concern for the ways the characters journey to and from their destinations.

This attention to travel is striking, because Highbury, ironically, is such a small locale. Moreover, Emma at twenty has never seen the sea and, before a June day in the novel, had never been to a celebrated Surrey landmark, Box Hill. Although other characters do travel—the Churchills move from Enscombe, in the north, to London and Richmond; the Campbells visit their daughter in Ireland by way of Holyhead in north Wales; and Frank Churchill goes to Weymouth, London, Richmond, and Highbury—Emma, like her father, stays close to home. From the first chapter, however, plans about how-to-get-there figure in the conversations:

> "Randalls is such a distance. I could not walk half so far."
> "No, papa, nobody thought of your walking. We must go in the carriage to be sure."
> "The carriage! But James will not like to put the horses to for such a little way;—and where are the poor horses to be while we are paying our visit?"   (8; 1: ch. 1)

In this exchange between Emma and her father, the decisions entailed in getting from place to place are succinctly summarized—distances are measured (we will read, just a little later, that Randalls is only half a mile from Hartfield), walking is compared with riding in a carriage, the convenience of a carriage is weighed against the inconvenience to horses and driver, and thought is given to the parking problem at the destination. Of course, what is important about this exchange is Emma's patient kindness with her father's excessive anxiety, and Mr. Woodhouse's odd solicitude for James and the horses.

But here as elsewhere, the book is laced with conversations that interweave information about various carriages with more lively matters. We learn about Mr. Knightley's arrival at the Coles' in his carriage (and his silence about the reason he has used it). The narrator notes that Emma disapproves of Mr. Knightley's preference for walking: "Mr. Knightley keeping no horses, having little spare money and a great deal of health, activity, and independence, was too apt, in Emma's opinion, to get about as he could, and not use his carriage so often as became the owner of Donwell Abbey" (213; 2: ch. 8). Likewise, whether or not Mr. Perry should buy a carriage is a matter of concern in the neighborhood: Mrs. Perry is reported to be worried about her husband's health—"she thought his being out in bad weather did him a great deal of harm." But discussion of the purchase lasted only three days (344–45, 346; 3: ch. 5), presumably because the expense of a carriage was too great.

We catch a glimpse of Mr. and Mrs. Elton forgetting to stop in their carriage to pick up Jane Fairfax and Miss Bates on the way to the Crown Inn ball, although Mrs. Elton claims, "Our coachman and horses are so extremely expeditious!" (320–21; 3: ch. 2). We hear about promises of a visit from the Sucklings in their barouche-landau (274; 2: ch. 14). We imagine the necessary traveling mode of the John Knightley family from London to the seaside or to Highbury in a carriage with their five children, servants, boxes, and bags. "Under a bright mid-day sun," we are told, "at almost Midsummer, Mr. Woodhouse was safely conveyed in his carriage, with one window down, to partake of this al-fresco party" at Donwell Abbey (357; 3: ch. 6). In reading about Emma's carriage ride home from Randalls, during which she is trapped alone with Mr. Elton, we of course focus on his breathless proposal and her firm refusal, as Celia Easton vividly describes in her essay in this volume. We do not worry, as Emma's father does, about the "dangers of a solitary drive from Vicarage-lane—turning a corner which he could never bear to think of—and in strange hands—a mere common coachman—no James" (133; 1: ch. 15). But although as readers we do not focus on these details of transportation, they remain a part of the novel's rich particularity and of our memory of specific scenes.

Just as important as the novel's attention to carriages is its attention to walking. Emma's perception, early in volume 1, that Harriet will be "useful" as "a walking companion" (26; 1: ch. 4) is analyzed, in this collection, by Devoney Looser and by Julia Prewitt Brown. Within the next few chapters of *Emma*, we see the two young women walking together—on the Donwell road (31; 1: ch. 4), near the vicarage (83; 1: ch. 10), and to town (155; 2: ch. 1). In fact, until the middle of December, "there [is] no weather to prevent the young ladies from tolerably regular exercise" (83; 1: ch. 10). Conversations between the two take place as they walk, and glimpses of their activity and of the landscape are interwoven with dialogue. For example, Emma is talking as she crosses "the low hedge, and tottering footstep which ended the narrow, slippery path through the cottage garden, and brought them into the lane again. . . . They walked on. The lane made a slight bend," and Emma has but a moment more to speak alone with Harriet before Mr. Elton joins them (87; 1: ch. 10). After the three "walked on together quietly," Emma contrives to dally behind, break her bootlace and throw it dexterously into a ditch, so as to get Harriet into Mr. Elton's house (89; 1: ch. 10).

There is a good deal of walking around the countryside of Surrey: Mr. Knightley's evening walks from Donwell to Hartfield; Emma's and the Westons' walks back and forth between Randalls and Hartfield; Mrs. Weston's and Miss Bates's trip across the street in Highbury (carefully examined by Bromberg in this volume); Harriet's little sojourns from Mrs. Goddard's to Hartfield, with stops in town at Ford's or the dressmaker's; Frank Churchill's walk from Hartfield to Highbury, where he will know how to jump over a puddle if he sees one; Jane Fairfax's solitary walk home from Donwell to Highbury on a hot afternoon in June. There are some horseback rides—Frank on his way to and from London or over to Highbury from Richmond, and Mr. Knightley (perhaps riding a horse from Mr. Cole's stable) on his way to Kingston to do an errand or making a "wet ride" home from London to see how Emma is taking the news of Frank's engagement. Austen's great editor, R. W. Chapman, even says: "The topography of Highbury is given in such detail that many attempts have been made to construct a map" ("Feigned Places").

Why does Austen meticulously record details that explain *how* characters make their way to and from their destinations? And why does she integrate the information into the fabric of conversation and feelings in the novel? A paper delivered by the critic Franco Moretti on nineteenth-century fiction suggests one answer. Moretti notes that realistic novels may seem to lack plot but have a superabundance of what might at first be thought of as "filler." A word that beginning readers might use as a synonym for "the boring parts," "filler," says Moretti, is prose about the ordinary things of life—not its grand or extraordinary moments. Attention to such everyday concerns as how to travel and where to park—the sort of issues we ourselves monitor, remember, organize, talk about, arrange, change, and reorganize—is part of what brings this novel to life. But because Austen has seamlessly woven such details into activities and thoughts that are more important to the characters, the kind of information about transportation I have extracted from the novel fades from view unless the reader concentrates on those details.

The opposite of "filler" is a "turning point," Moretti says, and the novel has a number of them. Perhaps the most significant ones are the three moments of awakening and reflection in which Emma recognizes her mistakes—in chapter 16 of volume 1, when Emma reviews her shock that Mr. Elton has proposed to her instead of to Harriet; in chapter 7 of volume 3, after the Box Hill episode, when Mr. Knightley chastises Emma for her cruel remark to Miss Bates; and in chapters 11 and 12 of volume 3, when Emma discovers that she loves Mr.

Knightley. But these key incidents are far fewer than the number of richly detailed moments that chronicle the stuff of everyday life.

Brown's essay in this volume, "The Everyday of *Emma*," suggests that perhaps the reason Austen's novels continue to enjoy such wide readership is her astounding patience and alertness in noting ordinary details. Sensitive readers discover in the novels the demands of the real world, and perhaps rediscover their importance in their own lives. Austen's attention to the everyday corroborates Elizabeth Bennet's remark, in *Pride and Prejudice*, that "there is something new to be observed . . . for ever" in the people one has known for years (43; 1: ch. 9). Echoing Elizabeth's comment is John Wiltshire's statement mentioned earlier: there is "something new and interesting to observe" in Highbury, whenever a reader enters its "close and intricate world." Austen's careful presentation of travel in Highbury is the sort of pattern that jumps out at the alert reader and that will reward a student who chooses to write about the topic.

But such motifs continue to intrigue thoughtful readers who seek to understand their significance, to speculate about what the details reveal about the novel's meaning, or at least to wonder what they contribute to its atmosphere. One answer is that rereading *Emma*, with its rich depiction of the everyday, suggests that vital clues to other people's lives and motives lie hidden in the details that we habitually ignore or consider routine. Many critics have noted, as the detective novelist P. D. James observes, that *Emma* is a kind of detective story, inviting readers to pay attention to seemingly unimportant details in order to discern hidden realities. James points out, "the detective story does not require murder. . . . What it does require is a mystery, facts which are hidden from the reader but which he or she should be able to discover by logical deduction from clues inserted in the novel with deceptive cunning but essential fairness" (243–44). In a talk she gave at Chawton to the Jane Austen Society in 1998, James examined the scenes in the novel in which Austen has laid the clues to the secret engagement of Frank Churchill and Jane Fairfax. As she explained, part of the joy of rereading the novel is to identify those clues, which were there but perhaps too subtle to be perceived on a first reading.

Another pleasure in rereading is to watch the characters—mostly Emma, of course, but others, too—trying to decipher that opaque surface of the everyday. Although the characters are alert to details of behavior, conversation, and expression as they attempt to read the motives of others, they often make incorrect deductions. For example, Emma, watching the conversation between Harriet and Mr. Elton, erroneously surmises that she is witnessing the preliminary stages of a proposal (87–88; 1: ch. 10). And Mrs. Weston draws a false conclusion about the significance of Mr. Knightley's arriving by carriage at the Coles' dinner party. Mr. Knightley is good at interpreting clues, although even he is not always right.

But the dense thicket of detail does not merely conceal clues about the novel's hidden plot or even about simple motives. As my study of the writer's attention to travel suggests, vivid presentation of everyday life sometimes represents nothing more than a realistic portrait of ordinary activity. At other times, a tiny detail can give the reader information of great significance. For example, when Miss Bates praises Mrs. Wallis's kind attention to her and her mother, she comments, "And it cannot be for the value of our custom now, for what is our consumption of bread, you know?" (237; 2: ch. 9) As Yasmine Gooneratne noted, the word "*now*" "simultaneously summarizes and dismisses the painful story of the family's descent in the world" (156). Almost any passage of dialogue or narration bristles with implied observations, richly imagined scenes, and barely articulated but identifiable assumptions. Its vibrant particularity contributes to the distinctive atmosphere of the novel, which both invites and resists interpretation. For this reason, student writers who engage deeply with the work and who trace a pattern through its pages may come up with insights that will surprise and inform their teachers.

Guest Lists and Invitations

Consider another pattern woven into the fabric of the novel. As the characters plan their various gatherings, the novel chronicles the social factors behind the invitations to the eight major events in *Emma*. Before each event, the narrator traces the considerations that determine the guest list; by pondering these preparations, a reader can catch a glimpse of the fluid and the rigid aspects of Highbury social life. Oddly enough, readers today often find that such debates have a familiar ring. Perhaps the funniest discussion about invitations occurs in the conversation between Frank Churchill and Emma about a ball—the one that does not actually occur:

> "You and Miss Smith, and Miss Fairfax, will be three, and the two Miss Coxes five," had been repeated many times over. "And there will be the two Gilberts, young Cox, my father, and myself, besides Mr. Knightley. Yes, that will be quite enough for pleasure. You and Miss Smith, and Miss Fairfax will be three, and the two Miss Coxes five; and for five couple there will be plenty of room."   (248; 2: ch. 11)

This passage, which amuses readers who recognize in it the repetitive, finger-counting patterns that are likely to occur when they plan parties, can serve as an introduction to the way the characters think through the inclusions and exclusions that determine who will be invited to an event. Just as the conversations about who will ride with whom shed light on friendship, kinship, and obligation, so also the delicate negotiations of courtesy or necessity that result in a guest list reveal who is "come-at-able," who will stay home, and who cannot be left out (20; 1: ch. 3).

For instructors organizing a class after students have read most of the novel, I offer, for each of the big scenes, questions for small-group discussions. This

exercise is intended not to check students' reading comprehension or their recollection but to encourage pairs or trios of students to examine passages and
talk about them. During such conversations students gain other insights into
Austen's artistry, and the close reading they do in class may help them find a
topic for an essay. Here are a number of questions, organized around the
novel's major social events, that emphasize the planning that precedes them.

1. Whom does Mr. Woodhouse not want to invite to the first evening dinner
at Hartfield, and how does Emma's "sense of right" overrule her father's wishes
(98; 1: ch. 12)? What is the effect of having both Knightley brothers present on
that evening? How does the party divide during the evening? What roles do
Emma and Mr. Knightley play during the dual (or dueling) conversations (101,
103, 107; 1: ch. 12)? In his essay on comedy in this volume, John Wiltshire suggests a way to understand the "comedy of cross-purposes" in the conversation
between Mr. Woodhouse and Isabella in this chapter.

2. Who is invited and who accepts the invitation to the Westons' dinner party
at Randalls (vol. 1, ch. 13)? How do different characters feel about the evening?
Consider the attitudes of Emma, Mr. Woodhouse, John Knightley, and Mr.
Elton toward the gathering. What is significant about Harriet Smith's being unable to attend? What arrangements have to be made about carriages, horses, and
directions to the house? How does each of the guests get to Randalls, and how
do they all get home? What does Emma's and Mr. Knightley's management of
the departures from Randalls reveal? Celia Easton's essay in this volume might
suggest ways to talk about Emma's ride home with Mr. Elton; Dorice Williams
Elliott's might suggest questions about Emma's thoughts after she gets home.

3. What is revealed about Emma in her shifting feelings about receiving an
invitation to the Coles' dinner party (206–09; 2: ch. 7)? What is significant
about the words in the invitation itself? What does Mr. Woodhouse direct
Emma to say in response to the invitation? Who is invited to arrive at what
times, and why? What is important about the way each guest arrives? The
essay by Joseph Wiesenfarth in this volume might structure questions about
the chapter itself—one of the most complex in the novel.

4. What considerations must Emma take into account in planning a dinner
party at Hartfield to honor Mrs. Elton (291; 2: ch. 16)? How do the feelings
and other obligations of her father and the various guests determine who actually attends and when each guest arrives? In what way do Emma's invitations to
Mrs. Elton and Jane Fairfax reveal the heroine's feelings? Teachers might construct questions about the conversations at the dinner party based on the discussion of the "duet" between Jane Fairfax and John Knightley or the "comic
dueling monologues" between Mr. Weston and Mrs. Elton (vol. 2, ch. 18) in
my introduction to this volume.

5. Who determines the guest list for the ball at the Crown Inn (vol. 2, ch. 11;
vol. 3, ch. 2)? What considerations about the setting and the guests' comfort
are discussed before the party (252–56; 2: ch. 11)? What preparations are
made before the ball (319; 3: ch. 2)? How do the characters arrive, and who

greets them? What plans for guests' transportation to the party are changed, and why? How is the reader informed about who attends the ball? The essay by Jonathan H. Grossman in this volume offers insights about Frank Churchill's exchanges with Mr. Woodhouse about the planned ball; Pamela Bromberg's might suggest ways of structuring discussion of the event itself.

6. In the gathering at Hartfield when Frank proposes a game with alphabet blocks, why does it happen that three groups of walkers converge (344–49; 3: ch. 5)? Why does Emma invite them all to visit her father at Hartfield? Why is Emma "out of hearing" when Mr. Weston addresses her? What parts of the conversation has she missed? What is significant about the ways members of the party enter and leave Hartfield?

7. Who plans the guest list for the strawberry picking at Donwell Abbey (354–57; 3: ch. 6)? Who wants to plan it? What considerations determine who will be invited? How might the guests travel to Donwell Abbey, and how are they actually conveyed to Mr. Knightley's residence? Why is a donkey "a sort of necessary" in a country life? What plans are proposed about the food to be served, who makes it, and where it will be eaten? Who invites Frank Churchill? Who is glad and who is sorry that Frank is invited? Why is he late? How does his lateness affect Mrs. Weston? Mr. Weston? Emma? Harriet Smith? Jane Fairfax? Frank himself? Discussion of this scene should provide insights into the reasons for tensions on the trip to Box Hill.

8. Who plans the guest list for the outing to Box Hill (352–53; 3: ch. 6)? Why are two parties combined into one? What does the arrangement reveal about life in Highbury? Why does Emma not complain about her dislike of the plans? What do we learn about Emma from the fact that she "denied none of it aloud, and agreed to none of it in private"? Who among the regular Highbury group does not go on the picnic, and why not? Jonathan Grossman's essay suggests ways of talking about the event itself.

Suggested Writing Assignments

One writing assignment—probably most appropriate for advanced students—is to focus on a pattern of Austen's presentation of "filler," as discussed by Moretti, in *Emma*. Students who become intrigued about the "surface and weight of the everyday" in the novel can select from a number of patterns to write about; no matter which one they choose, they will discover "something new and interesting." A part of the assignment might be to interpret the pattern, or at least to speculate about what it contributes to the novel's meaning or to its atmosphere.

Here is a list of some of these patterns.

Students might elaborate on the novel's attention to health and illness: conversations about who has a cold or something "amiss" with a tooth, about who is prone to respiratory illness, or which foods are dangerous to health; characters who are healthy (Emma's last illness seems to have been measles when she was a child); the role of the apothecary, Mr. Perry.

A paper could focus on letters, some of which we read and others we hear about. Characters expect letters, write letters, wait for letters, read and remember letters, and share letters aloud. Jane Fairfax "fills the whole page and crosses half" and Miss Bates has difficulty in reading such "chequer-work" (157; 2: ch. 1). We learn about some letters by hearing them talked about. We fathom Jane's suffering when she decides to return Frank's packet of letters to him. In one scene, Jane lavishly praises the post office. In *Emma* the post office represents both a link to the outside world and a site of intimate connection. Tracing its role in the book can inspire a thoughtful paper. A student might even consult a fine essay by David Wheeler, "The British Postal Service, Privacy, and Jane Austen's *Emma*," for social history on the topic.

A student might (like some critics) consider the novel's attention to pastimes like charades, riddles, anagrams, games, and entertainments. Or a student can trace the ways the novel introduces music, singing, dancing, pianos, piano playing, Italian songs, practicing, and a Broadwood piano into the lives of its characters. A topic some students enjoy writing about is the novel's attention to food—including the suppers at Hartfield, recommendations of a "basin of gruel," the hindquarters of pork, boiled eggs, an asparagus and sweetbreads casserole, a small glass of wine, a wedding cake, a cold collation, and some baked apples. Perhaps less obvious is the novel's richly developed sense of place; students may be surprised at how concretely Austen has imagined such details as the path through the Donwell estate, the walks between Hartfield and Randalls, the light snow on the path from Randalls, the sharp turn in the road at the vicarage, the street in front of Ford's, Mr. Coles' stables in town, the countryside where Gypsies camp and young ladies walk, the beautiful location of the Abbey Mill Farm, and the row of trees that "led to nothing," the strawberry beds, and the "English verdure, English culture, English comfort" of Donwell Abbey (360; 3: ch. 6).

An English major might look at the way this book reveals (and hides) its connections to other literature—Chapman's footnotes can help. In *Emma* Austen alludes to *A Midsummer Night's Dream* and *Romeo and Juliet*; Ann Radcliffe's *The Romance of the Forest*; Regina Roche's *The Children of the Abbey*; a riddle by David Garrick; the Book of Psalms; Milton's *L'Allegro*; William Cowper's *The Task*; Dr. Johnson's *Rambler* 107; John Gay's *Fables*; Oliver Goldsmith's *The Vicar of Wakefield*; Madame de Genlis's *Adelaide and Theodore*. Recent scholarship has traced these connections with erudition and imagination.

Yet another project is to trace the novel's repetition of certain distinctive words, as John Wiltshire, in his second essay in this volume, does with the word "comfort." He highlights both the allure of the word "comfort," which "springs to Austen's pen when she seeks to define something important, something to be treasured," and its potential danger—of people being trapped in too much contentment. The words "comfort" and "spirit" (about which

Wiltshire wrote in *Jane Austen and the Body*) seem to signal something important in *Emma*. But there are others, including "pleasure," "blessing," "duty," "perfection," "blunder," "happy," "change," "entertainment," and "secret" (and their cognates). As they reread the novel, students watching for one of these words and its relatives will find that it jumps from the page in many chapters. Wiltshire's essay can serve as a model for analyzing the way that a repeated word provides ambiguity and shifting valence in various passages. Probably a teacher should alert students that Austen does not use repeating words to enforce a consistent meaning.

Finally, an assignment I have used successfully is to have students choose one item from a list of scenes or episodes in volume 2 or volume 3. In a paper, students explore how they understood the scene or episode when they first encountered it (and how Emma understands it) and how they understood it after they had finished the book. Students should probably consider first the literal meaning of dialogue and narration and determine how Emma experiences the event; then, after completing the novel, they can explore hidden implications, as well as the experiences of other characters in the scene. The drawback of this assignment is that the student must cover the scene twice. The advantage is that it shows students how clearly Austen imagined each character's implied thoughts and experience of the scene. The assignment assures that students rereading a section of the book gain a deep understanding of one scene—an understanding that is not possible at a first reading. This exercise produces exclamations of wonder and pleasure, for students, by analogy, observe Austen's careful construction of the whole novel.

Events that especially reward this kind of attention are, in volume 2, the Coles' dinner party (ch. 8) (analyzed in this volume by Wiesenfarth); Miss Bates's invitation to hear the pianoforte (ch. 9) (decoded by Bromberg in this volume); the discussion of another ball and a subtle change in Emma's feelings (ch. 11) (analyzed by Grossman); Frank Churchill's farewell (ch. 12); Emma's review of her feelings (ch. 13) (see the sentence-by-sentence analysis demonstrated by Elliott); and the dinner at Hartfield (chs. 16–18) (partially unraveled in my "Challenges" essay). In volume 3, students can write about the ball at the Crown Inn (ch. 2) (also discussed by Bromberg); Harriet's confession and a new resolution (ch. 4); the game of alphabet blocks (ch. 5); the outing to Donwell Abbey (ch, 6); and the aftermath of the Box Hill outing (ch. 8). Writing such a paper—like reading *Emma*, like teaching *Emma* (and like working on this volume) tempts one to go on and on.

Health, Comfort, and Creativity:
A Reading of *Emma*

John Wiltshire

One of the chief challenges in teaching *Emma*, I've found—as with all Jane Austen's novels—is to persuade students to go beyond talking about characters and about the romance plot and to understand the novel's structure and its status as a work of art. Motivating student readers is all the more important in the wake of the recent films, which, for good reasons, replace Austen's artistic purposes and designs with their own intentions and ambitions and, perhaps inevitably, emphasize sexuality and romance. In the past, critics have made many attempts to read *Emma* by focusing on such moral or pedagogical matters as the education or humiliation of Emma's imagination or (more recently) on her relation to patriarchal society. In this essay I suggest an approach that, by picking up a little-noticed preoccupation of the text, the quotidian but salient notion of "comfort," calls attention to a vital aspect of the novel's underlying conceptual, or rather emotional and ethical, structure.

One way to begin discussion of *Emma*, especially with students who have read other Austen novels but also with those who are studying the writer for the first time, is to point out its densely populated textual space. A distinctive feature of *Emma* is the way it embeds its action convincingly in the small, circumscribed, but nevertheless detailed Highbury world. Austen does so, partly, through the passing mention—as if they were already known to the reader—of a number of figures who never actually make an appearance in the novel. The apparently casual citation of the names of Mrs. Goddard, Mrs. Perry, the Coles, and William Larkins, among others—students can profitably be asked to hunt for the references—persuades readers that they already know them and creates a narrator who is a denizen of the world on which she reports so familiarly. One of these figures, whose notice serves to populate Highbury and to thicken its description, is the apothecary, or local doctor.

Mr. Perry is, in fact, mentioned in *Emma* every twenty or so pages, in one connection or another: Mr. Woodhouse talks about him, he is seen passing through the town, or reports are given of his medical opinion. His presence is more than incidental to the novel, however. Of course a small town would have its local doctor, just as it would have a school and shopkeepers, many of whom are named, and even briefly characterized, in *Emma*—for instance, the obsequious Mrs. Ford, at the draper's shop, and Mrs. Wallis, the baker's wife, who can sometimes give a rude answer (236–37; 2: ch. 9). Mr. Perry is more important to the novel's main interests than these figures, as his close relation (perhaps a friendship) with Emma's father suggests. An active person, often glimpsed on the road, "walking hastily by," always coming back from somewhere or other, he is a familiar reference for the citizens of Highbury, but he is equally significant as a pointer to some of the novel's leading concerns. His very activity, which is also movement up the social scale, forms a telling contrast with the genteel inertia of his principal patient in the community, Mr. Woodhouse. "Why is Mr. Perry mentioned so often in this novel?," students may be asked.

The threading of Mr. Perry through the narrative suggests, perhaps, that Austen is interested in matters of health. Serious illness is rare in *Emma* (the distant Mrs. Churchill's medical emergencies are treated with skepticism), and Highbury's most dramatic bodily event—Mrs. Weston's pregnancy and the birth of little Anna—occurs with only the briefest of facetious mentions. But minor ailments and imagined illnesses—coughs, colds, biliousness, fever, fainting fits, putrid sore throat—are common occurrences in the novel and are matters of considerable importance to the community Austen depicts. In fact, one might say that talk about health is the idiolect—the characteristic mode of human exchange—in Highbury. People fuss over each other, over remedies and rhubarb, over taking cold, over drafts and diets, just as they do everywhere. While *Emma* reflects this ordinariness, the novel infuses it with extraordinary narrative tension and excitement. A good way of opening up these issues is for the class to examine the comic dialogue, in chapter 12 of the first volume, in which Isabella and her father dispute the rival virtues of their favorite doctors and health resorts. But health is more than a source of incidental humor in the novel: it has a larger and more important dimension.

Austen expects readers to understand the notion of health in a moral register as well as in a physical one, although the two are interconnected. The focus of this perspective is Emma herself. The reader is introduced to Emma by being privy to her consciousness, sharing her excitement at the pleasure, the game, that taking up Harriet Smith promises (23; 1: ch. 2). Instructors can use this scene as an opportunity to show how free indirect discourse works: through the irony that the technique allows, the reader necessarily is skeptical about Emma's reasoning and motives. (Free indirect discourse is examined in detail in Dorice Williams Elliott's essay in this volume.) The mixed response to Emma's enthusiasm for Harriet is soon taken up and spelled out in the conversation between Mr. Knightley and Mrs. Weston (ch. 5). One speaks of his reservations about Emma, the other replies by pointing out how lovely the young woman is—that she is "the complete picture of grown-up health" (39; 1: ch. 5). Mrs. Weston's response is illogical and doesn't meet Mr. Knightley's criticisms, but by speaking of Emma as the picture of health, Mrs. Weston indicates her sense of Emma's fundamental or ontological goodness—she is not only physically but also emotionally and morally sound (Wiltshire, *Body*).

The principle of health in Emma is the key to the novel's energy and warmth. For most of the book, spirited, capable, and active as she is, she has no difficulty in coping with the dogged timidity and resistances of her father. His ill health (real or presumed) is also understood in a moral as well as a physical sense. He is frightened of drafts, of even short journeys in the carriage, of anything unpredictable or unforeseen or hasty. As Mr. Knightley surmises, "to have any of them sitting down out of doors to eat would inevitably make him ill" (356; 3: ch. 6). It would be melodramatic, and out of harmony with the spirit of the novel, to say that he is afraid of life itself, but the idea suggests how high the stakes in *Emma* are. His invalidism can be thought of as an emotional or characterological constriction or failure. If *eager* is one of the novel's most frequent characterizing words for its heroine, then confronting that term with its opposites, invalidism and withdrawal, sets up a profound ethical conflict.

Another figure clearly contrasted with Emma is Jane Fairfax. "Bless me! poor Jane is ill!" is Miss Bates's first exclamation when reading the letter that introduces her into the novel (162; 2: ch. 1). The association of Jane with ill health shadows her, although in this instance students might share Emma's suspicion that Jane's cold is no more than a pretext for her return to Highbury. But the theme of Jane's liability to illness is continued when Mr. Knightley steps in to prevent her from singing herself hoarse (229; 2: ch. 8) or when his brother, John, comments on her walking in the rain. These chivalrous interventions, however, are not all they seem, for it is as if the motif of Jane's ill health encompasses a set of anxieties concerned specifically with female vulnerability. Jane, whose susceptibility to illness is the opposite of Emma's robustness—the heroine responds to Mrs. Weston's query "Are you well, my Emma?" with "Oh! perfectly. I am always well, you know" (420; 3: ch. 12)—can also represent something larger about the limits and conditions of a woman's life. Jane's ill health, or the threat of it, is also a way of defining the cloud that hangs over her, the confinement of her condition, the stresses and constrictions involved in dwelling with her aunt. Miss Fairfax is pale, subject to prolonged nervous tension and anxiety, and at the climax of the novel undergoes a collapse that is clearly more emotional than physical, as Mr. Perry—revealing himself, at this late stage of the book, as a wise and trustworthy clinician—perceives. His speech is still reported, not direct: "Her present home, he could not but observe, was unfavourable to a nervous disorder: confined always to one room;—he could have wished it otherwise" (389; 3: ch. 9). The class can be invited to think about Jane Fairfax's circumstances and to imagine her daily life from the information given. The victim of repression and anxiety, Jane is eventually cured, as Mrs. Elton archly remarks, by "a young physician from Richmond," Frank Churchill.

Frank's difficulties with the erratic and demanding hypochondriac Mrs. Churchill are a distant reflection of Emma's with Mr. Woodhouse. Mrs. Churchill's influence restricts and frustrates his erotic or emotional life in a way that parallels Mr. Woodhouse's effect on Emma, although in a more material, sharper way. Like Emma, Frank is never physically ill. He is a figure of energy, of a restless (and sexual) spiritedness that becomes the more frenetic, erratic, and reckless the more frustration it encounters. His teasing, ingenuity, and contrivance match Emma's and signal to the reader that her stratagems are similarly linked to her physicality. Initially his energy is diverted into schemes to snatch opportunities to be with Jane, as well as in hoodwinking the delightful but to him not sexually alluring Miss Woodhouse. His vitality is expressed not only in his physical activity (he rides about the countryside a lot) but also in his ingenious plans, like the ball at the Crown Inn. His behavior is characteristic when, blocked by Jane's apparent resolution to break off their engagement at Box Hill, he thinks of more movement, in a wider sphere, of travel abroad. His frustration communicates itself to Emma: "the young man's spirits now rose to a pitch almost unpleasant" (374; 3: ch. 7).

Frank and Mr. Woodhouse meet head-on over the plans for the ball at the Crown. Where the preparations for the dance are concerned, Mr. Woodhouse is as vocal and determined as he is anywhere in the novel. He is afraid they will all catch colds from the damp rooms inevitably found at an inn, and he says so. Frank cannot resist:

> "I was going to observe, sir," said Frank Churchill, "that one of the great recommendations of this change would be the very little danger of any body's catching cold—so much less danger at the Crown than at Randalls! Mr. Perry might have reason to regret the alteration, but nobody else could."
>
> "Sir," said Mr. Woodhouse, rather warmly, "you are very much mistaken if you suppose Mr. Perry to be that sort of character. Mr. Perry is extremely concerned when any of us are ill. But I do not understand how the room at the Crown can be safer for you than your father's house."
>
> "From the very circumstance of its being larger, sir. We shall have no occasion to open the windows at all—not once the whole evening; and it is that dreadful habit of opening the windows, letting in cold air upon heated bodies, which (as you well know, sir) does the mischief."
>
> "Open the windows!—but surely, Mr. Churchill, nobody would think of opening the windows at Randalls. Nobody could be so imprudent! I never heard of such a thing. Dancing with open windows!—I am sure, neither your father nor Mrs. Weston (poor Miss Taylor that was) would suffer it."
>
> "Ah! sir—but a thoughtless young person will sometimes step behind a window-curtain, and throw up a sash, without its being suspected. I have often known it done myself."
>
> "Have you indeed, sir—Bless me! I never could have supposed it. But I live out of the world, and am often astonished at what I hear."
>
> (251–52; 2: ch. 11)

Comic scenes like this one give *Emma* its distinctive quality. Ostensibly this dialogue is about physical health, but a class should readily observe that it is about much more than that. Frank's teasing is similar to but more amiable (if more persistent and inventive) than Mr. John Knightley's earlier taunting about the dangers of snow on the ground at Randalls (126; 1: ch. 15). At this point, the attributes that Frank represents—youth, energy, enterprise—most directly confront the conservatism of Mr. Woodhouse, who once again enlists Mr. Perry, the hidden center of the novel's circling concern with health.

Here, moreover, a key link between health, creativity, and the materially real, open environment is suggested. Oliver Sacks has remarked that the defining condition of "patienthood" is "the contraction in all realms (not least the moral realm)," and he has pointed, conversely, to "the spaciousness of health, of full being, of the real world" (125). The association of illness with contracture, of health with spaciousness, is translated, in *Emma*, into particular settings. The novel begins with scenes of confinement indoors that gradually diminish in frequency, as the seasons turn from winter to spring to summer, the action bells out, the pace heats up, with outings and expeditions. The symbolic freight of indoor and outdoor settings is hinted, too, in such declarations as "I love an open nature" and "Oh, if you knew how much I love everything that is decided and open!" (460; 3: ch. 16). In discussing the exchange between Frank and Mr. Woodhouse, some students may feel that the talk about opening windows is a cruel and irresponsible teasing of the old gentleman, but most, I think, will support Frank and will recognize that, for all his delight in mischief, he is speaking for health.

Health in *Emma*, then, has a spatial, or material, register as well. In many ways, the novel suggests, health may be a more problematic matter for women than for men, for ladies than for gentlemen. Men ride about freely, to London and back in a day, or walk three miles to pick walnuts. A lady cannot walk across the street to get letters in a light rain without attracting the kindly but interfering attention of her neighbors. Austen may be reflecting the manners and customs of her time, but the issue is deeper than mere social practice. The novel connects health and energy with activity and the outdoors; indoors is associated with the stifling of energies and enterprise. *Emma* sets up a connection between confinement and ill health (of the psychosomatic kind) and suggests how health has a necessary connection to outgoing, or openness, in all of its senses. The moments of freedom, when a woman is alone and able to walk at leisure outside, are treasured spaces in the novel: they define some of its highest points. "Oh, Miss Woodhouse, the comfort of being sometimes alone!" Jane Fairfax exclaims when, being pushed to extreme and unladylike measures, she flees the strawberry party at Donwell (363; 3: ch. 6).

This passage is not, by any means, the only one in the novel that emphasizes "comfort." Running alongside the novel's focus on health, in fact, is its attention to "comfort" (Rybczynski). Emma's "comfortable home" is mentioned in the very first sentence, and the word, or its cognates, recurs continually, making its unobtrusive contribution to the novel's ambience and network of ideas. No doubt it stands for something that Austen herself valued dearly. All three of the novels written, or completed, after she was settled at Chawton testify to the importance Austen attached to the notion of home and to the provision of domestic comfort. Once students have had their attention called to the frequency of this word, they should be asked to think about its range of meanings and to look it up in a good dictionary. (The associations of comfort are discussed illuminatingly by Joy Alexander.) In earlier centuries the noun *comfort* meant "assistance or support" and its associated verb took the same coloring: "Be comfortable to my mother, your mistress, and make much of her," are Bertram's parting words to Helena in *All's Well That Ends Well* (1.1.74–75) (c. 1602). In Johnson's *Dictionary* (1755), *comfort* is still defined as "consolation, support under calamity or danger." *Comfort* evolved its domestic meaning in the later eighteenth century in tandem with the development of a more leisured society: in this sense it is an indisputably middle-class, or bourgeois, notion, depending as it usually does on a material substrate, a steady income, for the security, placidity, and ease it evolved to denote. The word had certainly acquired its dominant modern senses by the time Austen wrote. Yet the word remains polysemous and multivalent, and Austen explores here some of its ambiguities and possibilities. In this novel, it is as if the strong, buoyant theme of health were accompanied by another theme, or riff, repeating and varying the notion of comfort—a lesser theme that at times seems to overwhelm, and at others to blend triumphantly with, the dominant one.

Among the dozens of references to comfort in *Emma*, the word is sometimes used with its secular, material, or financial meaning uppermost, as when Mrs. Weston's "comfortable provision" is mentioned or when Mr. Weston is said to have "fitted up his house so comfortably" (13; 1: ch. 1). But when Emma guiltily reflects that she has failed to add to "the stock of [the Bateses'] scanty comforts" (155; 2: ch. 1), by not visiting the two women as often as she should, the novelist employs the word to cover a broader range of meaning. If Emma thinks sardonically about Harriet's admiration for "the many comforts and wonders of Abbey Mill farm," she is using the word in one of its oldest senses, meaning, according to the *Oxford English Dictionary*, "enjoyment and delight." Frank Churchill, in front of the Eltons' house, comments that if it were to be shared with the woman he loved, the vicarage, though small, must have ample room "for every real comfort" (204; 2: ch. 6). We hear, too, of Mr. Woodhouse's "comfortable talk with his dear Isabella" (100; 1: ch. 12). Mr. Perry seems to dispense comfort in this sense, as well as medicines, in his consultations with Mr. Woodhouse (434; 3: ch. 14).

Comfort, then, is clearly a concept with a wide range of suggestiveness. While it points to a key value not only of the community depicted in the novel but of the novel itself, it also rings alarm bells. Younger readers will not need to be alerted to the idea that a world devoted to comfort, above all, has turned its back on risk, adventure, and excitement, and students might discuss the issue in class. Comfort can be a seductive and problematic value. It allows no conceptual space for movement, for enterprise, for the strong, the heroic, the romantic. If we were to say that *Emma* celebrates the values of comfort, we would be near to acquiescing in a view of Austen not unlike that notoriously expressed by Charlotte Brontë in her letter to Lewes of 1848: "No fresh air, no blue hill, no bonny beck. I should hardly like to live with her ladies and gentlemen, in their elegant but confined houses" (qtd. in Southam 126). Yet clearly the word springs to Austen's pen when she seeks to define something impor-

tant, something to be treasured. In one of the novel's more remarkable references, Emma thinks of it in salutation of the landscape before her at Donwell
Abbey: "It was a sweet view—sweet to the eye and to the mind. English verdure, English culture, English comfort, seen under a sun bright, without being
oppressive" (360; 3: ch. 6).

We are struck, once again, that Austen uses a word so much associated with
the indoors to define her heroine's deepest moment of affiliation with a
beloved landscape, as part of temperately phrased but nonetheless absolute
endorsement of her communion with the qualities that landscape bodies forth.
Even so, comfort is a value that might make a modern reader, so to speak, uncomfortable. Certainly the notion is, in some ways, difficult to reconcile with
that enhanced sense of health which, as I've been arguing, the novel makes
pivotal to its argument.

One primary focus of comfort in *Emma*, in fact, is on Mr. Woodhouse. "Her
father's comfort" is one of Emma's preoccupations, even when, with another
part of her mind, she is busily playing imaginative games with Harriet Smith
and Mr. Elton and later with Jane Fairfax and Mr. Dixon. "To her he looked for
comfort" (126–27; 1: ch. 15). "Comfort" to Mr. Woodhouse means only habit,
familiarity, safety, a reassurance premised on compensation for unacknowledged loss. It is a substitutive value, a consolation or solace, replacement for a
failure that cannot be defined. The quotation marks around "comfortable" are
prominent in John Knightley's unwillingness ever to leave home ("the folly of
not allowing people to be comfortable at home" [113; 1: ch. 13]) and in Mrs.
Elton's otiose pronouncement that "there is nothing like staying at home, for
real comfort" (274; 2: ch. 14).

The problematic side of this value emerges most sharply when Emma tells
Harriet, early in the novel, that she will never marry, since her nephews and
nieces will "supply every sort of sensation that declining life can need" and that
such attachments suit her "ideas of comfort better than what is warmer and
blinder" (86; 1: ch. 10). At this point, the class should understand that the culti-
vation of comfort (however broad a meaning the word may carry) can be self-
destroying, shutting down options and denying aspects of the personality that
are comically being demonstrated—as the instructor might point out—in
Emma's vigor and decisiveness even as she makes these pronouncements.
Comfort also suggests a kind of dependency, in contrast to that native energy
or creative spark that is signaled when Emma is described and indeed narra-
tively incarnated as the picture of health.

But Austen, rescuing the notion of comfort from the material and the debili-
tated, puts it into vital connection with ethical and psychological health at certain key moments of the novel, especially when Emma responds to the pleas of
Harriet and Jane Fairfax. These encounters are worth discussing in class.
Meeting Robert Martin and his sister by accident in Ford's shop, Harriet is seriously distressed: "Oh! dear, I thought it would have been the death of me!"
she cries. She turns to Emma for help: "Oh! Miss Woodhouse, do talk to me

and make me comfortable again" (179; 2: ch. 3). But in this instance, being "not thoroughly comfortable herself" (because she feels, but will not acknowledge, some guilt), Emma's attempts to reassure and calm Harriet fail. Discomposed by Harriet's vivid account of her experience, Emma cannot communicate reassurance. And so Harriet remains unhappy, agitated, unappeased—and continues to irritate Emma—until Emma finds the psychological and moral means to allay her distress. In chapter 13, volume 2, Harriet brings to Emma her renewed agitation over Mr. Elton's prospective wedding day. Why does Emma succeed here, when she failed earlier? This is an important question for a class to answer. At this point, composed in her own mind, sure of her ground, Emma goes directly to the point, appeals to Harriet's affection for her, and "the violence of grief was comforted away" (268; 2: ch. 13).

It is helpful, I've found, to elicit the implications of these encounters, and the concepts of "object relations" psychoanalytic thought can illuminate the processes taking place here, for Emma is, to some extent, in the position of mother to Harriet. To Donald Winnicott and to W. R. Bion, the mother's relation to her infant is of vital importance. If she is a normal, or what Winnicott terms "good enough," mother, she responds to the infant's distress or tantrum, not by denying it, by becoming angry or distressed herself, but by experiencing the emotion in herself yet moderating it with her own, more stable feelings (Winnicott 10; see also 112). The mother "contains" the child's unformed and inexpressible feelings (Bion 104). She can contain the distress—not in the sense of denying or curtailing it, but in the sense of taking it into herself, experiencing it for herself—and then, in an important part of the process, return the experience or feeling to the child, moderated and transformed through her wisdom. That way she teaches the infant to contain its own feelings, so that it can progress to understand its own emotions. This relation of mother and child, these analysts suggest, is a model for later productive relations between adults, especially between patient and therapist. The infant whose mother habitually responds in this way is assured of basic psychological health. Emma is thus a kind of good mother figure to Harriet when she is herself at ease, and not such a good one when she is pursuing her own schemes and living through her own fantasies.

Harriet's plea to Emma, "Oh! Miss Woodhouse, do talk to me and make me comfortable again," is followed later in the novel, and in a much graver key, by that appeal of Jane Fairfax's during the strawberry party at Donwell: "'Will you be so kind,' said she, 'when I am missed, as to say that I am gone home?'" At first, Emma demurs, but quickly understands: "She saw it all"—and helps Jane get away. At this point, Jane speaks openly for the first time: "Oh! Miss Woodhouse, the comfort of being sometimes alone!" It is not simply because Jane speaks involuntarily and not just because her words resonate with Emma's experience that Emma herself is here so open and responds so kindly and well; it is because she herself, as Austen has shown, has absorbed the "comfort" of Donwell Abbey. Emma thus "contains" both Harriet's and Jane's distress, and, in this sense, comfort is harmonically linked to health—as if an ancient potentiality of the bourgeois, commonplace meaning of "comfort" has been brought out and found to convey a profound idea.

What is striking about Emma's responses is her quick resourcefulness—so much the opposite of her father's instinctive deferral of decisions and pleasures. And it is with Mr. Woodhouse, of course, that Emma displays most engagingly the capacity to contain anxiety that I am discussing. As Edmund Wilson put it: "it is she who takes the place of the parent and Mr. Woodhouse who becomes the child" (*Classics* 201). She does not always succeed: one incident that provides a provocative instance for a class to discuss occurs when, rattled by her first confrontation with Mrs. Elton, Emma falters in talking to her father about visiting her. In my judgment, Mr. Woodhouse actually wins this round—wins the conversational and moral battle (vol. 2, ch. 14).

Comfort, then, is not inimical to health. Indeed, psychological comfort is the very basis of healthy living, of spontaneous receptivity to the world. In Winnicott's thought, only the infant who has been held, been comforted in the way I have described, will go on to live creatively. If the mother fails to hold the infant's distress, it has no means of emotional survival other than what he terms "compliance" with the mother's moods and behavior, an inveterate habit of adaptation to the world (Bion 65). (He goes on to suggest a continuum between the capacity to play, the small spontaneous gestures of everyday life, and the larger notion of creativity that we associate with works of art.) Emma's everyday creativity is fundamental to Austen's conception of her character—for instance, in her ability to replace the small Pembroke on which her father had taken his meals for many years with a large, round, modern table (347; 3: ch. 5). Yet this creativity, too, has its downside. Emma's other-than-compliant relation to reality is exemplified in her enterprising schemes for Harriet Smith's future. She is just as creative, in Winnicott's sense, when she breaks off her bootlace and throws it into the ditch, as an excuse for going into the vicarage, as when she finds a way of disposing of the Westons' wedding cake without upsetting the stomach or nerves of her father. Her enhancement (so to speak) of Harriet's portrait is almost a copybook illustration of creativity gone astray. Creativity, like comfort, then, cannot be an absolute value.

The novel's interest in health and illness, in activity and stasis, in the indoors and the outdoors, which are all linked and unifed, is demonstrated most movingly in Emma and Mr. Knightley's final reconciliation, in volume 3, chapter 13. When Harriet and Mr. Knightley seem to be on the verge of an engagement, Emma experiences her most melancholy evening, pacing about the drawing room at Hartfield, full of ominous thoughts, an evening during which her father "could only be kept tolerably comfortable by . . . exertions which had never cost her half so much before" (422; 3: ch. 12). Emma's energies are in danger here of being overtaxed, consumed by the domestic affections, so that while they are certainly part of those qualities in her that may be trusted (as Mrs. Weston has put it), they are in another sense the very avenues through which her young life's own project may be stemmed and frustrated. But the next day the weather clears:

> With all the eagerness which such a transition gives, Emma resolved to be out of doors as soon as possible. Never had the exquisite sight, smell, sensation of nature, tranquil, warm, and brilliant after a storm, been more attractive to her. She longed for the serenity they might gradually introduce; and on Mr. Perry's coming in soon after dinner, with a disengaged hour to give her father, she lost no time in hurrying into the shrubbery. (424; 3: ch. 13)

The claims of comfort and health are beautifully reconciled in this climactic scene. With her father indoors, taken care of, comfortably occupied with Mr. Perry, Emma is free to step outdoors, to be creative—to take those courageous, playful conversational initiatives that culminate in the clearing up of misunderstandings and lead Mr. Knightley toward his declaration of love. Emma's health is thus understood against a background of containing stability. Her creativity flourishes, as did Austen's as an artist, because her world—in Austen's case, cultural tradition and family loyalty—is in place reliably to hold and assist her. Winnicott makes no bones about the significance of the conception of psychological health he propounds, believing it to be essential to creativity (95–110). The reiterated notion of "comfort" in this novel, so easy to overlook, so contrary to romance, ultimately releases meanings that are central to its artistic design. There are many different ways in which the humor, the intricacy, the vigor of *Emma* can be brought out to new readers, and what I have suggested here is merely one way. But there is no way around the fact that *Emma* addresses issues of physical, psychological, even moral health that are vital to life itself.

Appendix:
"Opinions of *Emma*"

Capt[n]. Austen.[1]—liked it extremely, observing that though there might be more Wit in P & P—& an higher Morality in MP—yet altogether, on account of it's peculiar air of Nature throughout, he preferred it to either.

M[rs] F. A.[2]—liked & admired it very much indeed, but must still prefer P. & P.

M[rs] J. Bridges—preferred it to all the others.

Miss Sharp—better than M P.—but not so well as P. & P.—pleased with the Heroine for her Originality, delighted with M[r] K—& called M[rs] Elton beyond praise.—dissatisfied with Jane Fairfax.

Cassandra—better than P. & P.—but not so well as M. P.—

Fanny K.[3]—not so well as either P. & P. or M P.—could not bear *Emma* herself.—M[r] Knightley delightful.—Should like J. F.—if she knew more of her.—

M[r] & M[rs] J. A.[4]—did not like it so well as either of the 3 others. Language different from the others; not so easily read.—

Edward[5]—preferred it to M P.—*only*. —M[r] K. liked by every body.

Miss Bigg—not equal to either P & P.—or M P.—objected to the sameness of the subject (Match-making) all through.—Too much of M[r] Elton & H. Smith. Language superior to the others.—

My Mother—thought it more entertaining than M P.—but not so interesting as P. & P.—No characters in it equal to Ly Catherine & M[r] Collins.—

---

[1] Francis William; his brother Charles is below.

[2] Francis's wife.   [3] Knight.

[4] James Austen.   [5] James Edward (as p. 432).

Miss Lloyd[1]—thought it as *clever* as either of the others, but did not receive so much pleasure from it as from P. & P—& M P.—

M^rs & Miss Craven—liked it very much, but not so much as the others.—

Fanny Cage—liked it very much indeed & classed it between P & P.—& M P.—

Mr Sherer—did not think it equal to either M P—(which he liked the best of all) or P & P.—Displeased with my pictures of Clergymen.—

Miss Bigg—on reading it a second time, liked Miss Bates much better than at first, & expressed herself as liking all the people of Highbury in general, except Harriet Smith—but c^d not help still thinking *her* too silly in her Loves.

The family at Upton Gray—all very much amused with it. —Miss Bates a great favourite with Mrs Beaufoy.

M^r & Mrs Leigh Perrot—saw many beauties in it, but c^d not think it equal to P. & P.—Darcy & Eliz^th had spoilt them for anything else.—Mr K. however, an excellent Character; Emma better luck than a Matchmaker often has.—Pitied Jane Fairfax—thought Frank Churchill better treated than he deserved.—

Countess Craven—admired it very much, but did not think it equal to P & P.—which she ranked as the very first of it's sort.—

Mrs Guiton—thought it too natural to be interesting.

Mrs Digweed—did not like it so well as the others, in fact if she had not known the Author, could hardly have got through it.—

Miss Terry—admired it very much, particularly Mrs Elton.

Henry Sanford—very much pleased with it—delighted with Miss Bates, but thought Mrs Elton the best-drawn Character in the Book.—Mansfield Park however, still his favourite.

[1] Martha.

Mr Haden—*quite* delighted with it. Admired the Character
of Emma.—

Miss Isabella Herries—did not like it—objected to my
exposing the sex in the character of the Heroine—
convinced that I had meant M^rs & Miss Bates for some
acquaintance of theirs—People whom I never heard
of before.—

Miss Harriet Moore—admired it very much, but M. P. still
her favourite of all.—

Countess Morley—delighted with it.—

Mr Cockerelle—liked it so little, that Fanny w^d not send me
his opinion.—

Mrs Dickson–did not much like it—thought it *very* inferior
to P. & P.—Liked it the less, from there being a Mr.
& Mrs Dixon in it.—

Mrs Brandreth—thought the 3^d vol: superior to anything
I had ever written—quite beautiful!—

Mr B. Lefroy—thought that if there had been more Incident, it would be equal to any of the others.—The
Characters quite as well drawn & supported as in any,
& from being more everyday ones, the more entertaining.—Did not like the Heroine so well as any of the
others. Miss Bates excellent, but rather too much of
her. M^r & Mrs Elton admirable & John Knightley a
sensible Man.—

Mrs B. Lefroy—rank'd *Emma* as a composition with S & S.
—not so *Brilliant* as P. & P—nor so *equal* as M P.—
Preferred Emma herself to all the heroines.—The
Characters like all the others admirably well drawn &
supported—perhaps rather less strongly marked than
some, but only the more natural for that reason.—M^r
Knightley Mrs Elton & Miss Bates her favourites.—
Thought one or two of the conversations too long.—

Mrs Lefroy—preferred it to M P—but liked M P. the least
of all.

Mr Fowle—read only the first & last Chapters, because he had heard it was not interesting.

Mrs Lutley Sclater—liked it very much, better than M P— & thought I had "brought it all about very cleverly in the last volume."—

Mrs C. Cage wrote thus to Fanny—"A great many thanks for the loan of *Emma*, which I am delighted with. I like it better than any. Every character is thoroughly kept up. I must enjoy reading it again with Charles. Miss Bates is incomparable, but I was nearly killed with those precious treasures! They are Unique, & really with more fun than I can express. I am at Highbury all day, & I can't help feeling I have just got into a new set of acquaintance. No one writes such good sense. & so very comfortable.

Mrs Wroughton—did not like it so well as P.&P.—Thought the Authoress wrong, in such times as these, to draw such Clergymen as Mr Collins & Mr Elton.

Sir J. Langham—thought it much inferior to the others.—

Mr Jeffery (of the Edinburgh Review) was kept up by it three nights.

Miss Murden—certainly inferior to all the others.

Capt. C. Austen[1] wrote—"Emma arrived in time to a moment. I am delighted with her, more so I think than even with my favourite Pride & Prejudice, & have read it three times in the Passage."

Mrs D. Dundas—thought it very clever, but did not like it so well as either of the others.

[1] Charles John.

NOTE

Austen, "Opinions of Emma," *Minor Works*, ed. Chapman 436–39. Reprinted by permission of Oxford University Press.

NOTES ON CONTRIBUTORS

Pamela S. Bromberg is professor of English at Simmons College. She contributed an essay to the MLA's *Approaches to Teaching Austen's* Pride and Prejudice. She has published essays on Margaret Atwood, William Blake, Lillian Hellman, and Margaret Drabble in various books and journals. Her research and teaching interests include the development of the English novel, the postmodern and colonial novel, and critical theory.

Julia Prewitt Brown is professor of English at Boston University. Her books include *Jane Austen's Novels: Social Change and Literary Form* (Harvard UP, 1979), *A Reader's Guide to the Nineteenth-Century English Novel* (Macmillan, 1985), and *Cosmopolitan Criticism: Oscar Wilde's Philosophy of Art* (UP of Virginia, 1997). Her research and teaching interests include nineteenth-century British literature, the relations between literature and the visual arts, and the novel genre.

Lorna J. Clark teaches prose fiction at the University of Ottawa. She has published *The Letters of Sarah Harriet Burney* (U of Georgia P, 1997), as well as articles and reviews on women writers, including Mary Shelley, Frances Burney, and Jane Austen. A contributor to the *New Dictionary of National Biography*, Clark edits the *Burney Letter* and is currently working on a volume of essays and two volumes of Frances Burney's *Court Journals*.

Carol M. Dole is professor of English at Ursinus College. She has published essays including "The Gun and the Badge: Hollywood and the Female Lawman," "The Return of the Father in Spielberg's *The Color Purple*," and "Austen, Class, and the American Market" in Linda Troost and Sayre Greenfield's *Jane Austen in Hollywood*. Her current project is a study of how the film industry markets and internally references sources to present film adaptations as literary.

Celia A. Easton is associate professor of English at the State University of New York, College at Geneseo. She has published an essay on Austen and land reform and continues to work on a project about Austen and the enclosure movement in England. She has published essays about women's friendship. Her research and teaching interests include eighteenth-century British literature, Austen, literary theory, and writing.

Dorice Williams Elliott is associate professor of English at the University of Kansas. Her most recent publication is *The Angel out of the House: Philanthropy and Gender in Nineteenth-Century England* (UP of Virginia, 2002). She has published widely on the literature and culture of eighteenth- and nineteenth-century Britain, including essays on Elizabeth Gaskell, Joseph Conrad, Hannah More, Sarah Scott, and Victorian factory novels. She is working on a book called "Transporting Class: Reinventing Social Relations in Australian Convict Fiction."

Marcia McClintock Folsom is professor of literature at Wheelock College. She is the editor of the MLA's *Approaches to Teaching Austen's* Pride and Prejudice, to which she contributed an essay, "Taking Different Positions." She coedited *By Women: An Anthology of Literature* (Houghton, 1976). She has published essays on Virginia Woolf, including one in the MLA's *Approaches to Teaching Woolf's* To the Lighthouse, and on

Sarah Orne Jewett. Her current projects include writing about teaching and Austen's reading of Shakespeare.

Jonathan H. Grossman is associate professor of English at the University of California, Los Angeles. He wrote *The Art of Alibi: English Law Courts and the Novel* (Johns Hopkins UP 2002). His research and teaching interests include the history and theory of the nineteenth-century novel, and he is now working on a book called "Eccentricities of the Everyday: Dickens, Time, and Realism."

Annette M. LeClair is associate librarian at Schaffer Library of Union College. She has published and presented essays on Austen's *Emma* and is working on an annotated version of Austen's "The Beautifull Cassandra." She has also published and presented essays on library and information-management issues. She serves as library liaison with the English department, organizing special programming for students of literature.

Devoney Looser is assistant professor of English at the University of Missouri, Columbia. She is the author of *British Women Writers and the Writing of History* (Johns Hopkins UP, 2000), editor of *Jane Austen and the Discourses of Feminism* (St. Martin's, 1995), and coeditor of *Generations: Academic Feminists in Dialogue* (U of Minnesota P, 1997). Her teaching and research interests include Austen and her contemporaries, feminist theory, and the history of aging. Her current project is a book called "Garrulous Granddames: British Women Writers and Old Age, 1750–1850."

Patricia Howell Michaelson is associate professor of literary studies at the University of Texas, Dallas. She is the author of *Speaking Volumes: Women, Reading, and Speech in the Age of Austen* (Stanford UP, 2002) and articles about Austen, Wollstonecraft, and women readers. Her research and teaching interests include reading and speech and the eighteenth- and nineteenth-century English novel. She is working on two book projects: one on the Regency period, and one on teaching fiction.

Jo Alyson Parker is associate professor of English at Saint Joseph's University. She published *The Author's Inheritance: Henry Fielding, Jane Austen, and the Establishment of the Novel* (Northern Illinois UP, 1998). She has published essays on Sterne's *Tristram Shandy*, Faulkner's *Absalom, Absalom!*, Austen's *Pride and Prejudice*, as well as essays on science fiction. Her research and teaching interests include eighteenth- and early nineteenth-century novels, theories of narrative, gender studies, and literature and science.

Ruth Perry is professor of literature at the Massachusetts Institute of Technology. Her most recent book is *Novel Relations: The Transformation of Kinship in England, 1748–1818* (Cambridge UP, forthcoming). She is the author of *Women, Letters, and the Novel* (AMS, 1980) and *The Celebrated Mary Astell: An Early English Feminist, 1666–1731* (U of Chicago P, 1986). She has served as president of the American Society for Eighteenth-Century Studies and as director of women's studies at the Massachusetts Institute of Technology. Her teaching and research interests include Charlotte Lennox, Jane Austen, and Anglo-American ballads.

Laura Mooneyham White is associate professor of English at the University of Nebraska, Lincoln. She is the author of *Romance, Language, and Education in Jane Austen's Novels* (Palgrave Macmillan, 1988), the editor of *Critical Essays on Jane Austen* (Hall, 1998), and essays on nineteenth- and twentieth-century British literature.

Her research and teaching interests include the British novel, comic and genre theory, and cultural studies. She is working on a book provisionally titled "The Making of Literary Modernism and Religious Conversion."

Joseph Wiesenfarth is professor emeritus at the University of Wisconsin, Madison. He is the author of *The Errand of Form: An Assay of Jane Austen's Art* (Fordham UP, 1967); *Gothic Manners and the Classic English Novel* (U of Wisconsin P, 1988); and books on George Eliot, Henry James, and Ford Madox Ford. He has published over one hundred articles and reviews and edited Austen's "Jack and Alice" (U of Alberta P, 1991). His research interests include Jane Austen's juvenilia. He is working on a book called "Ford Madox Ford and the Regiment of Women."

John Wiltshire is reader in English at La Trobe University in Melbourne, Australia. He is the author of *Samuel Johnson in the Medical World: The Doctor and the Patient* (Cambridge UP, 1991), *Jane Austen and the Body: "The Picture of Health"* (Cambridge UP, 1992), and *Recreating Jane Austen* (Cambridge UP, 2001). He wrote the chapter on *Mansfield Park*, *Emma*, and *Persuasion* in *The Cambridge Companion to Jane Austen* (Cambridge UP, 1987). His teaching and research interests include eighteenth-century literature, literature and medicine, psychoanalytic theory, and the history of psychoanalysis.

SURVEY PARTICIPANTS

Birgitta Berglund, *Kristianstad University, Sweden*
Pamela S. Bromberg, *Simmons College*
Julia Prewitt Brown, *Boston University*
Charlene Bunnell, *West Chester University*
Ann Campbell, *Emory University*
James P. Carson, *Kenyon College*
Lorna J. Clark, *University of Ottawa*
Edward Copeland, *Pomona College*
Laura Dabundo. *Kennesaw State University*
Carol M. Dole, *Ursinus College*
Celia A. Easton, *State University of New York, Geneseo*
Dorice Williams Elliott, *University of Kansas*
Marcia McClintock Folsom, *Wheelock College*
Mark K. Fulk, *State University of New York, Buffalo*
William Galperin, *Rutgers University, New Brunswick*
Jonathan H. Grossman, *University of California, Los Angeles*
Lynda Hall, *Chapman University*
Lisa Hopkins, *Sheffield Hallam University, England*
Deborah Kennedy, *Saint Mary's University, Nova Scotia*
Victoria Kortes-Papp, *Quebec*
Annette M. LeClair, *Union College, Schenectady, New York*
Devoney Looser, *University of Missouri, Columbia*
Harriet Margolis, *Victoria University, New Zealand*
James McNally, *Old Dominion University*
Patricia Howell Michaelson, *University of Texas, Dallas*
Mark James Morreale, *Marist College*
Jo Alyson Parker, *Saint Joseph's University*
Ruth Perry, *Massachusetts Institute of Technology*
James Scannell, *Utica College of Syracuse University*
Linda Schlossberg, *Harvard University*
Barbara K. Seeber, *Brock University, Ontario*
Robert Sirabian, *Mississippi Valley State University*
Johanna M. Smith, *University of Texas, Arlington*
Louise Z. Smith, *University of Massachusetts, Boston*
Hilda Staels, *University of Leuven, Belgium*
Stuart Tave, *University of Chicago*
David Toise, *Long Island University*
Richard S. Tomlinson, *Saint Catherine's College, Oxford*
Karen Vaught-Alexander, *University of Portland*
Arthur J. Weitzman, *Northeastern University*
David Wheeler, *University of Southern Mississippi*
Laura Mooneyham White, *University of Nebraska, Lincoln*
Joseph Wiesenfarth, *University of Wisconsin, Madison*
John Wiltshire, *LaTrobe University, Australia*
Celestine Woo, *College of New Rochelle*

WORKS CITED

Addison, Joseph, and Richard Steele. *The Spectator*. Ed. Donald F. Bond. 5 vols. Oxford: Clarendon, 1965.

Alexander, Joy. "Anything Goes? Reading *Mansfield Park*." *Uses of English* 52.3 (2001): 239–51.

Aristotle. *Poetics*. *Aristotle's Theory of Poetry and Fine Art*. Trans. S. H. Butcher. 4th ed. New York: Dover, 1955.

Armstrong, Nancy. *Desire and Domestic Fiction: A Political History of the Novel*. New York: Oxford UP, 1987.

Astell, Mary. *Some Reflections upon Marriage*. London, 1700.

Austen, Henry. "Biographical Notice of the Author." Jane Austen, Northanger Abbey *and* Persuasion. 3–9.

Austen, Jane. "Catharine; or, The Bower." Austen, *Novels*, vol. 6: 192–240.

———. *Emma*. Austen, *Novels*, vol. 4.

———. *Emma*. Ed. Fiona Stafford. London: Penguin Classics, 1996.

———. *Emma*. Ed. James Kinsley. Introd. Terry Castle. Oxford: Oxford UP, 1998.

———. *Emma*. Ed. Stephen M. Parrish. Norton Critical Ed. 3rd ed. New York: Norton, 2000.

———. *Emma*. Ed. Alistair Duckworth. Case Studies in Contemporary Criticism. New York: Bedford-St. Martin's, 2002.

———. *Jane Austen's Letters*. Ed. Deirdre Le Faye. 3rd ed. Oxford: Oxford UP, 1995.

———. *Jane Austen's Letters to Her Sister Cassandra and Others*. Ed. R. W. Chapman. 2nd ed. Oxford: Oxford UP, 1952.

———. *Jane Austen's Manuscript Letters in Facsimile: Reproductions of Every Known Extant Letter, Fragment, and Autograph Copy with an Annotated List of All Known Letters*. Ed. Jo Modert. Carbondale: U of Southern Illinois P, 1990.

———. *Jane Austen's* Sir Charles Grandison. Ed. Brian Southam. Oxford: Oxford UP, 1980.

———. *Love and Friendship*. Austen, *Novels*, vol. 6: 76–109.

———. *Mansfield Park*. Austen, *Novels*, vol. 3.

———. Northanger Abbey *and* Persuasion. Austen, *Novels*, vol. 5.

———. *The Novels of Jane Austen*. Ed. R. W. Chapman. 3rd ed. 6 vols. 1932–54. Rev. Mary Lascelles and Brian C. Southam. 1963–69. Oxford: Oxford UP, 1987.

———. "Opinions of *Emma*." Austen, *Novels*, vol. 6: 436–39.

———. "Plan of a Novel." Austen, *Novels*, vol. 6: 428–30.

———. *Pride and Prejudice*. Austen, *Novels*, vol. 2.

———. "Sanditon." Austen, *Novels*, vol. 6: 363–427.

Austen-Leigh, J. E. *A Memoir of Jane Austen*. London: Bentley, 1880, 1883.

———. *A Memoir of Jane Austen*. Ed. R. W. Chapman. 2nd ed. Oxford: Clarendon, 1926.

———. *A Memoir of Jane Austen*. London: Folio, 1989.

———. *A Memoir of Jane Austen by Her Nephew*. 1870. Rpt. Persuasion, *with* A Memoir of Jane Austen. Ed. D. W. Harding. London: Penguin, 1965.

Austen-Leigh, William, and Richard Arthur Austen-Leigh. *Jane Austen, A Family Record*. Rev. and enl. Deirdre Le Faye. Boston: Hall, 1989. Rev. ed. of *Jane Austen, Her Life and Letters*. New York: Dutton, 1913.

Babb, Howard S. *Jane Austen's Novels: The Fabric of Dialogue*. Columbus: Ohio State UP, 1962.

Bakhtin, M. M. *The Dialogic Imagination*. Trans. Caryl Emerson and Michael Holquist. Austin: U of Texas P, 1981.

Bal, Mieke. *Narratology: An Introduction to the Theory of Narrative*. Trans. Christine van Boheemen. Toronto: U of Toronto P, 1985.

Banfield, Ann. *Unspeakable Sentences: Narration and Representation in the Language of Fiction*. Boston: Routledge, 1982.

Barthes, Roland. *S/Z*. Trans. Richard Miller. New York: Hill, 1974.

Benjamin, Jessica. "Master and Slave: The Fantasy of Erotic Domination." *The Bonds of Love*. New York: Pantheon, 1988. 51–84.

Bion, W. R. *Second Thoughts: Selected Papers on Psychoanalysis*. 1967. Northvale: Aronson, 1993.

Birtwistle, Sue, and Susie Conklin. *The Making of Jane Austen's* Emma. London: Penguin, 1996.

Bloom, Harold, ed. *Jane Austen's* Emma. New York: Chelsea, 1987.

———. *Fanny Burney's* Evelina. New York: Chelsea, 1988.

Booth, Wayne C. "Emma, *Emma*, and the Question of Feminism." *Persuasions* 5 (1983): 29–40.

———. *The Rhetoric of Fiction*. 2nd ed. Chicago: U of Chicago P, 1983.

Bordwell, David, and Kristin Thompson. *Film Art: An Introduction*. 6th ed. New York: McGraw, 2001.

Bourdieu, Pierre. *Outline of a Theory of Practice*. Trans. Richard Nice. Cambridge: Cambridge UP, 1977.

Bowers, Bege K., and Barbara Brothers, eds. *Reading and Writing Women's Lives: A Study of the Novel of Manners*. Ann Arbor: U of Michigan Research P, 1990.

Briggs, Asa. *A Social History of England: From the Ice Age to the Channel Tunnel*. London: Weidenfeld, 1994.

Brodie, Laura Fairchild. "Jane Austen and the Common Reader: 'Opinions of *Mansfield Park*,' 'Opinions of *Emma*,' and the Janeite Phenomenon." *Texas Studies in Literature and Language* 37 (1995): 54–71.

Brower, Reuben, and Richard Poirier, eds. *In Defense of Reading*. New York: Dutton, 1962.

Brown, Julia Prewitt. "The Feminist Depreciation of Jane Austen: A Polemical Reading." *Novel* 23 (1990): 303–13.

———. "The 'Social History' of *Pride and Prejudice*." Folsom 58–66.

Brown, Lloyd W. *Bits of Ivory: Narrative Techniques in Jane Austen's Fiction*. Baton Rouge: Louisiana State UP, 1973.

Burney, Frances. *Evelina; or, The History of a Young Lady's Entrance into the World.* Ed. Stewart J. Cooke. New York: Norton, 1998.

————. *The Journal and Letters of Fanny Burney (Madame d'Arbley).* Ed. Joyce Hemlow et al. 12 vols. Oxford: Clarendon, 1972–84.

Burrows, John F. "Style." Copeland and McMaster 170–88.

Butler, Marilyn. *Jane Austen and the War of Ideas.* Oxford: Clarendon, 1975.

Byrne, Paula. *Jane Austen and the Theatre.* London: Hambledon, 2001.

Cameron, Deborah. *Feminism and Linguistic Theory.* 2nd ed. London: Macmillan, 1992.

Carlyle, Thomas. *Selected Writings.* Middlesex: Penguin, 1971.

Cartmell, Deborah, and Imelda Whelehan, eds. *Adaptations: From Text to Screen, Screen to Text.* New York: Routledge, 1999.

Castle, Terry. Letter. *London Review of Books* 24 Aug. 1995: 4.

————. "Sister-Sister [Was Jane Austen Gay?]." Rev. of *Jane Austen's Letters,* ed. Deirdre Le Faye. *London Review of Books* 3 Aug. 1995: 4–6.

Chapman, R. W. "Appendixes: Chronology of *Emma*" Austen, *Novels,* vol. 4: 497–98.

————. "Feigned Places." *Novels,* vol. 4: 521.

————. "Introductory Note to *Emma.*" Austen, *Novels,* vol. 4: xi.

————. Preface. Austen, *Novels,* vol. 6: v–vi.

————. "Notes." Austen, *Novels,* vol. 4: 489–94.

Chatman, Seymour. *Story and Discourse: Narrative Structure in Fiction and Film.* Ithaca: Cornell UP, 1978.

Clarkson, Thomas. *The History of the Rise, Progress, and Accomplishment of the Abolition of the African Slave-Trade by the British Parliament.* 2 vols. London, 1808.

Clueless. Dir. and writer Amy Heckerling. With Alicia Silverstone and Paul Rudd. Paramount, 1995.

Coates, Jennifer. *Women, Men and Language: A Sociolinguistic Account of Gender Differences in Language.* 2nd ed. London: Longman, 1993.

Cohen, Michèle. *Fashioning Masculinity: National Identity and Language in the Eighteenth Century.* London: Routledge, 1996.

Cohn, Dorrit. *Transparent Minds: Narrative Modes for Presenting Consciousness in Fiction.* Princeton: Princeton UP, 1978.

Copeland, Edward. "The Economic Realities of Jane Austen's Day." Folsom 33–45.

————. "Money." Copeland and McMaster 131–48.

————. *Women Writing about Money: Women's Fiction in England, 1790–1820.* Cambridge: Cambridge UP, 1995.

Copeland, Edward, and Juliet McMaster, eds. *The Cambridge Companion to Jane Austen.* Cambridge: Cambridge UP, 1997.

Craig, G. Armour. "Jane Austen's *Emma*: The Truths and Disguises of Human Disclosure." Brower and Poirier 235–55.

Craik, W. A. *Jane Austen: The Six Novels.* London: Methuen, 1965.

Demers, Patricia. *The World of Hannah More.* Lexington: UP of Kentucky, 1996.

Dole, Carol. "Austen, Class, and the American Market." Troost and Greenfield 58–78.

Duckworth, Alistair, ed. "A Critical History of *Emma*." Austen, *Emma*, ed. Duckworth. 405–24.

Dussinger, John A. *In the Pride of the Moment: Encounters in Jane Austen's World*. Columbus: Ohio State UP, 1990.

Edgeworth, Maria. *Belinda*. Ed. Kathryn J. Kirkpatrick. Oxford: Oxford UP, 1994.

Elias, Norbert. *The Civilizing Process*. Trans. Edmund Jephcott. New York: Pantheon, 1978. Oxford: Blackwell, 1994.

———. *The History of Manners and State Formation and Civilization*. Vol. 1 of Elias, *Civilizing Process*.

Eliot, George. *Middlemarch*. Boston: Houghton-Riverside, 1956.

Emma. Dir. and writer Douglas McGrath. With Gwyneth Paltrow and Jeremy Northam. Miramax, 1996.

Emma. Dir. Diarmuid Lawrence. Writer Andrew Davies. With Kate Beckinsale and Mark Strong. 1996. A&E, 1998.

Epstein, Julia. *The Iron Pen: Frances Burney and the Politics of Women's Writing*. Bristol: Bristol Classical, 1989.

Farrer, Reginald. "Jane Austen, *ob*. July 18, 1917." *Quarterly Review* 228 (July 1917): 23–25. Rpt. *Emma*. Ed. Parrish 365–67.

Fergus, Jan. *Jane Austen: A Literary Life*. New York: St. Martin's, 1991.

Ferguson, Moira. *Eighteenth-Century Women Poets: Nation, Class, and Gender*. Albany: State U of New York P, 1995.

Ferriss, Suzanne. "Emma Becomes Clueless." Troost and Greenfield 122–29.

Fielding, Henry. "Essay on Conversation." *Miscellanies by Henry Fielding, Esq*. 1743. Ed. Henry Knight Miller. Vol. 1. Middletown: Wesleyan UP, 1972.

Finch, Casey, and Peter Bowen. "'The Tittle-Tattle of Highbury': Gossip and the Free Indirect Style in *Emma*." *Representations* 31 (1990): 1–18.

Fludernik, Monica. "Discourse Representation." *Encyclopedia of the Novel*. Ed. Paul Schellinger. 2 vols. Chicago: Fitzroy Dearborn, 1998.

Folsom, Marcia McClintock, ed. *Approaches to Teaching Austen's* Pride and Prejudice. New York: MLA, 1993.

Frye, Northrop. *The Double Vision: Language and Meaning in Religion*. Toronto: U of Toronto P, 1991.

Fussell, Paul. *Class: A Guide through the American Status System*. New York: Simon, 1983.

Gay, Penny. *Jane Austen and the Theatre*. Cambridge: Cambridge UP, 2002.

———. *Jane Austen's* Emma. Horizon Studies in Literature. Sydney: Sydney UP, 1995.

Geggus, David. "British Opinion and the Emergence of Haiti, 1791–1804." Walvin 123–49.

Genette, Gerard. *Narrative Discourse: An Essay in Method*. 1980. Trans. Jane E. Lewin. Ithaca: Cornell UP, 1983.

———. *Narrative Discourse Revisited*. Trans. Jane E. Lewin. Ithaca: Cornell UP, 1998.

Gibbon, Frank. "The Antiguan Connection." *Cambridge Quarterly* 11 (1982): 298–305.

Gilbert, Sandra M., and Susan Gubar. *The Madwoman in the Attic: The Woman Writer and the Nineteenth-Century Literary Imagination*. New Haven: Yale UP, 1979.

Gooneratne, Yasmine. *Jane Austen*. Cambridge: Cambridge UP, 1970.

Grey, J. David, A. Walton Litz, and Brian Southam, eds. *The Jane Austen Companion*. New York: Macmillan, 1986.

Grice, H. P. "Logic and Conversation." *Speech Acts*. Ed. Peter Cole and Jerry Morgan. Syntax and Semantics 3. New York: Academic, 1975.

Grimm, Jacob, and Wilhelm Grimm. "King Thrushbeard." *Fairy Tales by Jacob and Wilhelm Grimm*. Trans. Lucy Crane. Cleveland: World, 1947. 64–69.

Halperin, John, ed. *Jane Austen: Bicentenary Essays*. Cambridge: Cambridge UP, 1975.

Harding, D. W. "Regulated Hatred: An Aspect of the Work of Jane Austen." *Scrutiny* 8 (1939–40): 346–62. Rpt. Watt, *Austen* 166–79.

Harris, Jocelyn. "'As If They Had Been Living Friends': *Sir Charles Grandison* into *Mansfield Park*." *Bulletin of Research in the Humanities* 83 (1980): 360–405.

———. "The Influence of Richardson on *Pride and Prejudice*." Folsom 94–99.

Hemlow, Joyce. "Fanny Burney and the Courtesy Books." *PMLA* 65 (1950): 732–61.

Himmelfarb, Gertrude. "The Many Faces of Emma." *Civilization* (1996–97): 74–75.

Hough, Graham. "Narrative and Dialogue in Jane Austen." *Critical Quarterly* 12 (1970): 201–29.

Hubback, J. H., and Edith C. Hubback. *Jane Austen's Sailor Brothers*. London: Lane, 1906.

Inchbald, Elizabeth. *A Simple Story*. Ed. J. M. S. Tompkins. Introd. Jane Spencer. Oxford: Oxford UP, 1988.

Jackson, Shelley. *Patchwork Girl*. CD-ROM. Watertown: Eastgate Systems, 1995.

James, C. L. R. *The Black Jacobins: Toussaint L'Ouverture and the San Domingo Revolution*. 1938. New York: Random, 1963.

James, P. D. "*Emma* Considered as a Detective Story." *A Time to Be in Earnest: A Fragment of Autobiography*. New York: Knopf, 2000. 243–59.

Johnson, Claudia. *Equivocal Beings: Politics, Gender, and Sentimentality in the 1790s*. Chicago: U of Chicago P, 1995.

———. *Jane Austen: Women, Politics, and the Novel*. Chicago: U of Chicago P, 1988.

———. Letter. *London Review of Books* 5 Oct. 1995: 4.

Jones, Mary Gwladys. *Hannah More*. New York: Greenwood, 1968.

Jones, Vivien, ed. *Women in the Eighteenth Century: Constructions of Femininity*. New York: Routledge, 1990.

Kaplan, Deborah. *Jane Austen among Women*. Baltimore: Johns Hopkins UP, 1992.

Kestner, Joseph. "Jane Austen: Revolutionizing Masculinities." *Persuasions* 16 (1994): 147–60.

Kettle, Arnold. *An Introduction to the English Novel*. Vol. 1. London: Hutchinson's U Library, 1951.

Kirkham, Margaret. *Jane Austen, Feminism and Fiction*. New York: Methuen, 1986. 2nd ed. London: Athlone, 1997.

Korba, Susan M. "'Improper and Dangerous Distinctions': Female Relationships and Erotic Domination in *Emma*." *Studies in the Novel* 29 (1997): 139–63.

Kowaleski-Wallace, Beth. *Their Fathers' Daughters: Hannah More, Maria Edgeworth and Patriarchal Complicity*. Oxford: Oxford UP, 1991.

Kundera, Milan. *The Art of the Novel*. Trans. Linda Asher. New York: Harper, 1988.

Landry, Donna. *The Muses of Resistance: Laboring-Class Women's Poetry in Britain, 1739–1796*. Cambridge: Cambridge UP, 1991.

Lane, Anthony. "The Dumbing of Emma." *New Yorker* 5 Aug. 1996: 76–77.

Lanser, Susan Sniader. *The Narrative Act: Point of View in Prose Fiction*. Princeton: Princeton UP, 1981.

Lascelles, Mary. *Jane Austen and Her Art*. Oxford: Clarendon, 1939.

Leavis, F. R. *The Great Tradition: George Eliot, Henry James, Joseph Conrad*. New York: Steward, 1948.

Leavis, Q. D. "A Critical Theory of Jane Austen's Writings." *Scrutiny* 10 (1941–42): 61–87.

Le Faye, Deirdre. "Jane Austen and Her Hancock Relatives." *Review of English Studies* 30 (1979): 12–27.

Lennox, Charlotte. *The Female Quixote; or, The Adventures of Arabella*. Ed. Margaret Dalziel. Introd. Margaret Anne Doody. Oxford: Oxford UP, 1989.

Letwin, Shirley Robin. *The Gentleman in Trollope: Individuality and Moral Conduct*. Pleasantville: Akadine, 1982.

Lew, Joseph. "'That Abominable Traffic': *Mansfield Park* and the Dynamics of Slavery." B. Tobin 271–300.

Lewes, George Henry. "The Lady Novelists." *Westminster Review* 58 (1852): 129–41. Rpt. Austen, *Emma*. Ed. Parrish 359–60.

Litz, A. Walton. "Criticism, 1939–83." Grey, Litz, and Southam 110–17.

Looser, Devoney. "'The Duty of Woman by Woman': Reforming Feminism in *Emma*." Austen, *Emma*. Ed. Duckworth 577–93.

———. "Feminist Implications of the Silver Screen Austen." Troost and Greenfield 159–76.

———, ed. *Jane Austen and Discourses of Feminism*. New York: St. Martin's, 1995.

Marshall, Mary Gaither. "Jane Austen and the MTV Generation: Teaching *Emma* at a Community College." *Persuasions* 13 (1991): 104–07.

McMaster, Juliet. "Class." Copeland and McMaster 115–30.

———. "Love and Pedagogy." Weinsheimer 408–14.

———. "The Secret Languages of *Emma*." *Jane Austen the Novelist: Essays Past and Present*. Ed. McMaster. London: Macmillan, 1996. 90–105.

Mellor, Anne Kostelanetz. *Mothers of the Nation: Women's Political Writing in England, 1780–1830*. Bloomington: Indiana UP, 2000.

Menand, Louis. "What Jane Austen Doesn't Tell Us." *New York Review of Books* 1 Feb. 1996: 13–15.

Meyersohn, Marylea. "Jane Austen's Garrulous Speakers." Bowers and Brothers 35–48.

Mezei, Kathy. "Who Is Speaking Here?: Free Indirect Discourse, Gender and Authority in *Emma, Howards End,* and *Mrs. Dalloway." Ambiguous Discourse: Feminist Narratology and British Women Writers.* Ed. Mezei. Chapel Hill: U of North Carolina P, 1996. 66–92.

Michaelson, Patricia Howell. *Speaking Volumes: Women, Reading, and Speech in the Age of Austen.* Stanford: Stanford UP, 2002.

Miller, D. A. "The Late Jane Austen." *Raritan* 10 (1990): 55–79.

———. *Narrative and Its Discontents: Problems of Closure in the Traditional Novel.* Princeton: Princeton UP, 1981.

Modert, Jo. "Chronology within the Novels." Grey, Litz, and Southam 53–59.

Monaghan, David, ed. *Emma: Contemporary Critical Essays.* New York: St. Martin's, 1992.

———. *Jane Austen: Structure and Social Vision.* London: Macmillan, 1980.

Moore, Lisa L. *Dangerous Intimacies: Toward a Sapphic History of the British Novel.* Durham: Duke UP, 1997.

Morgan, Susan. "Why There's No Sex in Jane Austen's Fiction." *Studies in the Novel* 19 (1987): 346–56.

Moretti, Franco. "Fillers." Narrative Conference Center for the Study of Culture. Rice Univ. 8 Mar. 2001.

Mudrick, Marvin. *Jane Austen: Irony as Defense and Discovery.* Princeton: Princeton UP, 1952.

Myers, Mitzi. "Reform or Ruin: 'A Revolution in Female Manners.'" *Studies in Eighteenth-Century Culture* 11 (1982): 199–216.

Nachumi, Nora. "'As If!': Translating Austen's Ironic Narrator to Film." Troost and Greenfield 130–39.

Newton, Judith Lowder. "*Evelina*: A Chronicle of Assault." Bloom, *Evelina* 59–83.

Parker, Mark. "The End of *Emma*: Drawing the Boundaries of Class in Austen." *Journal of English and Germanic Philology* 91.3 (1992): 344–59.

Pascal, Roy. *The Dual Voice: Free Indirect Speech and Its Functioning in the Nineteenth-Century European Novel.* Manchester: Manchester UP; Totowa: Rowman, 1977.

Perry, Ruth. "Austen and Empire: A Thinking Woman's Guide to British Imperialism." *Persuasions* 16 (1994): 95–106.

———. "Interrupted Friendships in Jane Austen's *Emma." Tulsa Studies in Women's Literature* 5.2 (1986): 185–202.

Pinchbeck, Ivy, and Margaret Hewitt. *Children in English Society.* 2 vols. London: Routledge, 1969.

Polwhele, Richard, and Thomas James Mathias. *The Unsex'd Females: A Poem Addressed to the Author of* The Pursuants of Literature. *By the Rev. Richard Polwhele. To Which Is Added, a Sketch of the Private and Public Character of P. Pindar.* Rpt. Cobbett, 1800.

Pool, Daniel. *What Jane Austen Ate and Charles Dickens Knew: From Fox Hunting to Whist—the Facts of Daily Life in Nineteenth-Century England*. New York: Simon, 1993.

Poovey, Mary. "Fathers and Daughters: the Trauma of Growing up Female." Bloom, *Evelina* 85–98.

———. *The Proper Lady and the Woman Writer: Ideology as Style in the Works of Mary Wollstonecraft, Mary Shelley, and Jane Austen*. 1984. 2nd ed. with new introd. Chicago: U of Chicago P, 1987.

———. "The True English Style." *Persuasions* 5 (1983): 48–51. Rpt. *Emma*. Ed. Parrish 396–400.

Potter, Tiffany F. "'A Low but Very Feeling Tone': The Lesbian Continuum and Power Relations in Jane Austen's *Emma*." *English Studies in Canada* 20 (1994): 187–203.

Preus, Nicholas. "Sexuality in *Emma*: A Case History." *Studies in the Novel* 23 (1991): 196–216.

Prince, Gerald. *Narratology: The Form and Functioning of Narrative*. Berlin: Mouton, 1982.

Reissman, Leonard. *Class in American Society*. New York: Free, 1959.

Rich, Adrienne. "Compulsory Heterosexuality and Lesbian Existence." *Signs* 5 (1980): 631–60.

Richardson, Samuel. *The History of Sir Charles Grandison in a Series of Letters in Seven Volumes*. Philadelphia: Lippincott, 1902.

Rizzo, Betty. *Companions without Vows: Relationships among Eighteenth-Century British Women*. Athens: U of Georgia P, 1994.

Rybczynski, Witold. *Home: A Short History of an Idea*. New York: Viking-Penguin, 1986.

Sacks, Oliver. *A Leg to Stand On*. London: Picador, 1985.

Said, Edward. "Jane Austen and Empire." 1989. *Culture and Imperialism*. New York: Knopf, 1993. 80–97.

Scott, Walter. Rev. of *Emma*. *Quarterly Review* 14 (1815): 188–201. Rpt. *Emma*. Ed. Parrish 357–59.

Sedgwick, Eve Kosofsky. "Jane Austen and the Masturbating Girl." *Critical Inquiry* 17 (1991): 818–37.

Smiles, Samuel. *Life and Labour*. Chicago, 1890.

Smith, Johanna M. "'I Am a Gentleman's Daughter': A Marxist-Feminist Reading of *Pride and Prejudice*." Folsom 67–73.

Snow, Edward. *A Study of Vermeer*. Rev. ed. Los Angeles: U of California P, 1994.

Sonnet, Esther. "From *Emma* to *Clueless*: Taste, Pleasure and the Scene of History." Cartmell and Whelehan 51–62.

Southam, Brian. *Jane Austen: The Critical Heritage*. London: Routledge, 1968.

Spacks, Patricia Meyer. "Emma's Happiness." *ADE Bulletin* 84 (1986): 16–18.

———. "Dynamics of Fear: Fanny Burney." Bloom, *Evelina* 31–57.

Spender, Dale. *Mothers of the Novel: One Hundred Good Women Writers before Jane Austen*. London: Pandora, 1986.

Spring, David. "Interpreters of Jane Austen's Social World: Literary Critics and Historians." Todd, *New Perspectives* 53–72.

Staël-Holstein, A. L. G. de. *Letters on England*. London: Bentley, 1830.

Sulloway, Alison. *Jane Austen and the Province of Womanhood*. Philadelphia: U of Pennsylvania P, 1989.

Tannen, Deborah. *Talking Voices: Repetition, Dialogue, and Imagery in Conversational Discourse*. Cambridge: Cambridge UP, 1989.

Thompson, James. *Between Self and World: The Novels of Jane Austen*. University Park: Pennsylvania State UP, 1988.

Tobin, Beth Fowkes. *History, Gender and Eighteenth-Century Literature*. Athens: U of Georgia P, 1994.

Tobin, Mary Elizabeth Fowkes. "Aiding Impoverished Gentlewomen: Power and Class in *Emma*." *Criticism* 30 (1988): 413–30.

Todd, Janet, ed. *Jane Austen: New Perspectives*. New York: Holmes, 1983.

———. *Women's Friendship in Literature*. New York: Columbia UP, 1980.

Tomalin, Claire. *Jane Austen: A Life*. New York: Knopf, 1997.

Trilling, Lionel. "*Emma* and the Legend of Jane Austen." *Beyond Culture: Essays on Literature and Learning*. London: Secker, 1966. 31–55.

———. Introduction. *Emma*. By Jane Austen. Boston: Houghton-Riverside, 1956. v–xxvi.

Troost, Linda, and Sayre Greenfield, eds. *Jane Austen in Hollywood*. Lexington: UP of Kentucky, 1998.

Veblen, Thorstein. *The Theory of the Leisure Class*. 1899. Boston: Houghton, 1973.

Vermeer, Jan. *The Soldier and the Young Girl Smiling*. Frick Museum, New York.

Vorachek, Laura. "'The Instrument of the Century': The Piano as an Icon of Female Sexuality in the Nineteenth Century." *George Eliot–George Henry Lewes Studies* 34–35 (2000): 26–43.

Wald, Gayle. "Clueless in the Neocolonial World Order." *Camera Obscura* 42 (1999): 51–69.

Waldron, Mary. *Lactilla, Milkwoman of Clifton: The Life and Writings of Ann Yearsley, 1753–1806*. Athens: U of Georgia P, 1996.

Walvin, James, ed. *Slavery and British Society, 1776–1846*. Baton Rouge: Louisiana State UP, 1982.

Watt, Ian, ed. *Jane Austen: A Collection of Critical Essays*. Englewood Cliffs: Prentice, 1963.

———. *The Rise of the Novel*. London: Chatto, 1957.

Weinsheimer, Joel, ed. *Jane Austen Today*. Athens: U of Georgia P, 1975.

Wheeler, David. "The British Postal Service, Privacy, and Jane Austen's *Emma*." *South Atlantic Review* 63.4 (1998): 34–47.

White, Hayden. "Narrativity in the Representation of Reality." *The Content of the Form: Narrative Discourse and Historical Representation*. Baltimore: Johns Hopkins UP, 1987. 1–25.

White, James Boyd. *When Words Lose Their Meaning: Constitutions and Reconstitutions of Language, Character, and Community*. Chicago: U of Chicago P, 1984.

Wiesenfarth, Joseph. "*Emma*: Point Counter Point." Halperin 207–20.

Williams, Raymond. *The Country and the City*. New York: Oxford UP, 1973.

Williamson, Barbara Fisher. "Kudos for Emma, Thumbs Down on Becky." *Publishers Weekly* 24 July 1987: 159.

Wilson, Edmund. *Classics and Commercials*. New York: Farrar, 1950.

———. "A Long Talk about Jane Austen." *New Yorker* 13 Oct. 1945; Rpt. Watt, *Austen* 3–40.

Wiltshire, John. *Jane Austen and the Body: "The Picture of Health."* Cambridge: Cambridge UP, 1992.

———. "*Mansfield Park, Emma, Persuasion*." Copeland and McMaster 58–83.

———. *Recreating Jane Austen*. Cambridge: Cambridge UP, 2001.

———. "The World of Emma." *Critical Review* 27 (1985): 84–97.

Winnicott, D. W. *Playing and Reality*. 1971. London: Routledge, 1994.

Woolf, Virginia. *The Common Reader: First Series*. Ed. Andrew McNeillie. New York: Harcourt, 1984.

———. *A Room of One's Own*. 1929. New York: Harcourt, 1989.

Wordsworth, William, and Samuel Taylor Coleridge. *Lyrical Ballads 1798*. Ed. W. J. B. Owen. 2nd ed. Oxford: Oxford UP, 1969.

The World. Ed. Edward Moore. 4 vols. London, 1761.

Zaal, J. "Is *Emma* Still Teachable?" *Crux: A Journal on the Teaching of English* 22.3 (1988): 61–68.

Zeller, Tom. "Calculating One Kind of Middle Class." *New York Times* 29 Oct. 2000: A5.

INDEX

Modern Language Association of America
Approaches to Teaching World Literature
Joseph Gibaldi, series editor

Achebe's Things Fall Apart. Ed. Bernth Lindfors. 1991.
Arthurian Tradition. Ed. Maureen Fries and Jeanie Watson. 1992.
Atwood's The Handmaid's Tale *and Other Works.* Ed. Sharon R. Wilson, Thomas B. Friedman, and Shannon Hengen. 1996.
Austen's Emma. Ed. Marcia McClintock Folsom. 2004.
Austen's Pride and Prejudice. Ed. Marcia McClintock Folsom. 1993.
Balzac's Old Goriot. Ed. Michal Peled Ginsburg. 2000.
Baudelaire's Flowers of Evil. Ed. Laurence M. Porter. 2000.
Beckett's Waiting for Godot. Ed. June Schlueter and Enoch Brater. 1991.
Beowulf. Ed. Jess B. Bessinger, Jr., and Robert F. Yeager. 1984.
Blake's Songs of Innocence and of Experience. Ed. Robert F. Gleckner and Mark L. Greenberg. 1989.
Boccaccio's Decameron. Ed. James H. McGregor. 2000.
British Women Poets of the Romantic Period. Ed. Stephen C. Behrendt and Harriet Kramer Linkin. 1997.
Brontë's Jane Eyre. Ed. Diane Long Hoeveler and Beth Lau. 1993.
Byron's Poetry. Ed. Frederick W. Shilstone. 1991.
Camus's The Plague. Ed. Steven G. Kellman. 1985.
Cather's My Ántonia. Ed. Susan J. Rosowski. 1989.
Cervantes' Don Quixote. Ed. Richard Bjornson. 1984.
Chaucer's Canterbury Tales. Ed. Joseph Gibaldi. 1980.
Chopin's The Awakening. Ed. Bernard Koloski. 1988.
Coleridge's Poetry and Prose. Ed. Richard E. Matlak. 1991.
Conrad's "Heart of Darkness" and "The Secret Sharer." Ed. Hunt Hawkins and Brian W. Shaffer. 2002.
Dante's Divine Comedy. Ed. Carole Slade. 1982.
Dickens' David Copperfield. Ed. Richard J. Dunn. 1984.
Dickinson's Poetry. Ed. Robin Riley Fast and Christine Mack Gordon. 1989.
Narrative of the Life of Frederick Douglass. Ed. James C. Hall. 1999.
Eliot's Middlemarch. Ed. Kathleen Blake. 1990.
Eliot's Poetry and Plays. Ed. Jewel Spears Brooker. 1988.
Shorter Elizabethan Poetry. Ed. Patrick Cheney and Anne Lake Prescott. 2000.
Ellison's Invisible Man. Ed. Susan Resneck Parr and Pancho Savery. 1989.
English Renaissance Drama. Ed. Karen Bamford and Alexander Leggatt. 2002.
Dramas of Euripides. Ed. Robin Mitchell-Boyask. 2002.
Faulkner's The Sound and the Fury. Ed. Stephen Hahn and Arthur F. Kinney. 1996.
Flaubert's Madame Bovary. Ed. Laurence M. Porter and Eugene F. Gray. 1995.

García Márquez's One Hundred Years of Solitude. Ed. María Elena de Valdés and Mario J. Valdés. 1990.

Gilman's "The Yellow Wall-Paper" and Herland. Ed. Denise D. Knight and Cynthia J. Davis.

Goethe's Faust. Ed. Douglas J. McMillan. 1987.

Gothic Fiction: The British and American Traditions. Ed. Diane Long Hoeveler and Tamar Heller. 2003.

Hebrew Bible as Literature in Translation. Ed. Barry N. Olshen and Yael S. Feldman. 1989.

Homer's Iliad *and* Odyssey. Ed. Kostas Myrsiades. 1987.

Ibsen's A Doll House. Ed. Yvonne Shafer. 1985.

Works of Samuel Johnson. Ed. David R. Anderson and Gwin J. Kolb. 1993.

Joyce's Ulysses. Ed. Kathleen McCormick and Erwin R. Steinberg. 1993.

Kafka's Short Fiction. Ed. Richard T. Gray. 1995.

Keats's Poetry. Ed. Walter H. Evert and Jack W. Rhodes. 1991.

Kingston's The Woman Warrior. Ed. Shirley Geok-lin Lim. 1991.

Lafayette's The Princess of Clèves. Ed. Faith E. Beasley and Katharine Ann Jensen. 1998.

Works of D. H. Lawrence. Ed. M. Elizabeth Sargent and Garry Watson. 2001.

Lessing's The Golden Notebook. Ed. Carey Kaplan and Ellen Cronan Rose. 1989.

Mann's Death in Venice *and Other Short Fiction.* Ed. Jeffrey B. Berlin. 1992.

Medieval English Drama. Ed. Richard K. Emmerson. 1990.

Melville's Moby-Dick. Ed. Martin Bickman. 1985.

Metaphysical Poets. Ed. Sidney Gottlieb. 1990.

Miller's Death of a Salesman. Ed. Matthew C. Roudané. 1995.

Milton's Paradise Lost. Ed. Galbraith M. Crump. 1986.

Molière's Tartuffe *and Other Plays.* Ed. James F. Gaines and Michael S. Koppisch. 1995.

Momaday's The Way to Rainy Mountain. Ed. Kenneth M. Roemer. 1988.

Montaigne's Essays. Ed. Patrick Henry. 1994.

Novels of Toni Morrison. Ed. Nellie Y. McKay and Kathryn Earle. 1997.

Murasaki Shikibu's The Tale of Genji. Ed. Edward Kamens. 1993.

Pope's Poetry. Ed. Wallace Jackson and R. Paul Yoder. 1993.

Proust's Fiction and Criticism. Ed. Elyane Dezon-Jones and Inge Crosman Wimmers. 1993.

Rousseau's Confessions *and* Reveries of the Solitary Walker. Ed. John C. O'Neal and Ourida Mostefai. 2003.

Shakespeare's Hamlet. Ed. Bernice W. Kliman. 2001.

Shakespeare's King Lear. Ed. Robert H. Ray. 1986.

Shakespeare's Romeo and Juliet. Ed. Maurice Hunt. 2000.

Shakespeare's The Tempest *and Other Late Romances.* Ed. Maurice Hunt. 1992.

Shelley's Frankenstein. Ed. Stephen C. Behrendt. 1990.

Shelley's Poetry. Ed. Spencer Hall. 1990.

Sir Gawain and the Green Knight. Ed. Miriam Youngerman Miller and
    Jane Chance. 1986.

Spenser's Faerie Queene. Ed. David Lee Miller and Alexander Dunlop. 1994.

Stendhal's The Red and the Black. Ed. Dean de la Motte and Stirling Haig. 1999.

Sterne's Tristram Shandy. Ed. Melvyn New. 1989.

Stowe's Uncle Tom's Cabin. Ed. Elizabeth Ammons and Susan Belasco. 2000.

Swift's Gulliver's Travels. Ed. Edward J. Rielly. 1988.

Thoreau's Walden *and Other Works*. Ed. Richard J. Schneider. 1996.

Tolstoy's Anna Karenina. Ed. Liza Knapp and Amy Mandelker. 2003.

Vergil's Aeneid. Ed. William S. Anderson and Lorina N. Quartarone. 2002.

Voltaire's Candide. Ed. Renée Waldinger. 1987.

Whitman's Leaves of Grass. Ed. Donald D. Kummings. 1990.

Woolf's To the Lighthouse. Ed. Beth Rigel Daugherty and Mary Beth Pringle. 2001.

Wordsworth's Poetry. Ed. Spencer Hall, with Jonathan Ramsey. 1986.

Wright's Native Son. Ed. James A. Miller. 1997.